New York City 5 Borough

Pocket Atlas

FOURTH LARGE SCALE EDITION

Copyright 1997 Hagstrom Map Company, Inc.
46-35 54th Road, Maspeth, New York 11378
Printed in Canada

Key Map for Manhattan and The Bronx 3
Key Map for Brooklyn, Queens, and Staten Island 4-5
Main Through Routes 6-7
Manhattan Subways 8
Legend 9
Sectional Street Maps
    Manhattan 10-20
    The Bronx 16-37
    Queens 38-87
    Brooklyn 88-117
    Staten Island 118-139
Historical New York 140
Historical Highlights 141
Selected Points of Interest 142-145
Neighborhoods 146-147
New York City Statistics 147
Quick Building Number Guide 148-149
Zip Code Information 149
Index to Streets and Roads 150-190

Cover Photo of California Sea Lions at The Bronx Zoo by Michael Warren

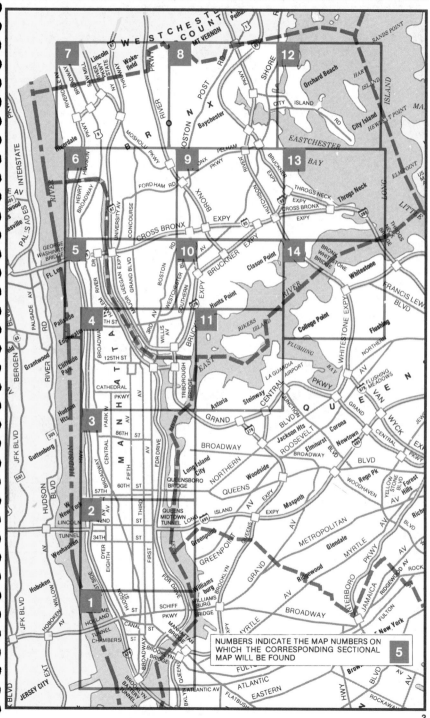

NUMBERS INDICATE THE MAP NUMBERS ON WHICH THE CORRESPONDING SECTIONAL MAP WILL BE FOUND 5

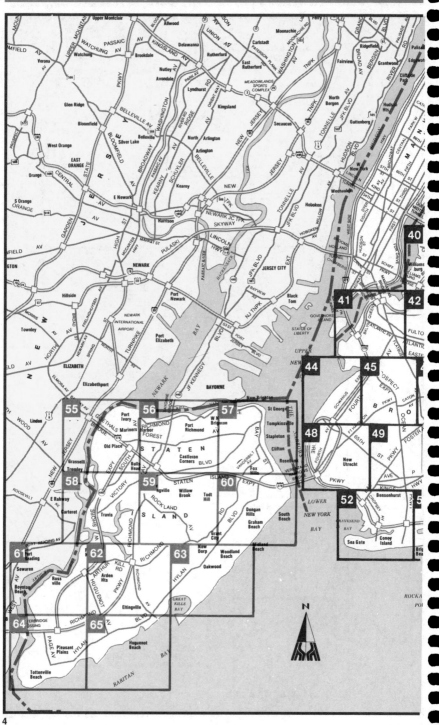

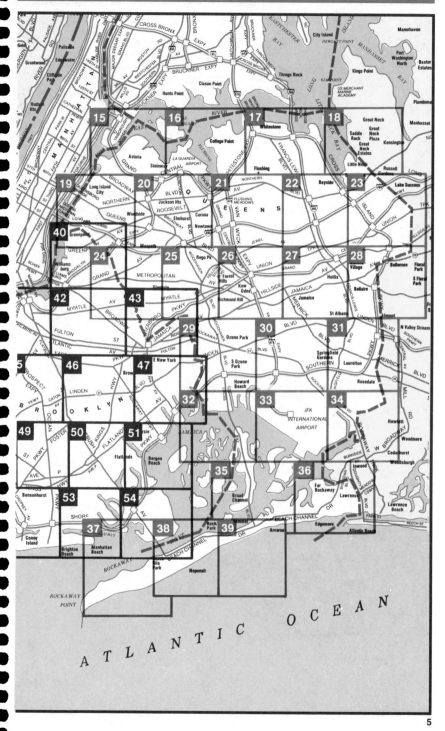

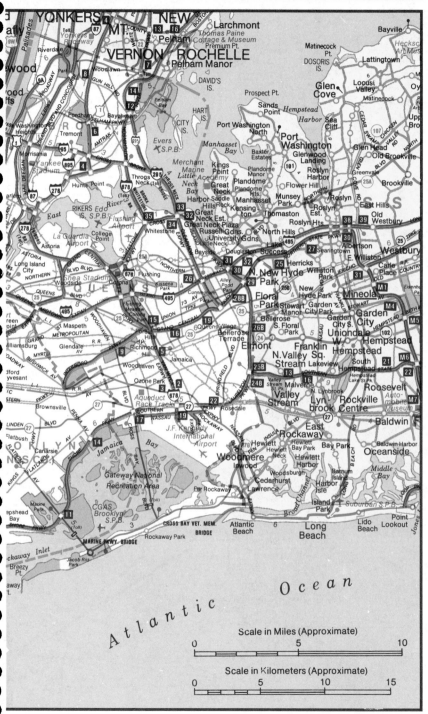

Scale in Miles (Approximate)

0   5   10

Scale in Kilometers (Approximate)

0   5   10   15

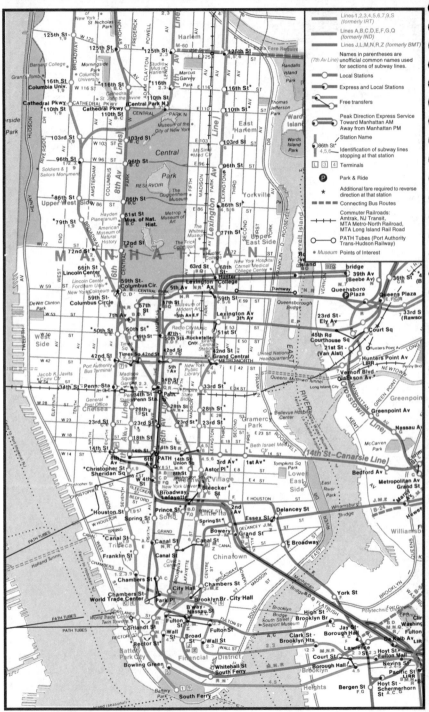

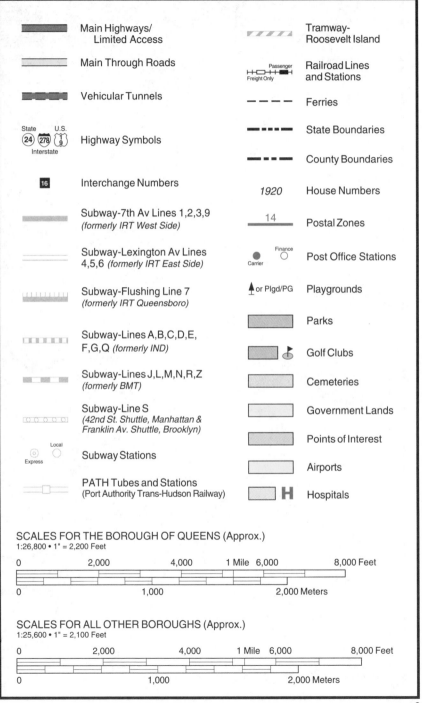

Main Highways/ Limited Access

Main Through Roads

Vehicular Tunnels

State (24) U.S. (278) Interstate (1 9) Highway Symbols

16 Interchange Numbers

Subway-7th Av Lines 1,2,3,9 (formerly IRT West Side)

Subway-Lexington Av Lines 4,5,6 (formerly IRT East Side)

Subway-Flushing Line 7 (formerly IRT Queensboro)

Subway-Lines A,B,C,D,E, F,G,Q (formerly IND)

Subway-Lines J,L,M,N,R,Z (formerly BMT)

Subway-Line S (42nd St. Shuttle, Manhattan & Franklin Av. Shuttle, Brooklyn)

Express Local Subway Stations

PATH Tubes and Stations (Port Authority Trans-Hudson Railway)

Tramway- Roosevelt Island

Passenger Freight Only Railroad Lines and Stations

Ferries

State Boundaries

County Boundaries

1920 House Numbers

14 Postal Zones

Carrier Finance Post Office Stations

or Plgd/PG Playgrounds

Parks

Golf Clubs

Cemeteries

Government Lands

Points of Interest

Airports

H Hospitals

SCALES FOR THE BOROUGH OF QUEENS (Approx.)
1:26,800 • 1" = 2,200 Feet

0   2,000   4,000   1 Mile 6,000   8,000 Feet

0   1,000   2,000 Meters

SCALES FOR ALL OTHER BOROUGHS (Approx.)
1:25,600 • 1" = 2,100 Feet

0   2,000   4,000   1 Mile 6,000   8,000 Feet

0   1,000   2,000 Meters

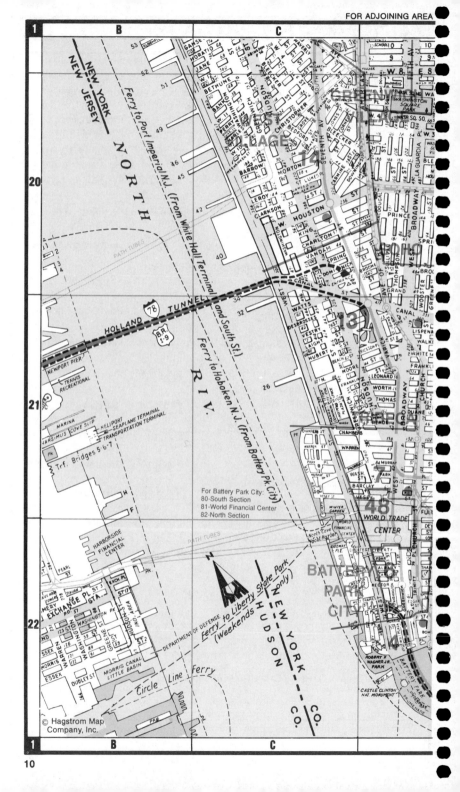

© Hagstrom Map Company, Inc.

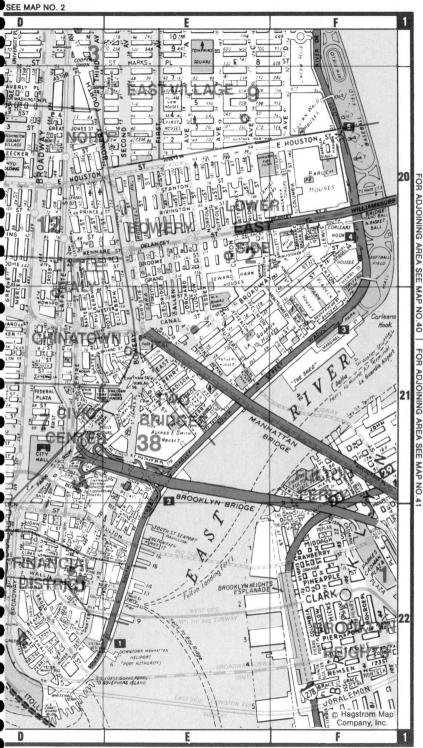

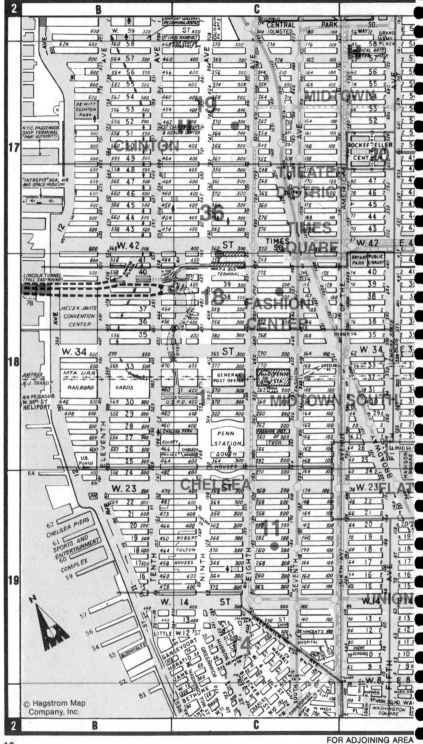

© Hagstrom Map Company, Inc.

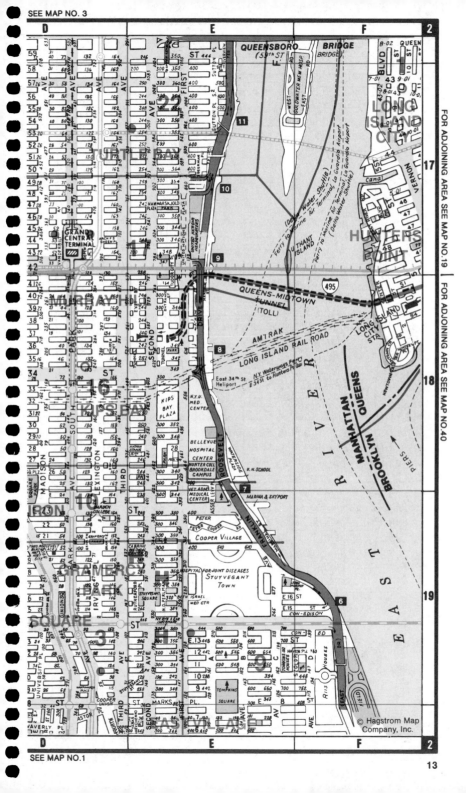

3

B   C

MANHATTAN VALLEY

CENTRAL

PARK

UPPER WEST SIDE

LINCOLN SQUARE

LINCOLN
TOWERS

LINCOLN
CENTER

FORDHAM
UNIVERSITY

AMSTERDAM
HOUSES

JOHN JAY COLLEGE
OF CRIMINAL JUSTICE

RIVERSIDE PARK

HENRY HUDSON PARKWAY

HUDSON RIVER

HAYDEN
PLANE-
TARIUM
AMERICAN
MUSEUM OF
NATURAL
HISTORY

RESERVOIR

THE GREAT LAWN

MET
MUSEUM OF ART

BELVEDERE
LAKE

BELVEDERE
CASTLE

THE RAMBLE

BOAT
HOUSE

CONSERVATORY
WATER

THE LAKE

BETHESDA

STRAW-
BERRY
FIELDS

CHERRY HILL

BANDSHELL

THE MALL

SHEEP
MEADOW

CHILDRENS
ZOO

HECKSCHER
PLAYGROUND

THE
ZOO

THE DAIRY
INFO CENTER

WOLLMAN
RINK

THE
POND

THE GREAT
HILL

THE LOCH

CONSERVATORY
GARDEN

NORTH MEADOW
BALL FIELD

RECREATION
HOUSE

THE
POOL

97 ST TRANSVERSE

SOUTH MEADOW
TENNIS COURTS

86 ST TRANSVERSE

65 ST TRANSVERSE

CENTRAL   PARK   SO.

GRAND
ARMY
PLAZA

MEDICAL ARTS
CENTER

W. 106   ELLINGTON BLVD. (DUKE)   ST

W. 96   ST

W. 86   ST

W. 72   ST

W. 59   ST

STRAUS
PARK

POMANDER WALK

SOLDIERS
SAILORS

EDGAR ALLAN POE ST

RIVERSIDE AMSTERDAM
HOUSES

SHERMAN

DANTE

OLMSTED

RIVERSIDE DR

WEST END AVE

BROADWAY

AMSTERDAM AVE

COLUMBUS AVE

CENTRAL PARK WEST

MANHATTAN AVE

FIFTH AVE

MUSEUM AVE

EAST DRIVE

WEST DRIVE

HUDSON PARKWAY

AMTRAK

14

15

16

B   C

3

D · E · F · 3

E. 106 AV

WARDS ISLAND 278 PARK

35

HELL GATE

MILL ROCK PARK

29

14

METROPOLITAN HOSPITAL CENTER

ASTORIA

2

CARNEGIE HILL

YORKVILLE

28

ENVIRONMENTAL EDUCATION CENTER
GRACIE MANSION

HALLETS COVE

LIGHTHOUSE PARK

UPPER EAST SIDE

23

GRACIE TER

WEST CHANNEL

BIRD S COLER MEM. HOSP.

EAST CHANNEL

RAINEY PARK

15

JOHN JAY PARK

44

ROOSEVELT ISLAND

MOTORGATE PLZ ROOSEVELT ISLAND BR

MARYMOUNT MANHATTAN COLLEGE

21

LENOX HILL

13

THE HOSP. FOR SPECIAL SURGERY

N.Y. HOSPITAL CORNELL MEDICAL CENTER

ROOSEVELT ISLAND

VERNON

16

ROCKEFELLER UNIVERSITY

MEM. SLOAN KETTERING CANCER CENTER

Ferry to Marine Air Terminal La Guardia Airport

CON-EDISON

E. 60th ST METROPORT

12

22

QUEENSBORO BRIDGE (59th ST BRIDGE)

© Hagstrom Map Company, inc.

D · E · F · 3

FOR ADJOINING AREA SEE MAP NO.15 / FOR ADJOINING AREA SEE MAP NO.19

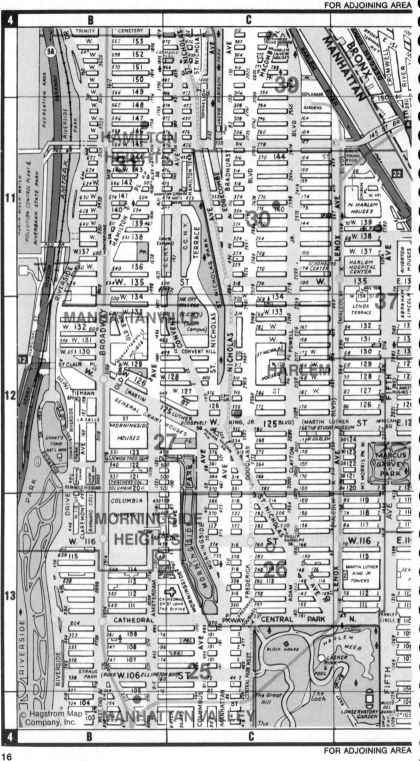

© Hagstrom Map Company, Inc.

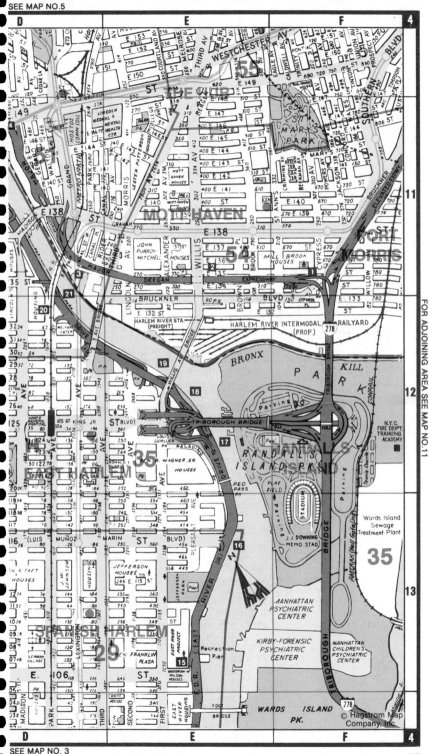

SHERMAN CREEK

FORT TRYON PARK

THE CLOISTERS

MORRIS HEIGHTS

FORT GEORGE

WASHINGTON BRIDGE

GEORGE WASHINGTON BRIDGE

TRANS-MANHATTAN EXPWY.

WASHINGTON HEIGHTS

HIGH BRIDGE

HARLEM RIVER

N.Y.S. PSYCHIATRIC INSTITUTE

COLUMBIA PRESBYTERIAN MEDICAL CENTER

MORRIS JUMEL MANSION

POLO GROUND HOUSES

AUDUBON TERRACE

TRINITY CEMETERY

W. 155 ST

MAHER CIRCLE

HARLEM RIVER DRIVE

HENRY HUDSON PARKWAY

RIVERSIDE DRIVE

FORT WASHINGTON AVE

BROADWAY

AMSTERDAM AVE

ST. NICHOLAS AVE

AUDUBON AVE

EDGECOMBE AVE

MACOMBS

JACKIE ROBINSON PARK

POWELL

© Hagstrom Map Company, Inc.

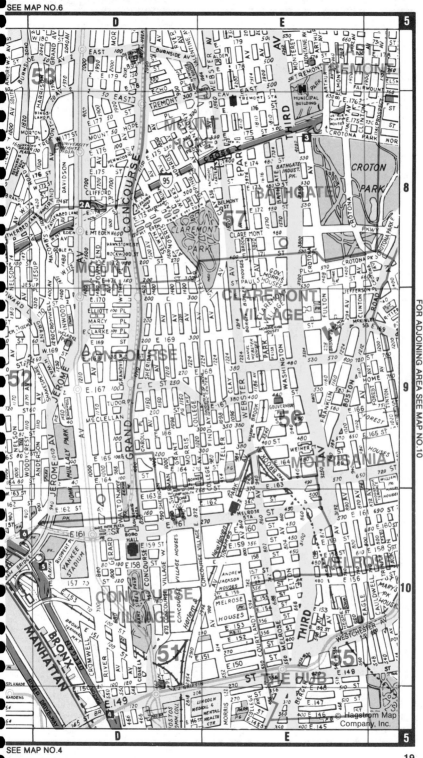

© Hagstrom Map Company, Inc.

FOR ADJOINING AREA SEE MAP NO.9

© Hagstrom Map Company, Inc.

WESTCHESTER CO.
BRONX CO.

COLLEGE OF
MOUNT ST. VINCENT

NORTH RIVERDALE

V A N

THE FRANK KELLY FIELD

DAVID SHERIDAN PLAZA

STABLE

71

WAVE HILL

PLOUGHMAN'S BUSH

FIELDSTON

PARADE GROUNDS

VAN CORTLANDT MANSION AND MUSEUM

MANHATTAN COLLEGE

NYCT SHOPS

RIVERDALE

(Hudson Line)

RIVERDALE STA.

PARK

N

C   D   E   **7**

YONKERS

HILLVIEW RESERVOIR
(CITY OF NEW YORK WATER SUPPLY)

WAKEFIELD

2

WOODLAWN

70

C O R T L A N D T

VAN CORTLANDT

GOLF COURSE

3

W O O D L A W N   C E M E T E R Y

ALLEN SHANDLER REC. AREA

MOSHOLU
K
GOLF COURSE

4

67

87

NORWOOD

DE WITT CLINTON HIGH SCH.

© Hagstrom Map Company, Inc.

C   D   E   **7**

MOUNT VERNON

MOUNT ST. MICHAEL SCHOOL

NYCT SUBWAY SHOPS & YARDS

WAKEFIELD

EASTCHESTER

SETON FALLS PARK

EDENWALD

BRONXWOOD TOWERS HOUSING

WILLIAMSBRIDGE

EASTCHESTER GARDENS PK.

BRONX RIVER PARKWAY

WILLIAMS BRIDGE STA.

PLAINS RD

66

67

69

© Hagstrom Map Company, Inc.

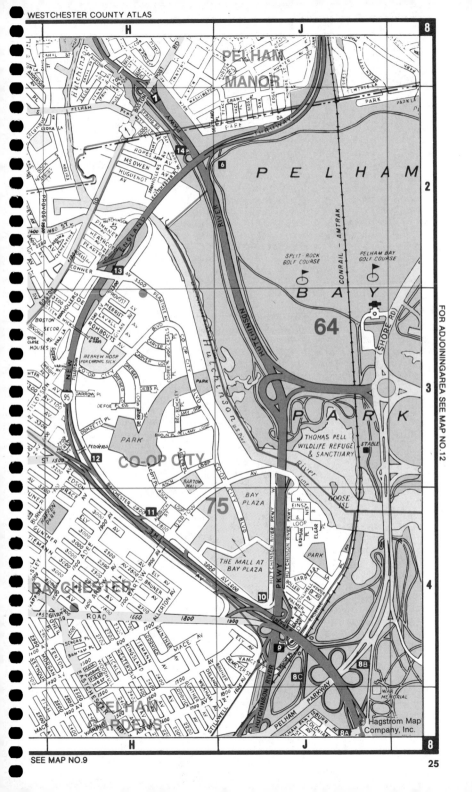

FOR ADJOINING AREA SEE MAP NO.12

FOR ADJOINING AREA

FOR ADJOINING AREA SEE MAP NO.6

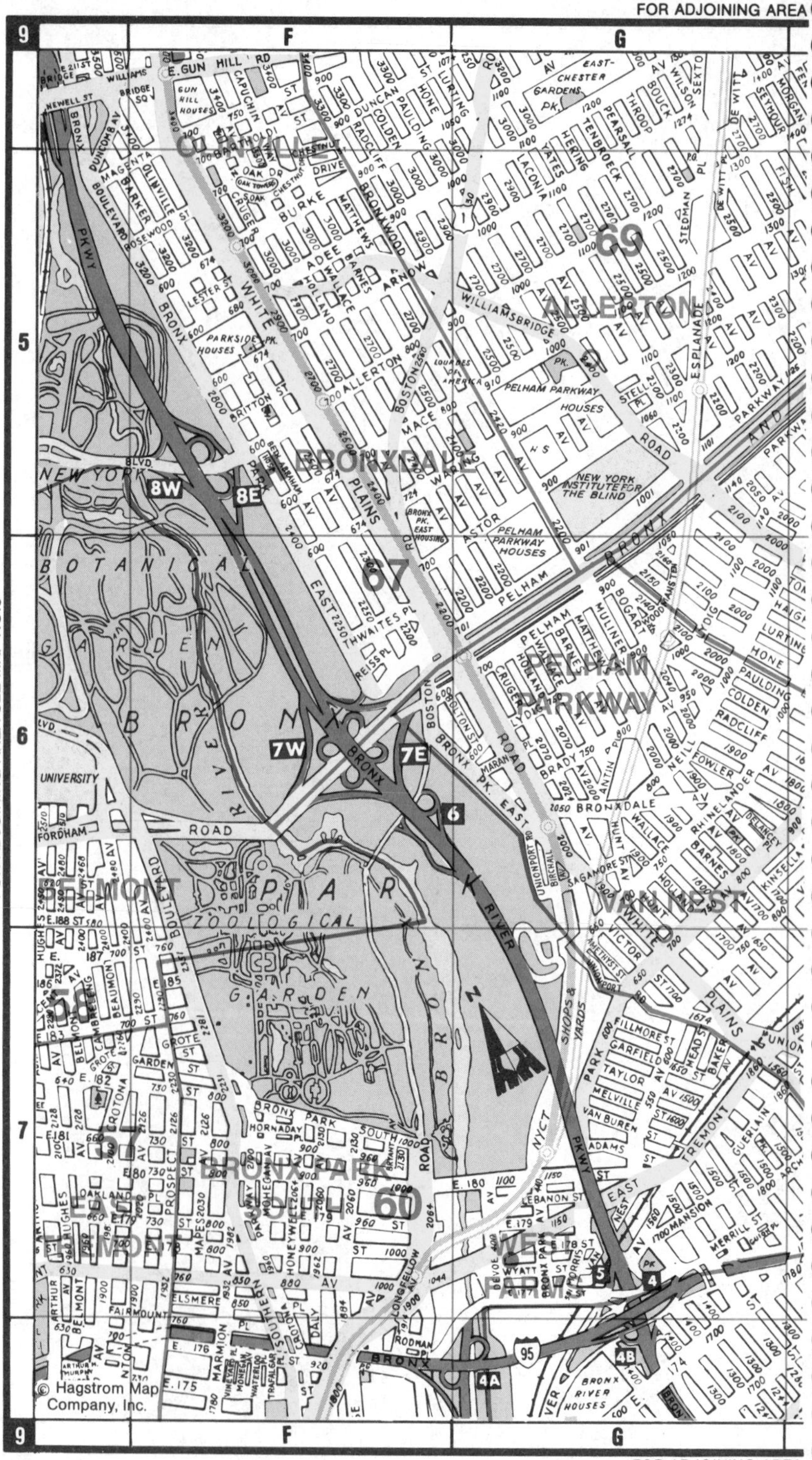

69

PELHAM GARDENS

PELHAM PKWY

North

Pelham Pkwy South

RHINELANDER

STILLWELL

BRONX MUNICIPAL HOSP. CENTER

SEMINOLE

WILKINSON AV

BRONX PSYCHIATRIC CENTER

HUTCHINSON RIVER PKWY

HUTCHINSON RIVER

65

PELHAM BAY PARK

PICNIC

MEMORIAL

8B

8C

9

8A

PARKCHESTER **61**

ST. THERESA

WILLIAMSBRIDGE

TENBROECK

HERING

YATES

TOMLINSON

BRONX MUNICIPAL HOSP.

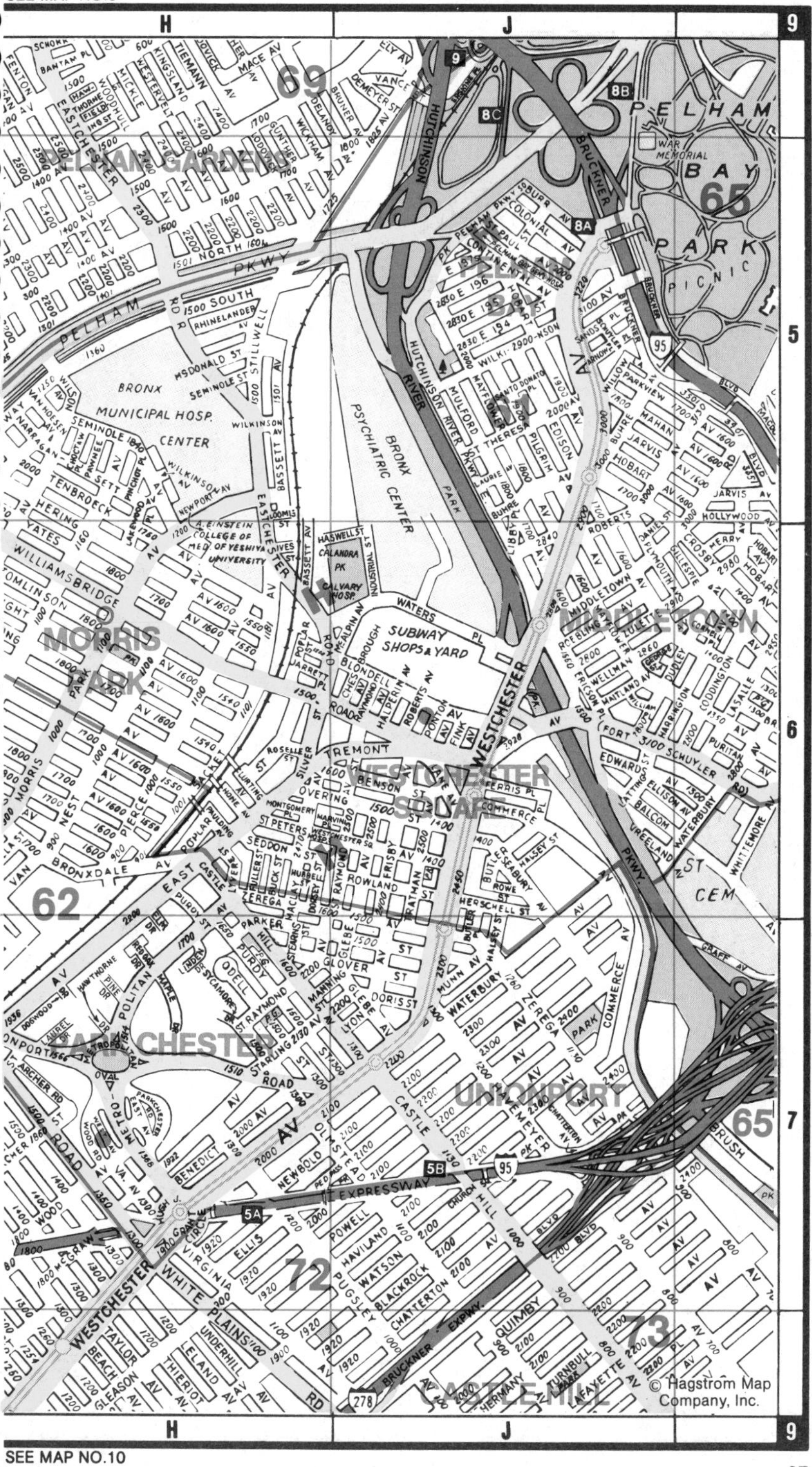

ALBERT EINSTEIN COLLEGE OF MED OF YESHIVA UNIVERSITY

HASWELLS
CALANDRA PK
CALVARY HOSP

WATERS PL

SUBWAY SHOPS & YARD

MIDDLETOWN

WELLMAN

EDISON

ROBERTS

HOBART

JARVIS

HOLLYWOOD

CROSBY

HOBART

MORRIS PARK

MORRIS AV

WEST

BRONXDALE AV

62

VAN

POPLAR

TREMONT

WESTCHESTER SQUARE

BENSON
OVERING

WESTCHESTER AV

COMMERCE

ST PETERS
SEDDON
CEREGA

GLEBE

DORIS

WATERBURY

COMMERCE

ST CEM

65

POLITAN

ODELL

RAYMOND

WESTCHESTER ROAD

METROPOLITAN OVAL

ARCHER RD

CASTLE

UNIONPORT

ZEREGA AV

BRUSH

PK

7

BENEDICT

NEWBOLD

EXPRESSWAY

5B

5A

95

POWELL
HAVILAND
WATSON
PUGSLEY
BLACKROCK
CHATTERTON

ORCHARD

HILL

ELLIS

VIRGINIA

UNDERHILL

LELAND

THIERIOT

GLEASON AV

72

WHITE PLAINS RD

WESTCHESTER

TAYLOR
BEACH

QUIMBY

HERMANY

TURNBULL

LAFAYETTE

73

EAST EMILE

SACKNER EXPWY

278

© Hagstrom Map Company, Inc.

5

6

7

EAST TREMONT

WEST FARMS

CROTONA PARK

CROTONA PARK EAST

BRONX RIVER

MORRISANIA

LONGWOOD

MELROSE

WESTCHESTER

HUNTS POINT

OAK POINT FREIGHT YARD

FOR ADJOINING AREA SEE MAP NO.5

© Hagstrom Map Company, Inc.

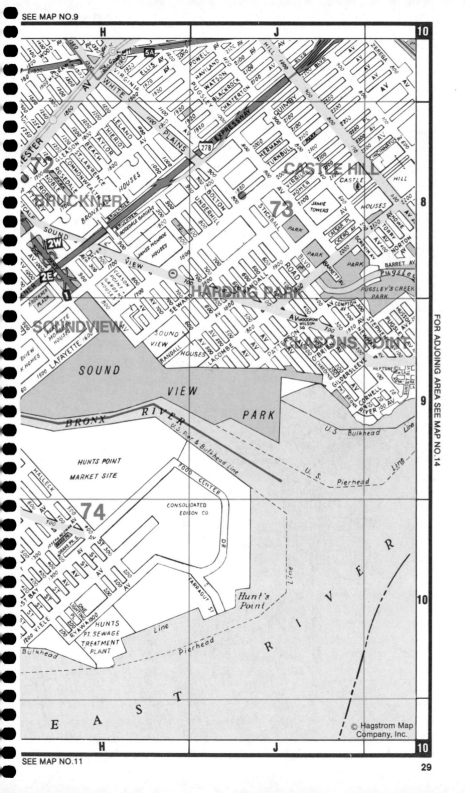

74

OAK POINT
FREIGHT YARD

U.S.

WESTCHESTER AV
MARY'S PARK
MOTT HAVEN

SOUTHERN BLVD
BRUCKNER
ELEVATED
BRUCKNER EXPWY
AMTRAK
CONRAIL
PORT MORRIS STA.

E.151 ST
E.150 ST
E.147 ST
E.146 ST
E.145 ST
E.144 ST
E.143 ST
E.141 ST
E.140 ST
E.138 ST
E.137 ST
E.136 ST
E.135

ST ANN'S AV
CRAINS
BECK AV
BEEKMAN AV
JACKSON AV
CYPRESS AV
WALNUT AV
WILLOW AV
LOCUST AV

PORT MORRIS

NORTH BROTHER ISLAND

U.S. Bulkhead Line
U.S. Pier & Bulkhead Ln.

SOUTH BROTHER ISLAND

U.S. Pier & B

N

MILL BROOK HOUSES
EXPRESSWAY
BROWN PL
BRUCKNER BLVD.
E.133 ST
E.132

HARLEM RIVER INTERMODAL
(PROP.)   RAILYARD
278

BRONX CO.
QUEENS CO.

BRONX KILL
PARK
CONRAIL

TRIBOROUGH BRIDGE

N.Y.C.
Fire Dep't.
Training
Academy

MANHATTAN
QUEENS

BEI

CON - EDISON

Parking
TRIBOROUGH BRIDGE
RANDALL'S ISLAND PK.
RANDALL'S ISLAND
Pool
PED PASS PK
PLAY FIELD
STADIUM
J.J. DOWNING MEMO. STAD.
Parking
Tennis Courts

35

Wards Island
Sewage
Treatment Plant

AMTRAK (Hell Gate line)

18 02
20-02
19-20 ST
20 ST
25-01
19-01
21-02
DITMARS
21
21-02
21-02
DITMARS
5

RALPH DEMARCO PARK

MANHATTAN
PSYCHIATRIC
CENTER

KIRBY-FORENSIC
PSYCHIATRIC
CENTER

MANHATTAN
CHILDREN'S
PSYCHIATRIC
CENTER

TRIBOROUGH BRIDGE
HELLGATE BRIDGE
La Guardia Airport
Marine Air Terminal

AMTRAK
22 RD
22 DR
23 RD
23 DR
23 TER
24-01
23-02
24
CRESCENT
26
29

WARDS
ISLAND
278
PARK

© Hagstrom Map
Company, Inc.

FOR ADJOINING AREA SEE MAP NO.4

55
54
35

11
12
13

F
G

H

J

HUNTS PT.
SEWAGE
TREATMENT
WORKS

Pierhead

Bulkhead

E A S T

R I V E R

TH
HER
ND

PENITENTIARY

& Bulkhead Line

R I K E R ' S   I S L A N D

70

U.S. Pier and Bulkhead Line

FOR ADJOINING AREA SEE MAP NO.16

O.

BRIDGE

RIKERS ISLAND

U. S. Pierhead Line

71

12

ERRIAN'S ISL.

Luyster Creek

SEWAGE
TREATMENT
PLANT

RIKERS

BOWERY

BAY

LAGUAR

MARINE AIR TERMINAL
DELTA SHUTTLE

BERRIAN

BLVD

STEINWAY PL

18-02

19

ST

ST

ST

AV

RD

19.02

AV

51 ST

MED.
OFFICE

LOT 9

LOT
7

MARINE TERMINAL RD

13

PK ST

ST

ST

ST

ST

20-02

40-01

45-01

ST

AV

49 00

ST

ST

RD

DR

AV

50

78

79

77

75

73

BLVD

68 01

5

21-02

33-01

32

5

21-02

21-02

21-02

ST

76 02

75

75

STEINWAY

AV

73

70

75

MARINE TERMINAL

22-02

PK

22-02

82-02

33-01

27-02

40-01

STEINWAY

BLVD

HAZEN

DITMARS

75

4

24-02

24-02

AV

31

29-02

36-01

40-01

AV

NORTH

WHITE OAK CT

PK

23-02

3-02

PW

SOUTH

MICHAEL'S

39

PK

© Hagstrom Map
Company, Inc.

H

J

12

K

L

WESTCHESTER CO
BRONX CO.

HOG ISLAND

PELHAM WOODS

PARK LA ROOSEVELT LA

CAT BRIAR

P E L H A M

HUNTER ISL

PICNIC GROVE

2

TWIN ISLAND

ENVIRONM. CENTER

CONRAIL — AMTRAK

PELHAM BAY GOLF COURSE

B A Y

Lagoon

PELHAM BRIDGE

SHORE RD

PARKING
64

ORCHARD BEACH

SHORE RD

BARTOW-PELL MANSION AND MUSEUM

PARK DR

3

PARK

THOMAS PELL WILDLIFE REFUGE & SANCTUARY

STABLE

PICNIC PLAY AREA

C I T Y   I S L A N D

RD

CITY I. BRIDGE

GOOSE ISL

Turtle Cove

PARKING

ELGAR PARK

75

RODMAN'S NECK
NYC POLICE DEPT
FIRING RANGE

4

U. S.

E A S T -

C H E S T E R

B A Y

N

65

U. S.

Pierhead

8B

BRUCKNER

P E L H A M

WAR MEMORIAL

B A Y   P K.

Bulkhead

© Hagstrom Map Company, Inc.

12

K

L

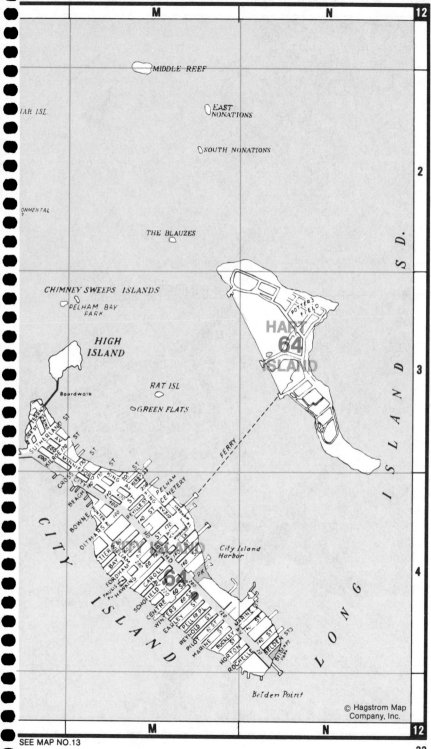

MIDDLE REEF

EAST NONATIONS

SOUTH NONATIONS

THE BLAUZES

CHIMNEY SWEEPS ISLANDS

PELHAM BAY PARK

HIGH ISLAND

RAT ISL

GREEN FLATS

Boardwalk

POTTER'S FIELD

HART 64 ISLAND

S D.

I S L A N D

FERRY

CITY ISLAND

City Island Harbor

CITY ISLAND 64

L O N G

Belden Point

SEE MAP NO.13

13 K L

PELHAM BAY PARK

WAR MEMORIAL

PICNIC AREA

CUBAN LEDGE

N

BRUCKNER

I-95

SPENCER ESTATES

PELHAM BAY

5

WESTCHESTER

MIDDLETOWN

61

COUNTRY CLUB

WATERBURY CLUB

THROGS NECK EXPRESSWAY

EASTCHESTER BAY

6

I-695

SCHUYLERVILLE

EAST

ST. RAYMOND'S CEMETERY

7C

TREMONT

65

UNIONPORT

62

I-295 CROSS BRONX EXPRESSWY

THROG'S NECK HOUSES

63

7

ST. RAYMOND'S CEMETERY

FERRY POINT PARK

HUTCHINSON

72

73

CASTLE HILL

BRONX RIVER

© Hagstrom Map Company, Inc.

13 K L

M   N   13

CITY ISLAND

L. I. S.

Belden Point

BIG TOM

L O N G   I S L A N D   S D.

5

6

Weir Creek

SOUND VIEW

EDGEWATER PARK

Locust Point

PARK

I 295

THROGS NECK BRIDGE (TOLL)

THROGS NECK EXPWY

LOCUST POINT DR

LONGSTREET AV

65

THROGS NECK BLVD

KEARNEY AV

HOLLYWOOD AV

LOGAN AV

SCHURZ AV

PHILIP AV

INDIAN

STATE UNIVERSITY OF NEW YORK MARITIME COLLEGE

PARK

Line

Pierhead

Bulkhead

U.S.

MARINA DR

THROGS NECK

7

BRONX CO.
QUEENS CO.

Line

© Hagstrom Map Company, Inc.

M   N   13

FOR ADJOINING AREA

FOR ADJOINING AREA SEE MAP NO.10

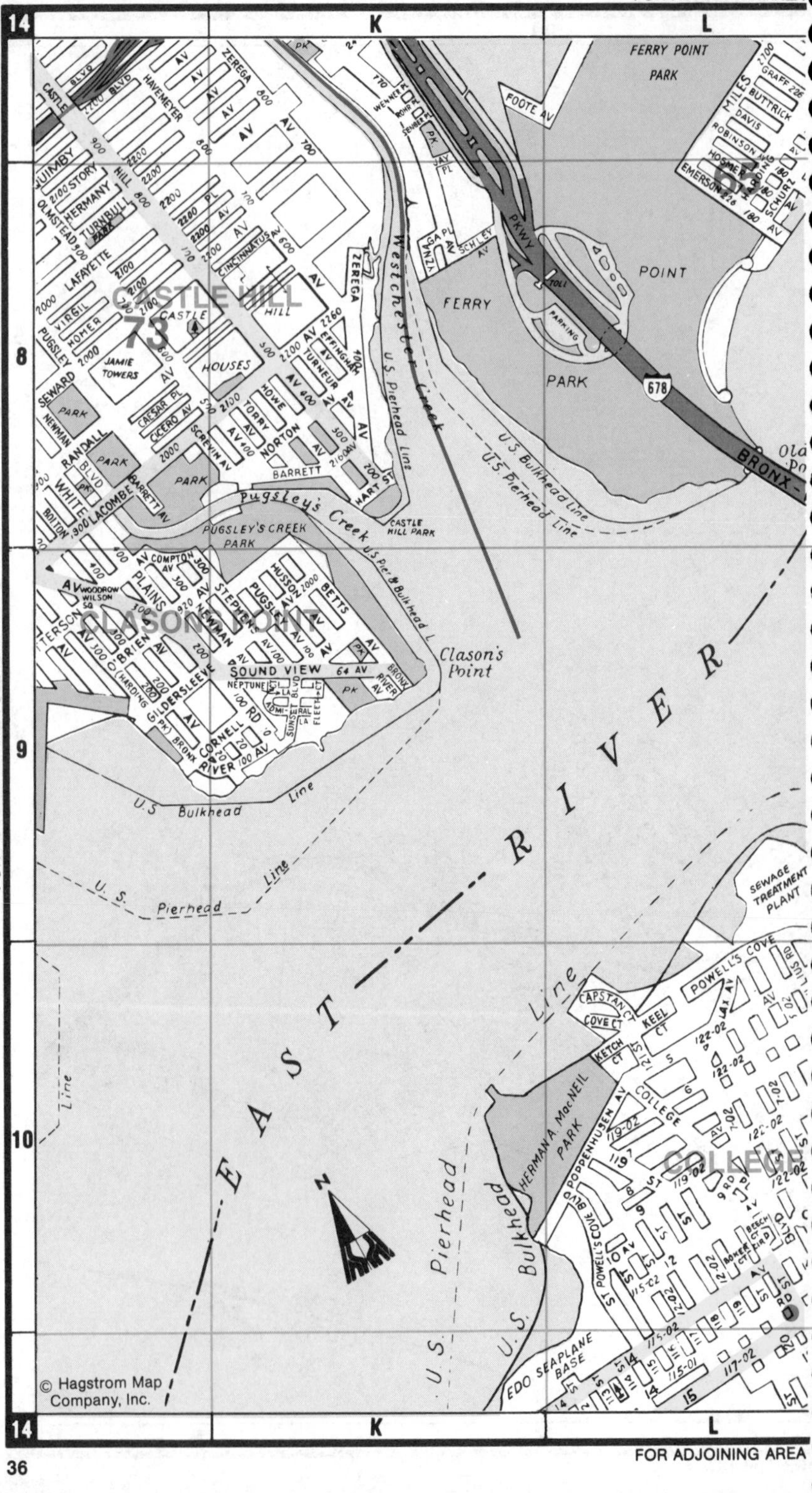

FOR ADJOINING AREA

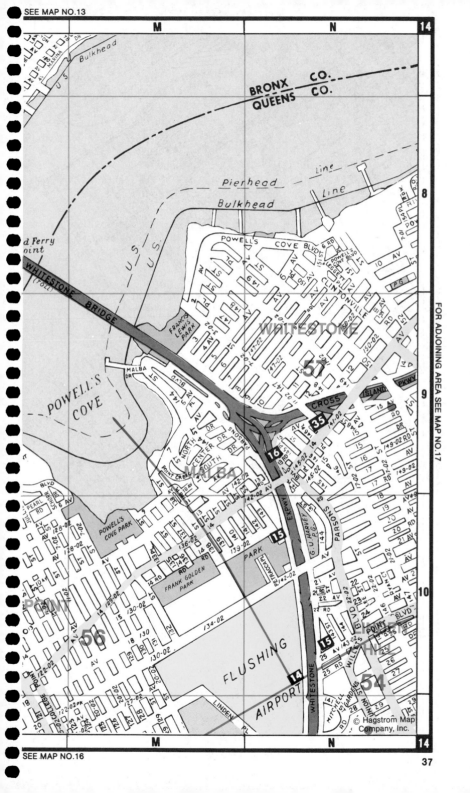

© Hagstrom Map Company, Inc.

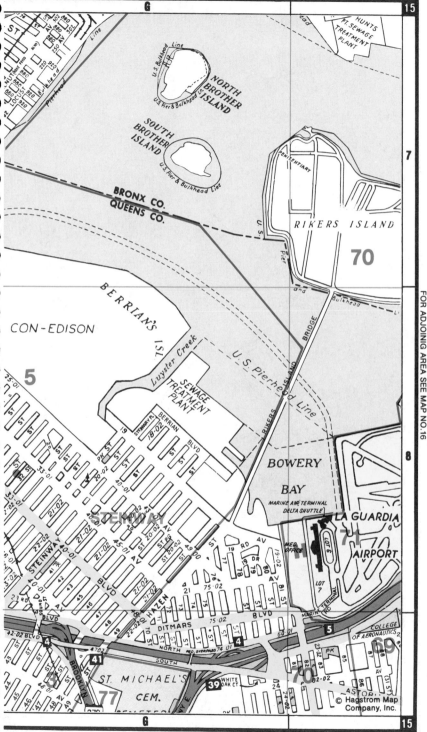

© Hagstrom Map Company, Inc.

16 H J

7

RIKERS ISLAND 70

EAST

HUNTS PT. SEWAGE TREATMENT PLANT

FARRAGUT ST

Hunt's Point

Pierhead Line

Pierhead Line

HERMAN A. PA

EDO SEAPLANE BASE

U.S. Pierhead

U.S. Bulkhead

ST POWELLS COVE BLVD

8

N

LAGUARDIA AIRPORT

FLUSHING

CENTRAL BLDG
AMERICAN
UNITED
TWA/CONTINENTAL
AMERICA WEST

LOT 1
LOT 2
LOT 3

US AIR

US AIR SHUTTLE

DELTA/NORTHWEST LOT 5

BAY

GRAND

94 ST

7

DITMARS BLVD 6

COLLEGE OF AERONAUTICS 23

PARK

JACKSON MILL RD

DITMARS

CENTRAL

PED OVERPASS

PRWY

69

ASTORIA

© Hagstrom Map Company, Inc.

16 H J

K

16

R I V E R

Line

BRONX - WHITESTONE BRIDGE
(TOLL)
Ferry Point

U.S.
U.S.

678

7

POWELL'S COVE

SEWAGE TREATMENT PLANT

FRANCIS LEWIS PARK

MALBA

MALBA DR

POWELL'S COVE

CAPSTAN CT
KETCH CT
KEEL CT

MacNEIL PARK

PENHUSEN AV

POWELL'S COVE

JULIUS RD
PEARL RD
SCHORR DR
BLVD
LA PZ AV

POWELL'S COVE PARK

COLLEGE POINT

NORTH DR
SOUTH DR
POINT CRESC

57

56

16

FRANK GOLDEN PARK

PETRACCA PL

PARK

PARSONS

EXPWY

G.U. HARVEY
P.G.

15

FLUSHING AIRPORT

WHITESTONE

WILLETS

BLVD

LEE ST

PARSONS

14

15

14

COLLEGE POINT

COLLEGE POINT

GRAHAM CT

LINDEN

COLLEGE POINT

MITCHELL
GARDENS

LINDEN HILL

INDUSTRIAL PARK

678

54

UNION

PARSONS

NORTH

HIGGINS

BARRINGTON

LEVITTS ATHLETIC FIELD

PRINCE ST
LATIMER PL
LINEAUS PL
CARLTON
LEAVITT
COLLINS ST

FLUSHING HOSP MED CENTER (N DIV)

8

WORLD'S FAIR MARINA

13

© Hagstrom Map Company, Inc.

K

16

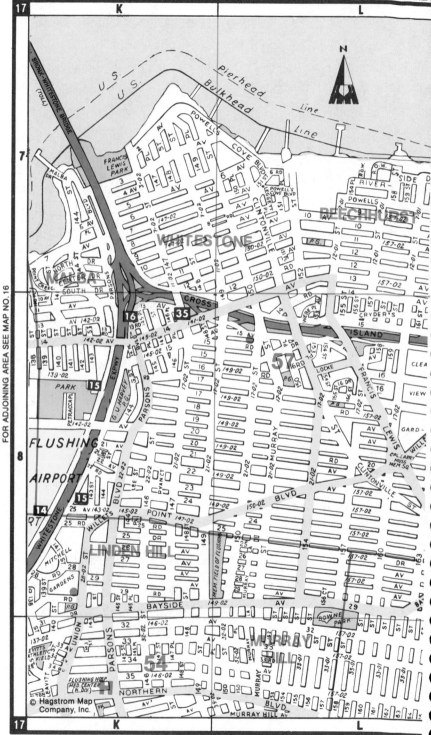

FOR ADJOINING AREA SEE MAP NO.16

FOR ADJOINING AREA SEEMAP NO. 21

© Hagstrom Map Company, Inc.

M

17

1 WILLETS ST
2 LITTLE BAY RD
3 CIRCLE DRIVE
4 BAYSIDE ST
5 CHAPEL RD
6 ABBOT RD
7 NORTH LOOP
8 LEE RD
9 ORDNANCE RD
10 SHORE RD
11 WHISTLER AV
12 WALTER REED RD
13 JARMAN RD
14 SYLVESTER LA
15 MURRAY AV
16 WEAVER AV
17 OFFICER'S DR
18 UNDERHILL RD
19 STORY AV
20 SPILLER RD
21 WESTAWAY RD
22 PRATT AV
23 EAST LOOP
24 RED CROSS LA
25 THEATER RD
26 DUANE RD
27 BOUNDARY RD
28 SGT. BEERS AV
29 SGT. BEERS LA
30 GEN. R.W. BERRY RD

1. BRIAN CRESCENT
2. EMILY RD
3. ROBIN LA
4. LORI DR
5. ESTATES LA
6. MELISSA CT
7. DARREN DR
8. DIANE PL
9. ROBERT RD
10. MICHAEL CT
11. MICHAEL PL
12. ESTATES DR
13. BONNIE LA
14. JORDAN DR
15. JORDAN CT

Willets Point

FORT TOTTEN

7

L I T T L E   B A Y

PARADE GROUND

THROGS NECK (TOLL) BRIDGE

295

COVE BLVD

LITTLE BAY PARK

33

32

CROSS

CLEARVIEW PARK

CLEARVIEW GOLF COURSE

32

34

BAY TERRACE

BELL

ISLAND PKWY

60

BAY TERRACE SHOPPING CENTER

UTOPIA

CLEARVIEW

CORP KENNEDY

BAY CLUB DR

PG

6B

BAYSIDE H.S.

PL PARK BAYSIDE ATHLET FIELD

PK

58

6A

51

BAYSIDE

© Hagstrom Map Company, Inc.

M

17

FOR ADJOINING AREA SEE MAP NO.18

8

18   M   N

1 WILLETS ST.
2 LITTLE BAY RD.
3 CIRCLE DRIVE
4 BAYSIDE ST.
5 CHAPEL RD.
6 ABBOT RD.
7 NORTH LOOP
8 LEE RD.
9 ORDNANCE RD.
10 SHORE RD.
11 WHISTLER AV.
12 WALTER REED RD.
13 JARMAN RD.
14 SYLVESTER LA.
15 MURRAY AV.
16 WEAVER AV.
17 OFFICER'S DR.
18 UNDERHILL RD.
19 STORY AV.
20 SPILLER RD.
21 WESTAWAY RD.
22 PRATT AV.
23 EAST LOOP
24 RED CROSS LA.
25 THEATER RD.
26 DUANE RD.
27 BOUNDARY RD.
28 SGT. BEERS AV.
29 SGT. BEERS LA.
30 GEN. R.W. BERRY RD.

N

FORT TOTTEN

PARADE GROUND

TOWN OF NORTH HEMPSTEAD

SADDLE ROCK

GREAT

L I T T L E

N E C K

B A Y

NASSAU CO.
QUEENS CO.

FOR ADJOINING AREA SEE MAP NO.17

CROSS ISLAND

WATER EDGE DR.
LITTLE NECK

60

BELL

LITTLE NECK PKWY

ST. MARYS HOSP. FOR CHILDREN

DOUGLAS MANOR

BAYVIEW
KENMORE
KNOLLWOOD
RICHMOND
WARWICK
GROSVENOR
BEVERLY
WESTMORELAND PL.
MANOR
HOLLYWOOD
ARLEIGH
PARK
RIDGE
ALSTON PL.
MELROSE

63

JOHN GOLDEN PARK

CROCHERON PARK

237-02

DEPEW AV

CORBETT RD.

61

BAYSIDE

DOUGLASTON

DOUGLASTON ST.

© Hagstrom Map Company, Inc.

PARK

18   M   N

44

GREAT NECK ESTATES

KENSINGTON

THOMASTON

GREAT NECK PLAZA

GREAT NECK STA.

RUSSELL GARDENS

UNIVERSITY GARDENS

LITTLE NECK STA.

LITTLE NECK

FOR ADJOINING AREA SEE NASSAU COUNTY ATLAS

FOR ADJOINING AREA SEE MAP NO. 23

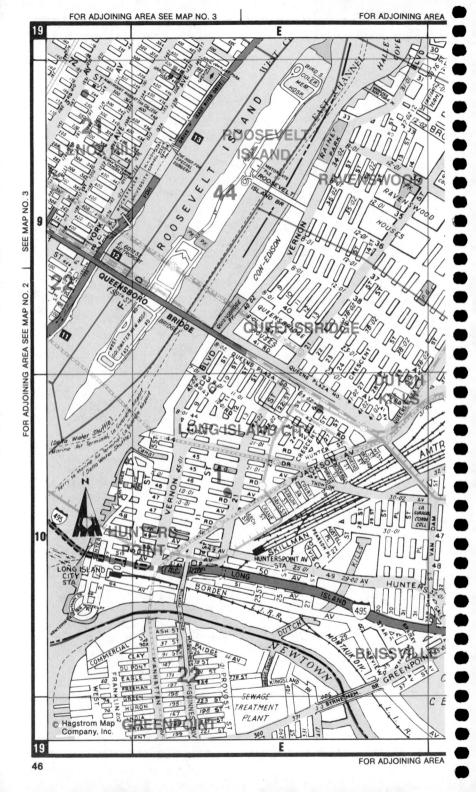

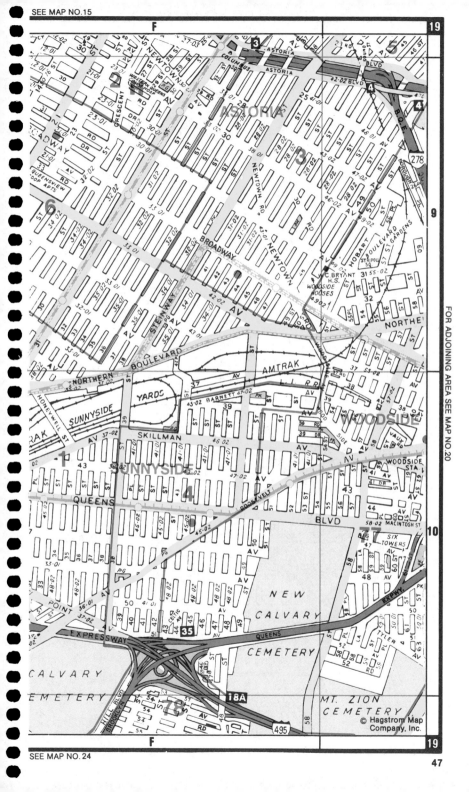

ASTORIA BLVD

HAZEN ST

DITMARS BLVD

NORTH

SOUTH

ST. MICHAEL'S CEMETERY

WHITE OAK CT

278

BROOKLYN QUEENS EXPWY

HOBART

BOULEVARD

STRIPOLI SQ

W.C. BRYANT H.S.

WOODSIDE HOUSES

NORTHERN

BROADWAY

WOODSIDE

ROOSEVELT

JACKSON HEIGHTS

ELMHURST HOSP CENTER

WOODSIDE STA

MACINTOSH ST

SIX TOWERS

QUEENS

EXPRESSWAY

OVERPASS

LAUREL HILL BLVD

NEW

CALVARY

BKLYN-QUEENS

CEM

GARFIELD

HENRY ST

CALAMUS

KNEELAND

CONRAIL

MT. ZION CEMETERY

RIDGEWOOD GARDENS

MAURICE

© Hagstrom Map Company, Inc.

H   J   20

FOR ADJOINING AREA SEE MAP NO.21

COLLEGE OF AERONAUTICS

69

EAST ELMHURST

ASTORIA

HEIGHTS

25A

OTTMARS AV

GRAND CENTRAL PARKWAY

PED OVERPASS

8

9

BLVD

JUNCTION BLVD

ELMHURST AV

WARREN AV

68

CORONA

NICOLLS

ALSTYNE AV

L.I.R.R.

CORONA

73

ELMHURST

JAMES

BROADWAY

QUEENS BLVD

JUSTICE AV

QUEENS CENTER

PARKING FIELD

ST. JOHN'S HOSP.

QUEENS

LEFRAK CITY

20

LONG ISLAND JCT

HORACE HARDING DR

74

SAUNDERS

BOOTH

BLVD

REGO PARK

9

10

20

© Hagstrom Map Company, Inc.

19

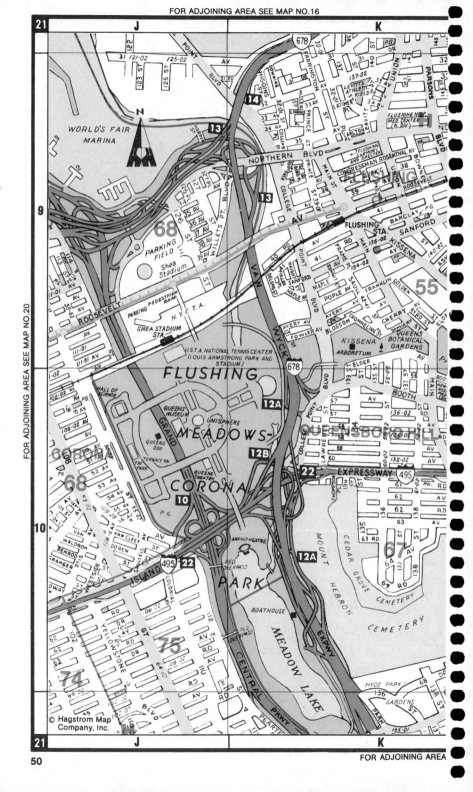

© Hagstrom Map Company, Inc.

L

21

BAYSIDE

MURRAY HILL

54

58

NORTHERN

MURRAY HILL STA.

25A

ROOSEVELT

BOWNE PARK

CROCHERON

DEPOT STATION

BROADWAY STA.

DEPOT STATION

NORTHERN BLVD

9

ASH AV

BEECH

CHERRY

DELAWARE

ELM

HAWTHORNE

HOLLYWOOD AV

FLUSHING HOSP. MED CENTER

GEORGIA

JASMINE

KALMIA

LABURNUM

OAK

FLUSHING CEMETERY

PIDGEON

MEADOW

AUBURNDALE

ASHBY

BOGLEY

COURTH

47 AV

EFFING

FAIRCHI

GLADWI

CORRIDOR

KISSENA L

KISSENA PARK

LITHONIA

METCALF

UNDERHILL

PECK

50 PL

BICYCLE TRACK

MEMORIAL

160-02

KISSENA PARK - GOLF COURSE

HIGH SCHOOL

23

160-02 AV

ST. MARY'S CEMETERY

24

LONG

REEVES

ISLAND EXPWY

10

QUEENS COLLEGE C.U.N.Y.

GRAVETT RD

MELBOURNE

67

GEORGETOWN

MEWS

POMONOK

POMONOK HOUSING

ELECTCHESTER HOUSES

65

VAN ARSDALE Jr.

AGUILAR

PARSONS

© Hagstrom Map Company, Inc.

L

21

22 L M

FOR ADJOINING AREA SEE MAP NO. 21

58

6A

CROCHERON

BROADWAY STA.
NORTHERN BLVD

AUBURNDALE STA.

AUBURNDALE

NORTHERN

FLUSHING CEMETERY

KISSENA PARK

LITHONIA
METCALF

KISSENA PARK - GOLF COURSE

BOOTH MEMORIAL

HIGH SCHOOL

ST. MARY'S CEMETERY

65

POMONOK

HARRY VAN ARSDALE Jr.

25

26

22

FRESH MEADOWS

66

© Hagstrom Map Company, Inc

22 L M

FOR ADJOINING AREA SEE MAP NO.18

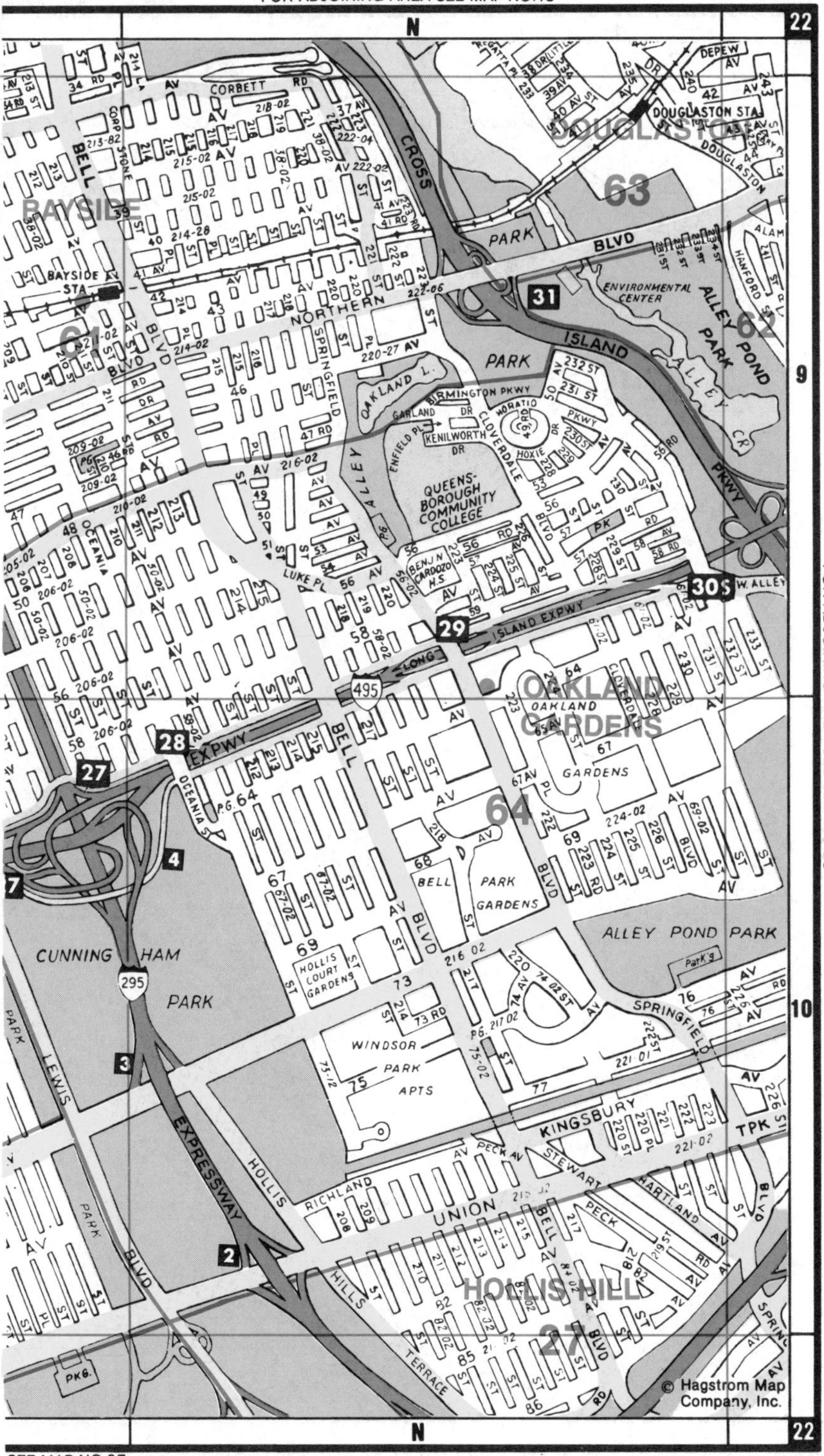

FOR ADJOINING AREA SEE MAP NO.23

SEE MAP NO.27

© Hagstrom Map Company, Inc.

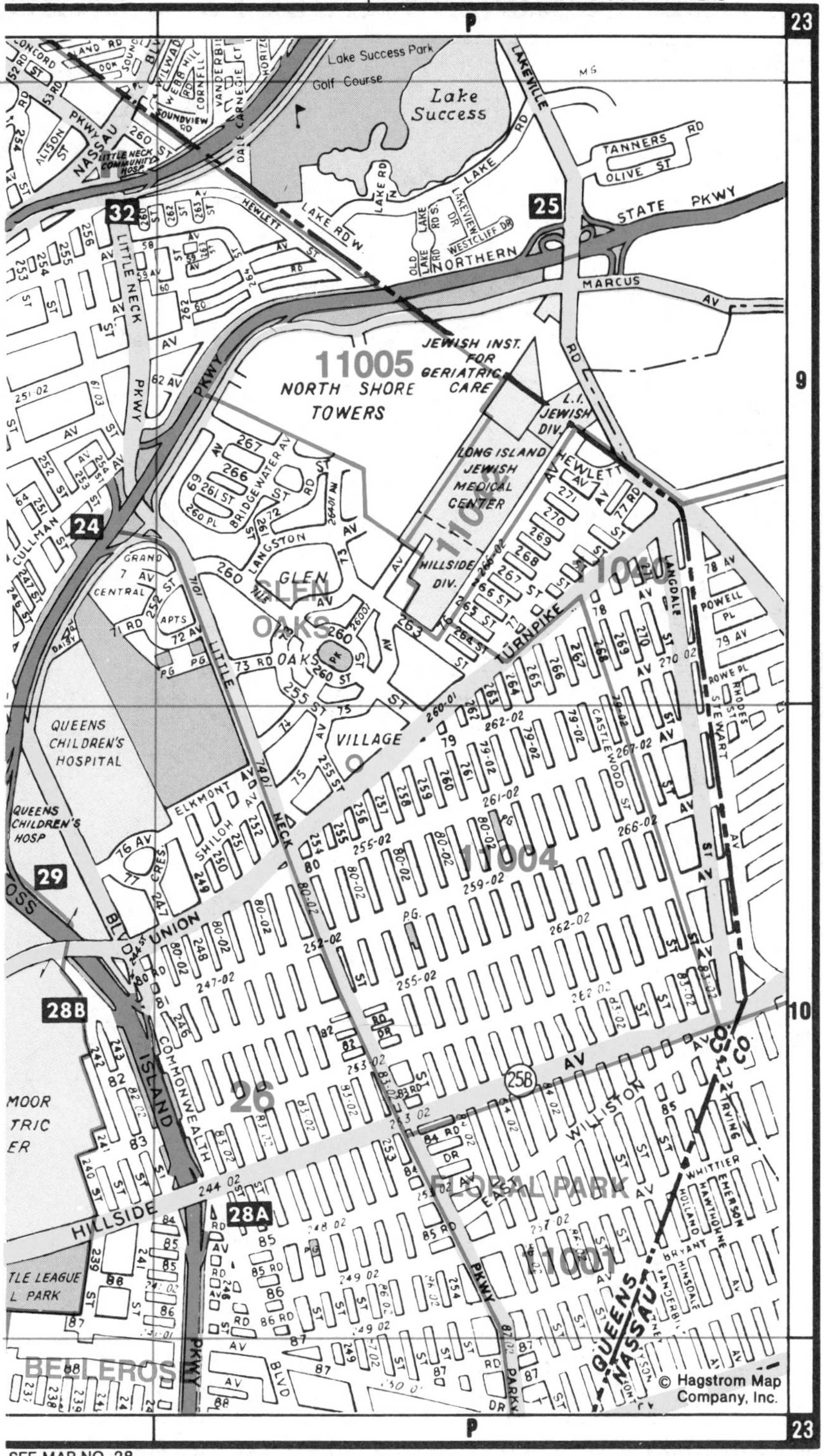

Lake Success Park
Golf Course

Lake
Success

Lake Success

TANNERS RD
OLIVE ST

STATE PKWY

NORTHERN

MARCUS AV

11005
NORTH SHORE TOWERS

JEWISH INST. FOR GERIATRIC CARE

L.I. JEWISH DIV.

LONG ISLAND JEWISH MEDICAL CENTER

HILLSIDE DIV.

HEWLETT

11040

GLEN OAKS

VILLAGE

QUEENS CHILDREN'S HOSPITAL

QUEENS CHILDREN'S HOSP

11004

CASTLEWOOD AV

26

MOOR TRIC ER

FLORAL PARK

11001

HILLSIDE

WHITTIER
EMERSON
HAWTHORNE

LITTLE LEAGUE L PARK

QUEENS
NASSAU

BELLEROS

© Hagstrom Map Company, Inc.

FOR ADJOINING AREA SEE MAP NO.40

FOR ADJOINING AREA SEE MAP NO.42

© Hagstrom Map Company, Inc.

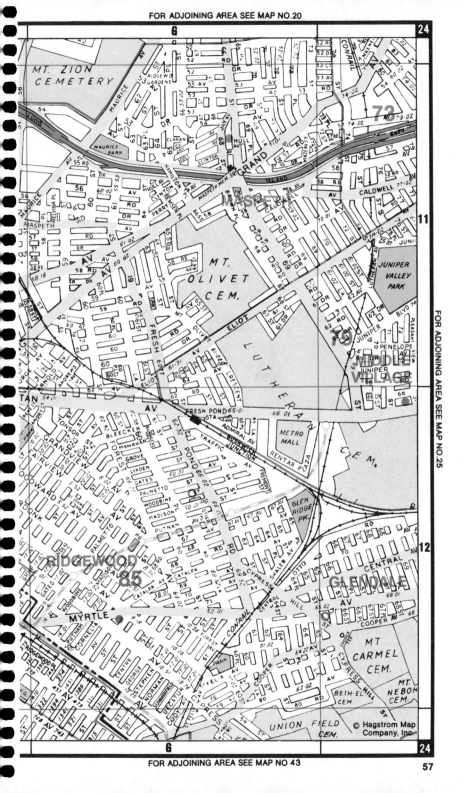

© Hagstrom Map Company, Inc.

© Hagstrom Map Company, Inc.

J

25

REGO PARK
74

75

11

WOODHAVEN

QUEENS

ST. JOHN'S CEMETERY

BOULEVARD

YELLOWSTONE

FOREST HILLS STADIUM

FOREST HILLS

FOREST HI. STA.

LA GUARDIA HOSP.

BURNS
CLYDE
DARTMOUTH
EXETER
FLEET
GROTON
HARROW
INGRAM
JUNO
KESSEL
LOUBET
MANSE
NAMSEN
OLCOTT

CONTINENTAL (71 AV)

85

AUBREY AV
DORAN
RUTLEDGE

SYBILLA
URSULA

TPK

MYRTLE

INTERBOROUGH

UNION

WOODHAVEN

PARK

18

12

PKWY

LEBANON CEMETERY

FOR EST PARK

FOREST PARK GOLF COURSE

VICTORY FIELD

TWIN FIELD

5

4

21

WOODHAVEN

JAMAICA

© Hagstrom Map Company, Inc.

J

25

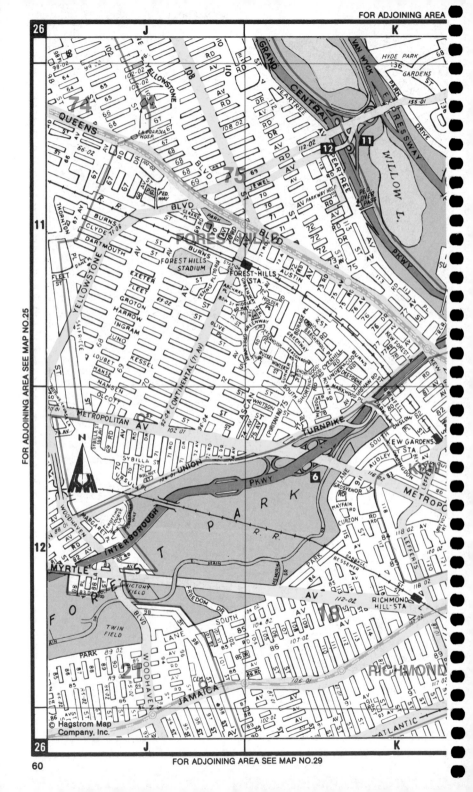

© Hagstrom Map Company, Inc.

L

26

65

66
HILLCREST

67

11

678

VAN WYCK

IND.
SUBWAY
YARD

10

14

13

UNION

CHARTER

VILLAGE RD PVT.

GRAND CENTRAL

15

16

St. JOSEPH'S HOSP.

GOETHALS
Queens
HOSPITAL
CENTER

PKWY

JAMAICA
HILLS

COOLIDGE
HOOVER
HOOVER

BORO
HALL

QUEENS

9

PERSHING

PLAIN

MANTON

BURDEN

BRIARWOOD

82

PARSONS

MAPLE
GROVE
CEMETERY

JAMES J.
CREEGAN

8

7

NEW GARDENS

GARDENS

HILLSIDE

WESTBRIDGE

18

L.I.R.R. YARDS

L.I.R.R.

EXPRESSWAY

6

JAMAICA
HOSPITAL

STA.

JAMAICA

ARCHER

JAMAICA STA.

35

ALLENDALE
WALTHAM
BRISBIN
CRESSHILL
SANDERS
LIVERPOOL

33

GUNZBERG

5

REMINGTON

ATLANTIC

P.G.

LLOYD RD

LIBERTY

PRINCE

YORK
COLLEGE

BEAVER

12

GRACE CEM.

MARY
IMMACULATE
HOSP.

RUFUS KING AV
KINGPARK
KING PARK

BURDETTE PL

SUTPHIN

© Hagstrom Map
Company, Inc.

L

26

27 L M

N

65

66

UTOPIA PKWY.

TURNPIKE

ST. JOHNS UNIVERSITY

UNION

U.S. ARMY RESERVE

CENTRAL

JAMAICA ESTATES

17 18

GRAND

CHARLECOTE

CROYDON

KENDRICK PL

DEVONSHIRE RD

IMMAC. CONC. MONAST.

DALNY

HILLSIDE

EGERTON

MIDLAND

RADNOR

CHEVY

PERTH

TUDOR

ABERDEEN

AVON

ST. JOSEPH'S HOSP.

GOETHALS

QUEENS HOSPITAL CENTER

JAMAICA HILLS

82

CHAPIN PKWY

GOTHIC

HIGHLAND

HILLSIDE

BRIARWOOD

PARSONS

PK.

MERRICK

BUS TERM.

88

89

90

93

LIBERTY PARK

12

SUTPHIN

JAMAICA

JAMAICA STA.

YORK COLLEGE

GRACE CEM.

RUFUS KING PARK

ARCHER

DOUGLAS

LIBERTY

MERRICK

39

GUNZBERG RD

SOUTH

BREWER

JAMAICA HOUSES

MARCONI MEM. FIELD

SUTPHIN

LIBERTY

BLVD

13

© Hagstrom Map Company, Inc.

27 L M

FOR ADJOINING AREA SEE MAP NO.28

© Hagstrom Map
Company, Inc.

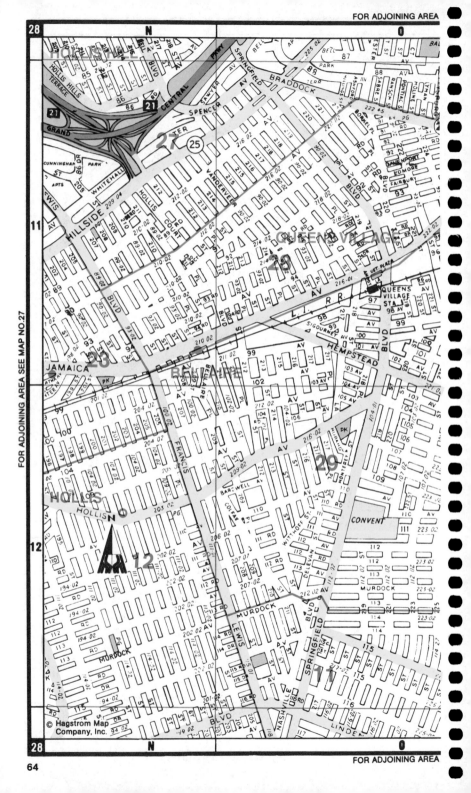

FOR ADJOINING AREA SEE MAP NO.27

© Hagstrom Map Company, Inc.

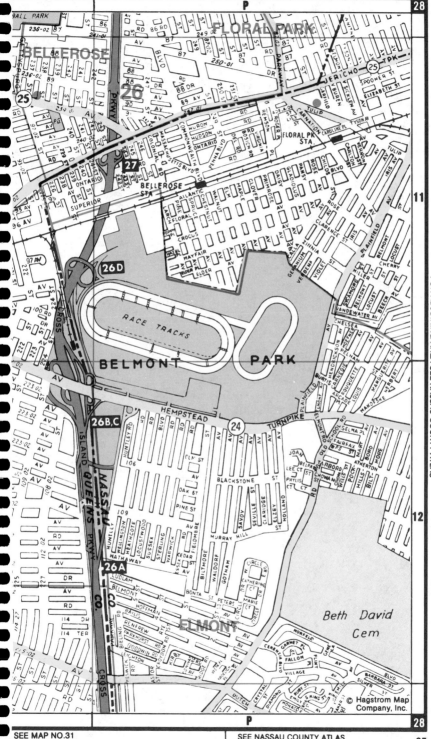

BELLEROSE

FLORAL PARK

BELMONT PARK

RACE TRACKS

ELMONT

Beth David Cem

© Hagstrom Map Company, Inc.

29 H J

CYPRESS HILLS

CEMETERY

MT. HOPE CEM.

SALEM FIELD CEM

CYPRESS HILLS

JAMAICA

WOODHAVEN

21

HIGHLAND PARK

8

13

FULTON

L.I.R.R.

ATLANTIC

ROCKAWAY

LIBERTY

GLENMORE AV

PITKIN

ACACIA CEM

BAYSIDE CEM

SUTTER

CITY LINE

PITKIN

SUTTER

NYCT PITKIN SUBWAY YARD

N. CONDUIT

S. CONDUIT

SO. CONDUIT

FORBELL

LINDEN PITKIN HOUSES

133

EAST NEW YORK

CYPRESS HILLS P.G.

HOUSING

BLAKE

DUMONT AV

LOUIS H. PINK

DUMONT

MEDICAL

BLVD

27

8

NEW LOTS

LORING

HOUSING

STANLEY

STANLEY P.G.

HEMLOCK

AUTUMN LA

WORTMAN

U.S. P.O.

WORTMAN

N

149

151

153

155

156

157

158

FLATLANDS AV

COZINE

© Hagstrom Map Company, Inc.

29 H J

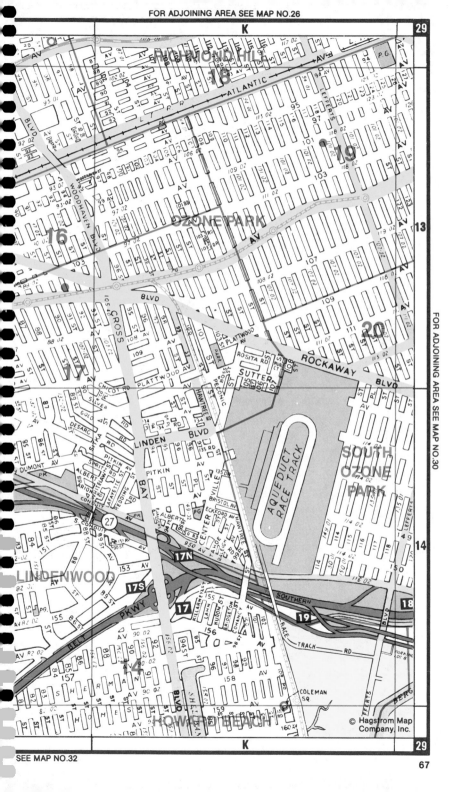

© Hagstrom Map Company, Inc.

30 K L

ATLANTIC AV

19

OZONE PARK

LIBERTY AV

13

SOUTH JAMAICA

35

678

ROCKAWAY

LINDEN BLVD

20

SOUTH OZONE PARK

AQUEDUCT RACE TRACK

N

14

SUTTER AV

18

NORTH BELT PARKWAY

SOUTHERN

19

18B

27

CONDUIT

RACE

TRACK RD

NASSAU

157 AV

158 AV

159 AV

14

COLEMAN SQ

BERGEN BASIN

BERGEN RD

30

VISCOUNT HOTEL

678

CARGO

© Hagstrom Map Company, Inc.

30 K L

© Hagstrom Map Company, Inc.

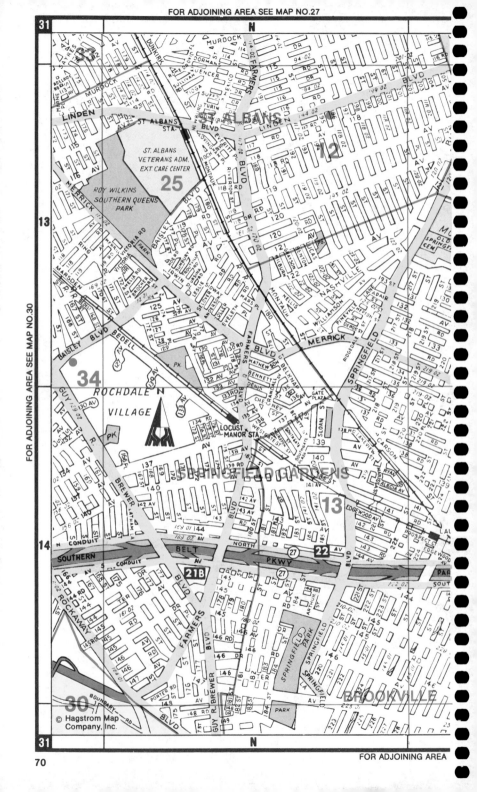

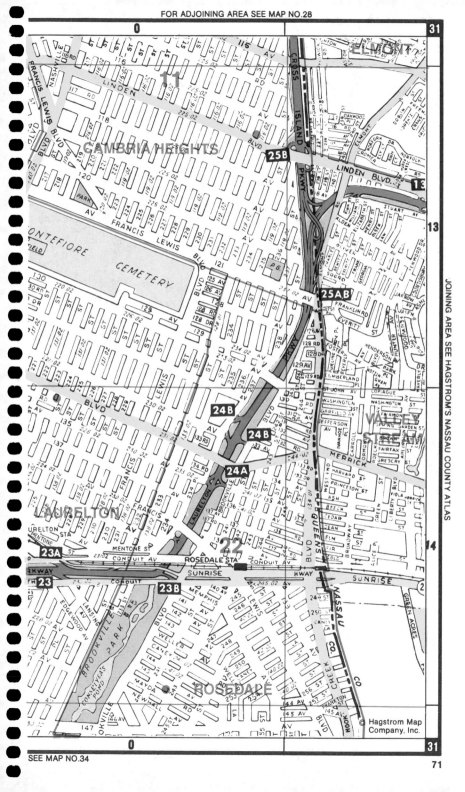

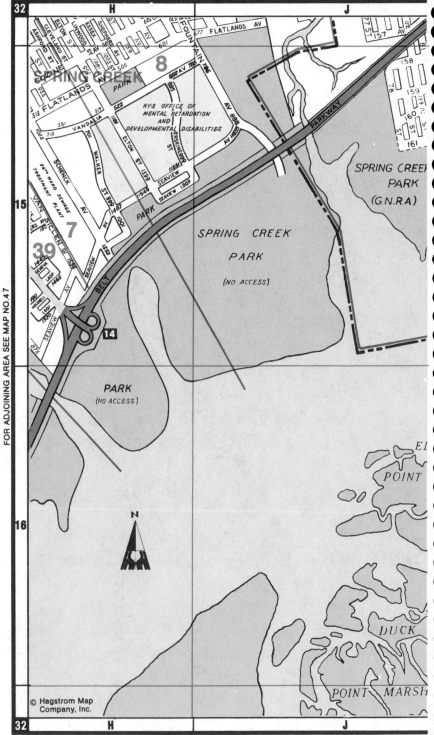

FOR ADJOINING AREA SEE MAP NO.47

SPRING CREEK

8

FLATLANDS AV

FLATLANDS

VANDALIA

NYS OFFICE OF
MENTAL RETARDATION
AND
DEVELOPMENTAL DISABILITIES

SCHENCK

WALKER

ELTON ST

SEAVIEW
SEAVIEW LOOP

26TH WARD SEWAGE
TREATMENT PLANT

VAN CLEN AV

7

39

HOWELL

SEAVIEW

BELT

PARK

14

PARKWAY

157

158

159

160

161

SPRING CREEK
PARK
(G.N.R.A)

SPRING CREEK
PARK
(NO ACCESS)

PARK
(NO ACCESS)

N

ELD
POINT

DUCK

POINT MARSH

© Hagstrom Map
Company, Inc.

K

32

158

COLEMAN SQ

159

160 AV

RUSSELL ST

HOWARD BEACH
14

CROSS

SHELLBANK

BAY BASIN

AV

161

161.02

162

162.02

163

164

165

165 AV

30

15

157

BRI 1ST
BAULT
DAVENPORT ST
163 DR
164 AV
164 RD
164 DR
HAWTREE

162

163

164

165

FRANK
M. CHARLES
MEMORIAL
PARK

PARK

BASIN

(G.N.R.A.)

(G.N.R.A)

BLVD

AV

G R A S S Y B A Y

CONGRESSMAN

JOSEPH P ADDABBO
BRIDGE

LEFFERTS

BRIDGE

LDERS

MARSH

PUMPKIN PATCH
MARSH

34

PUMPKIN PATCH CHANNEL

CROSS

BAY

BLACK

BANK

MARSH

BAR

HASSOCK

East
Pond

WILDLIFE REFUGE

BLVD

16

32

HES

K

© Hagstrom Map
Company, Inc.

© Hagstrom Map Company, Inc.

FOR ADJOINING AREA SEE MAP NO.33

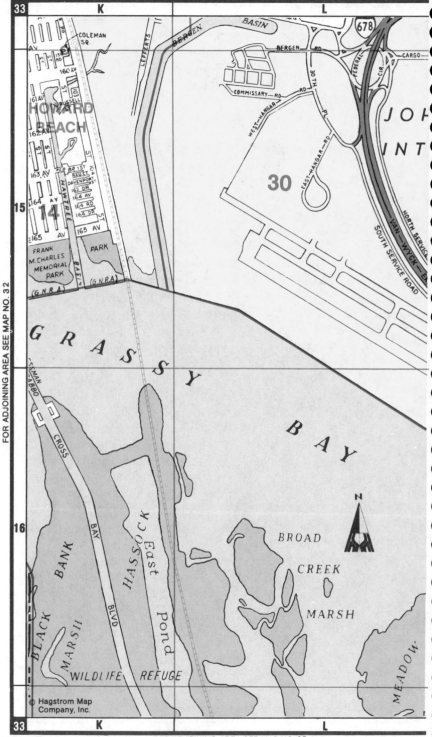

33

K

L

678

COLEMAN SQ.

AV

160 AV

BERGEN

BASIN

BERGEN RD.

CARGO

FEDERAL CIR.

COMMISSARY RD.

30TH

161AV

RUSSELL

HOWARD BEACH

162 AV

WEST-HANGAR-RD

RD.

J O H

I N T

163 AV

163 DR

DAVENPORT

164 AV

164 RD

30

EAST-HANGAR-RD.

164 DR

15

14

165

165 AV

NORTH SERVICE

SOUTH SERVICE ROAD

VAN WYCK

FRANK M.CHARLES MEMORIAL PARK

PARK

(G.N.R.A.)

(G.N.R.A.)

G R A S S Y

B A Y

CROSS BAY BLVD

16

BROAD

N

BLACK BANK MARSH

HASSOCK

East Pond

CREEK

MARSH

MEADOW

WILDLIFE REFUGE

© Hagstrom Map Company, Inc.

33

K

L

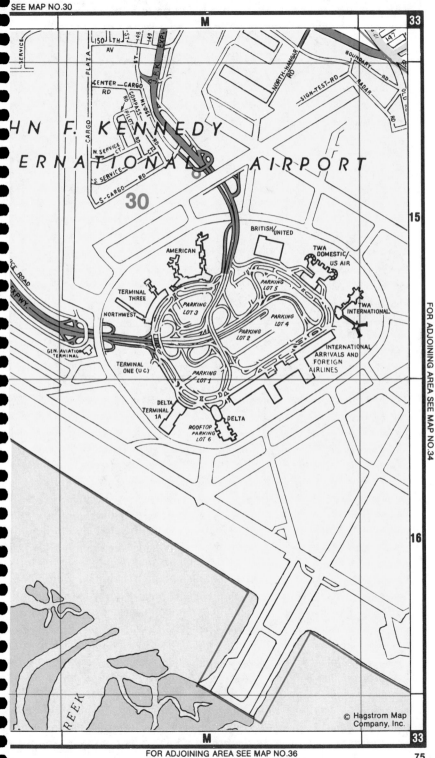

JOHN F. KENNEDY INTERNATIONAL AIRPORT

30

150 TH AV
148 ST
149 ST
147

PLAZA
J.E.K. EXPWY
BOUNDARY RD
OLD RD
RADAR RD

CENTER RD
CARGO RD
COMPASS RD
PILOT RD
N. SERVICE CT.
S. SERVICE CT.
S-CARGO RD
N. SERVICE RD
S SERVICE RD
NORTH-HANGAR RD
SIGN-TEST-RD

CARGO

BRITISH/UNITED

AMERICAN

TWA DOMESTIC/US AIR

TERMINAL THREE

PARKING LOT 3

PARKING LOT 5

TWA INTERNATIONAL

NORTHWEST

PARKING LOT 4

PARKING LOT 2

GEN. AVIATION TERMINAL

TERMINAL ONE (U.C.)

PARKING LOT 1

INTERNATIONAL ARRIVALS AND FOREIGN AIRLINES

DELTA TERMINAL 1A

DELTA

ROOFTOP PARKING LOT 6

SERVICE ROAD

CREEK

15

16

33

33

FOR ADJOINING AREA SEE MAP NO.34

34

878

34

BROOKVILLE

13

BOUNDARY RD

RADAR RD

OLD ROCKAWAY BLVD

PORTER RD

ROCKAWAY

GUY R BREWER

SPRINGFIELD AV

LA

PARK

147 AV

148 AV

148 RD

175 ST

149

150 AV

182 ST

183 ST

150 DR

151 DR

223

148 AV

149 AV

JOHN F.

15

BROOKVILLE

PARK

BLVD

THURSTON

TWA DOMESTIC US AIR

KENNEDY

TWA INTERNATIONAL

INTERNATIONAL ARRIVALS AND FOREIGN AIRLINES

30

INTERNATIONAL

AIRPORT

N

16

HEAD OF BA

TOWN OF HEMPSTEAD

TOWN OF HEMPSTEAD

93

91

INWOOD COUNTRY CLUB

© Hagstrom Map Company, Inc.

34

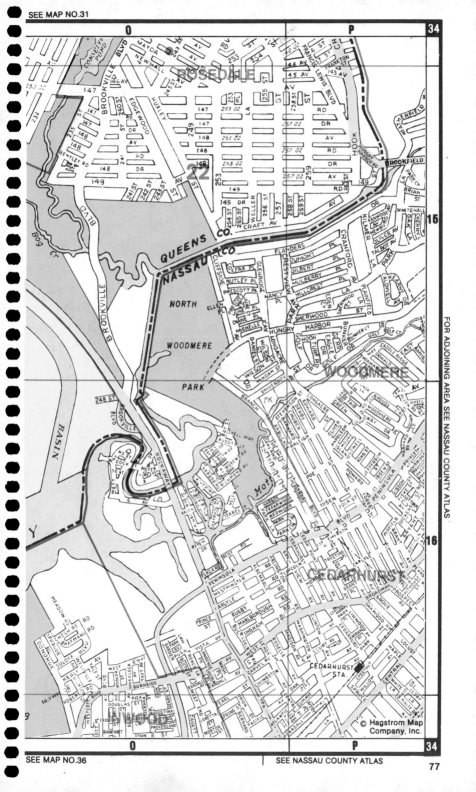

35 K

WILDLIFE REFUGE

BLACK

RULERS BAR

West Pond

VISITOR CENTER

93

17

J A M A I C A

GATEWAY NATIONAL RECREATION

YELLOW BAR

34

AREA

RULERS BAR

BROAD CHANNEL

HASSOCK

BLACK WALL CHANNEL

BLACK WALL MARSH

N

JAMAICA BAY UNIT

BIG

EGG MARSH

SHAD CREEK RD

TOLL

18

LITTLE EGG

MARSH

GIANT BAR MARSH

CROSS BAY VETERANS MEM BRIDGE

BROAD

© Hagstrom Map Company, Inc.

Pierhead Line
lkhead Line

PARK SEAS

94

99 01

SEAWAY

ROCKAWAY

35 K

35

L

M

C H A N N E L

EAST HIGH MEADOW

HASSOCK CREEK

JAMAICA BAY

JO COS

B A Y UNIT

M A R S H

17

BIG MUCK CREEK

WINHOLE HASSOCK

SILVER HOLE

M A R S H

G R A S S   H A S S O C K

U.S. Bulkhead Line

DUBOS POINT WILDLIFE SANCTUARY

BARBADOES DR

BAYFIELD AV

DE COSTA AV

HILLMEYER

SOMERVILLE

BURCHELL RD

ELIZABETH AV

ELIZABETH AV

VERNAM BASIN

THURSBY

HESSLER

GOUVERNEUR AV

92

CHANNEL

ARVERNE B

BARBADOES BASIN

ROCKAWAY INDUSTRIAL PARK

SCHEER ST

AMSTEL BLVD

18

BEACH 54-01

PARVINE

BARBADOES DR

BEACH ST

ROCKAWAY

FREEWAY

CHANNEL

BEACH DRIVE

CARLTON

R.F.W.

BLVD

SEAFOAM

ARVERNE

SWAN RD

STORY

LARKIN

HAMMELS

BEACH 90

93

HOLLAND AV

PKWY

BOARDWALK

PUBLIC BEACH

© Hagstrom Map Company, Inc.

L

M

35

SEE MAP NO. 39

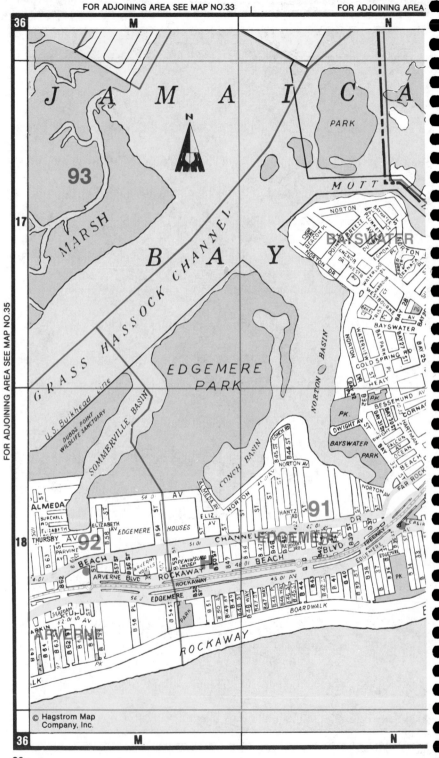

JAMAICA

93

MARSH

BAY

PARK

MOTT

BAYSWATER

GRASS HASSOCK CHANNEL

U.S. Bulkhead Line

DUBOS POINT
WILDLIFE SANCTUARY

SOMMERVILLE BASIN

EDGEMERE
PARK

NORTON BASIN

CONCH BASIN

BAYSWATER

BESSEMUND AV

DWIGHT AV

BAYSWATER
PARK

ALMEDA

BURCHELL
ELIZABETH

THURSBY AV

92

ALMEDA AV

ELIZABETH

EDGEMERE HOUSES

PARVINE AV

BEACH

ARVERNE BLVD

ROCKAWAY

PENINSULA
HOSP

CHANNEL

ALMEDA AV

ELIZ.
AV

91

EDGEMERE

BLVD

BEACH

NORTON AV

HANTZ
RD

GREENWAY DR

EDGEMERE

BOARDWALK

ARVERNE

ROCKAWAY

SEAGIRT

INWOOD COUNTRY CLUB

CEDARHURST

INWOOD

Athletic Field

LAWRENCE

LAWRENCE STA.

INWOOD STA.

REDFERN HOUSES

FAR ROCKAWAY STA.

FAR ROCKAWAY

CENTRAL

ST. JOHN'S EPISCOPAL HOSP.

WAVECREST

O'DONOHUE PARK

SEAGIRT BLVD

(PUBLIC)

BEACH

QUEENS CO.
NASSAU CO.

U.S. Coast Guard Station

ATLANTIC BEACH BRIDGE (Toll)

ATLANTIC BEACH

ATLANTIC BLVD

SILVER POINT PARK

FOR ADJOINING AREA SEE HAGSTROM'S NASSAU COUNTY ATLAS

© Hagstrom Map Company, Inc.

37

F

GERRITSEN BEACH

SHEEPSHEAD BAY

35

9A

KNAPP

SEWAGE TREATMENT PLANT

COYLE

PARK

BROWN

FORD

NOSTRAND

SHELL BANK CREEK

CANAL

GERRITSEN AV

29

9B

HARKNESS

BRAGG

BRIGHAM ST

SHORE

EMMONS AV

PLUM BEACH CHANNEL

PLUM BEACH PKWY.

SHEEPSHEAD BAY

Line

PLUMB BEACH
(G.N.R.A.)

Bulkhead Line

LEVARD

MANHATTAN BEACH

NORFOLK ST

OXFORD ST

PEMBROKE ST

GATE

KINGSBOROUGH
COMMUNITY
COLLEGE

PARK

U.S. Pierhead   and   Bulkhead

ORIENTAL
BEACH

N

Borough

R O C K A W A Y

BREEZY
POINT

PALMER AV

B 216 ST

DENVILLE WK
CLINTON WK
BATH WK
BAYWAY WK

ROCKAWAY

5 AV WK

AV

OCEAN AV

BREEZY POINT

19

20

BREEZY
POINT BLVD.

B 222 ST
B 221 ST
B 220 ST
B 219 ST
B 217 ST
B 216 ST
B 215 ST
B 214 ST

JETTY

ROCKAWAY
POINT

© Hagstrom Map
Company, Inc.

GATEWAY

37

F

G   H   37

FLOYD
BENNETT
FIELD
GATEWAY NATIONAL
RECREATION AREA

U.S.
COAST GUARD

PARK HQ

UNIT HQ

34

BARREN ISLAND MARINA

Dead Horse Bay

AVIATION RD

U.S. NAVY
RESERVE

DEAD HORSE INLET
(GERRITSEN INLET)

TOLL AV

City   Bulkhead   Line   U.S. Pierhead   and

Line

Line

BRIDGE (Toll)

MARINE PKWY

19

Line

I N L E T

ROXBURY

U.S.
COAST GUAR

RD

CHAPEL WK
BAYSIDE DR
MARSHALL AV
LIBERTY LA
BEDFORD AV
HIGHLAND PL

ROCKAWAY
POINT
COMM.

BAYSIDE AV
ROXBURY AV
AV

ROXBURY
HILLSIDE

97

MARKET
ST
ROCKAWAY
MARKET ST
BREEZY

BLVD

STATE

HIGHLAND PL
COURTNEY LA
NEPTUNE WK
MANVILLE LA
THETFORD LA
DORIS LA
JANET LA

SEABREEZE
HILLSIDE
BAYSIDE
AV

BROWNSV
HARFORD
OCEANVIEW
CENTER

RD
UNI
H

FORT   TILDE

95

20

CRESTES WK
ARCADIA WK
BEDFORD PL
GRAHAM PL
REID AV
B 201 ST

NATIONAL

RECREATION   AREA

BREEZY
POINT   UNIT

© Hagstrom Map
Company, Inc.

G   H   37

38

H

FLOYD
BENNETT
FIELD
GATEWAY NATIONAL
RECREATION AREA

COAST GUARD

N

PARK HQ

UNIT HQ

34

U.S. NAVY
RESERVE

FLATBUSH

JAMAICA
BAY
UNIT

TOLL

AVIATION RD.

AV.

Pierhead and Bulkhead

Line

head

U.S.

MARINE

Toll

PKWY. BRIDGE

Line

FOR ADJOINING AREA SEE MAP NO. 37

19

ROCKAW

ROCKAW

ROXBURY

PARKING FIELD

RIIS PARK

U.S. COAST GUARD RD.

97

ROXBURY AV.

BAYSIDE AV.

SEABREEZE AV.

HILLSIDE AV.

HILLSIDE

ROXBURY

BEACH AV.

BROWNS

STATE

FORT TILDEN

95

JACOB

B 169

B 169

ST.

UNIT HQ.

BOARD

WALK

BOARD

BOARD

OCEANVIEW

B 193 ST.

GATEWAY NATIONAL RECREATION AREA

UNIT

BREEZY

POINT

ATLANT

20

38

H

84

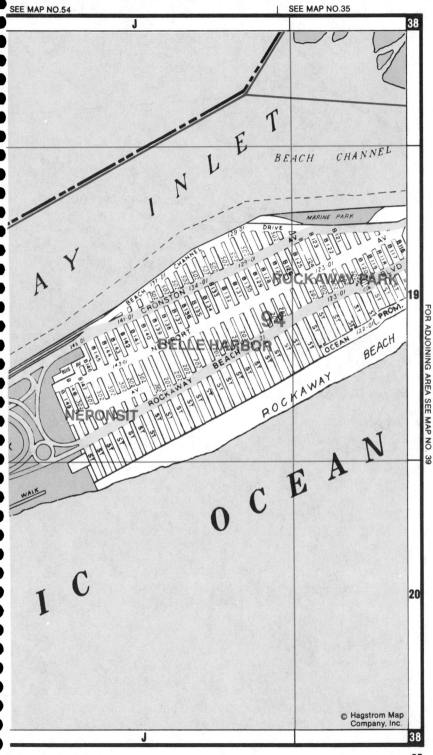

39 | K

GIANT BAY MARSH

BEACH CHANNEL

U.S. Pierhead Li
U.S. Bulkhead

BEACH

CHANNEL
PARK

ROCKAWAY

ROCKAWAY BEACH

SEASIDE

CHANNEL DRIVE

CRONSTON

NEWPORT

BELLE HARBOR

ROCKAWAY

ROCKAWAY PARK

94

BEACH

OCEAN

PROMENADE

(BOARDWALK)

MEMORIAL CIR

ROCKAWAY

19

20

ATLANTIC

N

© Hagstrom Map
Company, Inc.

39 | K

OCEAN

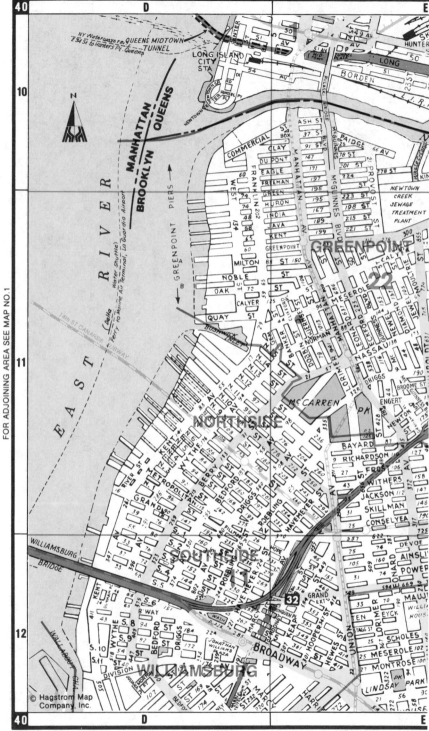

FOR ADJOINING AREA SEE MAP NO. 24

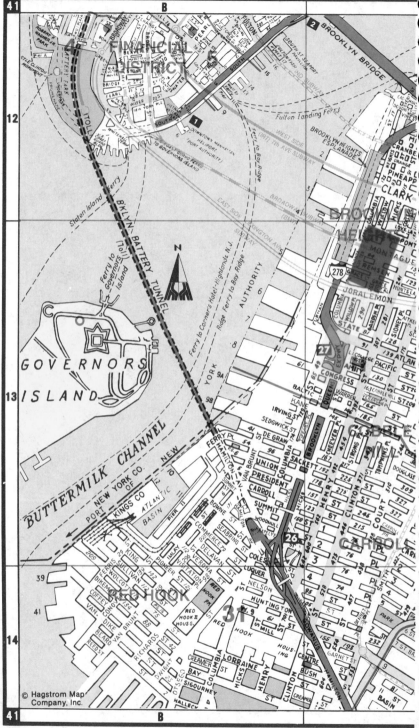

© Hagstrom Map Company, Inc.

FOR ADJOINING AREA SEE MAP NO. 42

© Hagstrom Map Company, Inc.

WILLIAMSBURG

U.S. NAVAL STATION

CLINTON HILL

PRATT INST

THE QUADRANGLES

LAFAYETTE GARDENS

MYRTLE

PARK HOUSING

WILLOUGHBY WALK

WOODHULL MEDICAL & MENTAL CENTER

MARTIN LUTHER KING JR PL

TOMPKINS HOUSES

BEDFORD-

TOMPKINS PARK

LEXINGTON

QUINCY

GATES

MONROE

MADISON

PUTNAM

JEFFERSON

HANCOCK

HALSEY

FULTON

ATLANTIC

PROSPECT HEIGHTS

CROWN HEIGHTS

ST. JOHNS

RESTORATION

NOSTRAND AV STA.

© Hagstrom Map Company, Inc.

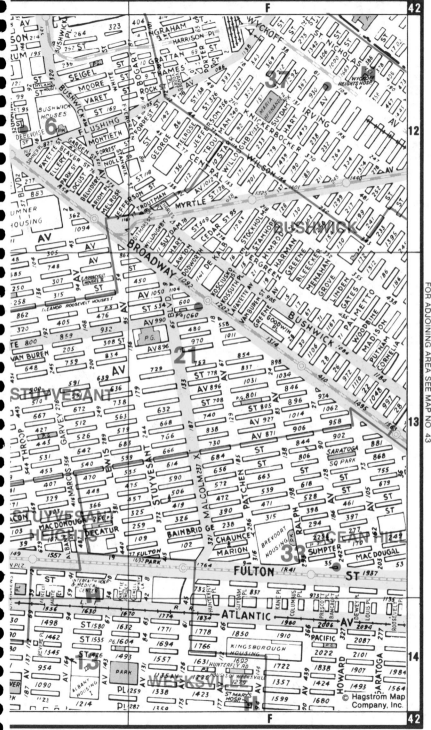

RIDGEWOOD

MYRTLE

WYCKOFF

KNICKERBOCKER

WILSON

CENTRAL

BUSHWICK

MADISON

FOR ADJOINING AREA SEE MAP NO 42

CONRAIL

UNION

MOUNT JUDAH CEM.

KNOLLWOOD PK. CEM.

JUDAH CEM.

TRINITY CEM.

CEMETERY OF THE EVERGREENS

BROADWAY

OCEAN HILL

MACDOUGAL

HULL

SOMERS

BROADWAY JUNCTION

FULTON

INTERBOROUGH

JAMAICA

SUNNYSIDE

SARATOGA

HOPKINSON AV.

EASTERN

PARKWAY

ATLANTIC

PITKIN

PITKIN

© Hagstrom Map Company, Inc.

GLENDALE

MT. LEBANON CEMETERY

MT. CARMEL CEM.

CYPRESS

BETH-EL CEM

MT. NEBOH CEM.

MACH-PELAH CEM.

MT. CARMEL CEM.

HILLS

PKWY

FOREST PKWY

PARK

CEMETERY

MT. HOPE CEM.

MAIMONIDES CEM.

INTERBOROUGH

CEM. OF THE B'NAI JESHURUM AND SHERETH ISRAEL

SALEM FIELD CEMETERY

RIDGEWOOD RESERVOIR

NATIONAL CEMETERY

HIGHLAND PARK

CYPRESS HILLS

RIDGEWOOD

HIGHLAND PARK

LIRR

PARK

PITKIN

CITY LINE

GLENMORE

LIBERTY

EAST NEW YORK

CYPRESS HILLS P.G.

CYPRESS HILLS HOUSING

DUMONT AV

BLVD

NYCT PITKIN AV. SUBWAY YARD

LINDEN PLAZA HOUSES

27

© Hagstrom Map Company, Inc.

FOR ADJOINING AREA SEE MAP NO. 29

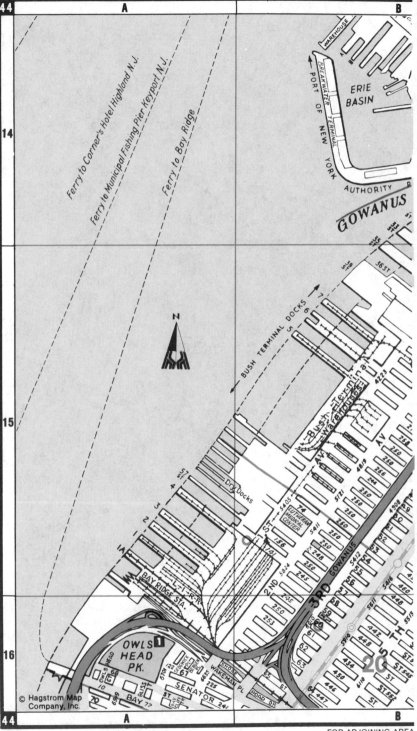

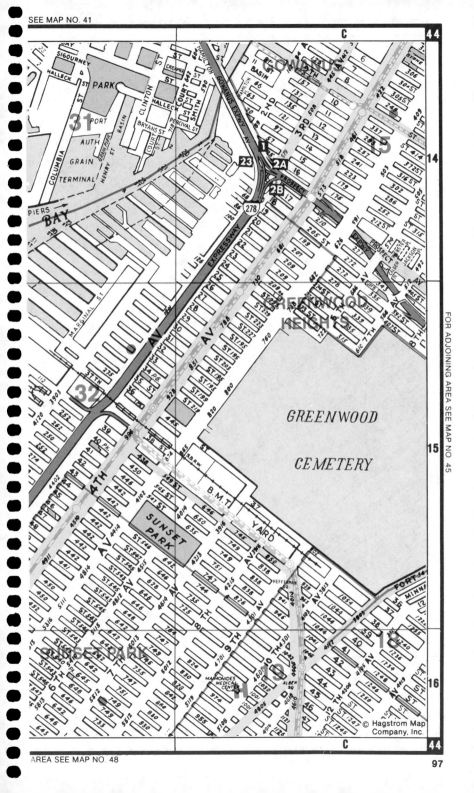

GOWANUS

PARK SLOPE

GREENWOOD HEIGHTS

GREENWOOD CEMETERY

SUNSET PARK

SUNSET PARK

MAIMONIDES MEDICAL CENTER

B.M.T. YARD

© Hagstrom Map Company, Inc.

D E 45

GRAND ARMY PLAZA

ST. JOHNS PL
LINCOLN
EASTERN PARKWAY

Brooklyn Central Library
Brooklyn Museum
Brooklyn Botanic Garden

LEFFERT'S HOMESTEAD

Litchfield Villa

PROSPECT

PARK

BOATHOUSE

PROSPECT LAKE

WINDSOR TERRACE

SOUTHWEST

PARK CIRCLE

PARKSIDE
PARADE
GROUNDS

CATON

PROSPECT PARK SOUTH

ALBEMARLE ROAD

BEVERLY

TURNER PL

CHURCH

KENSINGTON

AVENUE

OCEAN

CARROLL ST
WEST

PROSPECT PARK

CARROLL

PROS PECT PARK WEST

VANDERBILT

GREENWOOD
CATON
PARKWAY

CORTELYOU
DORCHESTER

PROSPECT-LEFFERTS GARDENS

FRANKLIN
BEDFORD
ROGERS

WASHINGTON

SULLIVAN
McKEEVER PL

EMPIRE BLVD
STERLING
LEFFERTS AV
LINCOLN ROAD
MAPLE
MIDWOOD
RUTLAND
KENMORE
HAWTHORNE
WINTHROP

PARKSIDE
CLARKSON
LENOX

BEEKMAN
CHESTER CT
WESTBURY CT

CALEDONIAN HOSP.

WOODRUFF AV
CROOKE

PARADE PL

FLATBUSH
CATON AV
LINDEN
MARTENSE
CHURCH AV
SNYDER
ALBEMARLE
TILDEN
BEVERLEY

ERASMUS

KENMORE TER
ALBEMARLE TER

CLARENDON RD

FLATBUSH

DITMAS PARK

OCEAN

PROSPECT

14

25

15

26

16

FOR ADJOINING AREA SEE MAP NO. 46

D E 45

46 E

PROSPECT
PARK
STERLING
ST. JOHNS
LINCOLN

BROWER
PARK

ALBANY
HOUSING
PARK

CROWN HEIGHTS

EASTERN PARKWAY

FRANKLIN
BEDFORD
ROGERS

UNION
PRESIDENT
CARROLL
CROWN
MONTGOMERY
MALBONE ST.

SULLIVAN
EMPIRE
STERLING
LEFFERTS
LINCOLN
MAPLE
MIDWOOD
RUTLAND
FENIMORE
HAWTHORNE
WINTHROP
PARKSIDE
CLARKSON
LENOX

BOULEVARD
WINGATE
EAST NEW YORK

EMPIRE BOULEVARD

ATHLETIC
FIELD

KINGSBROOK
JEWISH
MEDICAL
CENTER

KINGS
COUNTY
HOSPITAL

KINGS CO. HOSPITAL

KINGSBORO PSYCHIATRIC CENTER

SUNY HEALTH
SCIENCE CENTER
AT BROOKLYN

LENOX
ALBANY
TROY

FLATBUSH
BEDFORD
LINDEN
MARTENSE
CHURCH
ERASMUS
SNYDER
ALBEMARLE
TILDEN

NOSTRAND

HOLY CROSS
CEMETERY

N

CHURCH
SNYDER

LOTT
BEVERLEY
CORTELYOU
CLARENDON

VANDERVEER
FLATBUSH
AVENUE
NEWKIRK
FOSTER

NEW YORK

BROOKLYN

ALBANY
TROY

SNYDER

FOSTER

© Hagstrom Map
Company, Inc.

100

46 E

F   G   46

WEEKSVILLE

HOUSES OF WEEKSVILLE
ST MARYS HOSP

EASTERN

LINCOUNTER PARK
LINCOLN TER
PARK

NEW YORK

UTICA

ROCHESTER

BUFFALO

RALPH

PARK

PITKIN

SUTTER

BLAKE

DUMONT

BROWNSVILLE

PARKWAY

GLENMORE

HOWARD

WATKINS

MOTHER

SETHLOW HOUSES

BELMONT

HUGHES APTS

LANGSTON

HOUSING

SARATOGA

HOPKINSON

LIVONIA

RIVERDALE

NEWPORT

LOTT

AMBOY

HEGEMAN

OSBORN

WATKINS

CHESTER

GASTON PK

ROCKAWAY

EAST RD

RUTLAND

WINTHROP

CLARKSON

LENOX

REMSEN

WILLMOHR

PARKWAY

LINDEN

CHURCH

REMSEN VILLAGE

TILDEN

BEVERLY

CLARENDON

SCHENECTADY

AVENUE

UTICA

KINGS

JODIE

WHITTY LA

PRESTON

FOSTER

L.I.R.R.

KINGSWAY

CHASE CT
PRESTON CT

COVENTRY

LINDA

RALPH

FARRAGUT

FLATLANDS

GLENWOOD

BROOKLYN TERMINAL MARKET

DITMAS

FOSTER

CONARSIE

ROCKAWAY

BROOKDALE HOSP

BLVD

ST JOHNS
S.J. TILDEN HOUSES

HOUSING

PLAY GROUND

PORTAL

GRAFTON

LEGION

HOWARD

TAPSCOTT

UNION

PARKWAY

HIGHWAY

27

© Hagstrom Map Company, Inc.

14

15

16

46

12

33

36

H

47 G

PITKIN AV

BROWNSVILLE

12

DUMONT

S. J. TILDEN HOUSES

LIVONIA

HEGEMAN AV

LINDEN BLVD

DEWITT

BREUKELEN HOUSING

36

CANARSIE

FLATLANDS AVENUE

GLENWOOD

Fresh Creek

FRESH CREEK PARK

© Hagstrom Map Company, Inc.

47 G

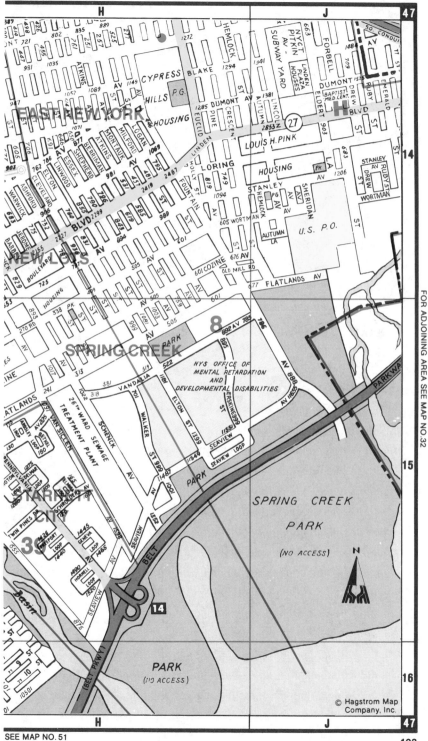

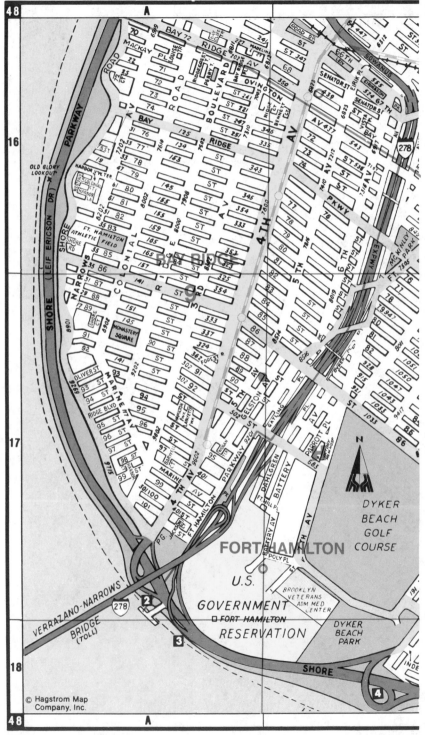

© Hagstrom Map Company, Inc.

FOR ADJOINING AREA SEE MAP NO 49

© Hagstrom Map Company, Inc.

49

C

MAIMONIDES MEDICAL CENTER

BOROUGH PARK

19

16

17

26

NEW UTRECHT

MAPLETON

4

WASHINGTON

BENSONHURST

14

AVENUE

KINGS

QUENT

© Hagstrom Map
Company, Inc.

49

C

FOR ADJOINING AREA SEE MAP NO.49

50 D E

BROOKLYN COLLEGE

DITMAS PARK

FLATBUSH

MIDWOOD

OCEAN PARKWAY

Streets and avenues visible: VANDERVEER, AVENUE D, NEWKIRK, FOSTER, FARRAGUT, GLENWOOD, KENILWORTH PL, AMERSFORT PL, CAMPUS RD, BEDFORD, NOSTRAND AV, VICTOR RD, B'LYN RD, FARR PL, PED BRIDGE, AURELIA CT, NEW YORK AV, KINGS HIGHWAY, MARINE, MADISON, QUENTIN, BURNETT ST, GERRITSEN AV, STUART ST, MOORE, CONEY, LOCUST, CHESTNUT, BAY, DELEMERE, MANSFIELD, DE KOVEN CT, WALDORF CT, WELLINGTON CT, IRVINGTON PL, STEPHENS, ALBANY

50 D E

F   G   **50**

EAST FLATBUSH

GEORGETOWN

FLATLANDS

MARINE PARK

MILL BASIN

MILL ISLAND

MARINE PARK

Kings Plaza S.C. and Marina

Glenwood Housing

Paerdegat

FOSTER AV

GLENWOOD ROAD

FARRAGUT ROAD

KINGS AVENUE

AVENUE K

FLATBUSH AVENUE

UTICA AVENUE

FILLMORE AVENUE

Bulkhead Line

16

34

36

17

50

FOR ADJOINING AREA SEE MAP NO. 51

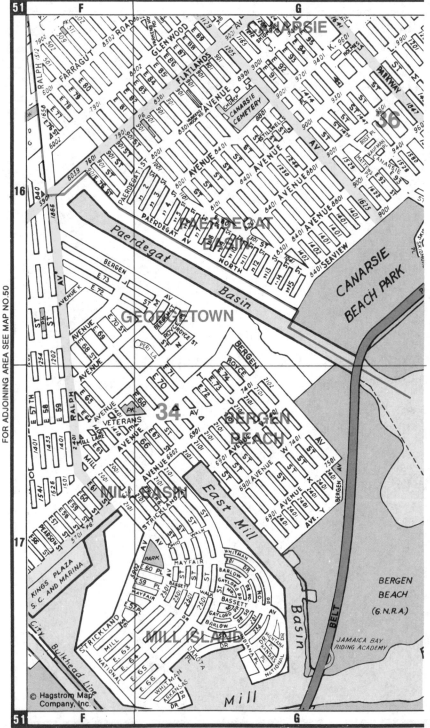

CANARSIE

PAERDEGAT BASIN

CANARSIE BEACH PARK

GEORGETOWN

BERGEN BEACH

MILL BASIN

BERGEN BEACH (G.N.R.A.)

KINGS PLAZA S.C. AND MARINA

MILL ISLAND

JAMAICA BAY RIDING ACADEMY

BELT

Mill

Bulkhead Line

© Hagstrom Map Company, Inc.

FOR ADJOINING AREA SEE MAP NO. 50

H

51

PARK
(NO ACCESS)

BAY VIEW
HOUSES

N

98OI AV

SKIDMORE

SKIDMORE AV

E 93 ST

SCHENCK

E 93 ST

E 91 ST

PARKWAY

13

CANARSIE
PIER
(G.N.R.A.)

16

GATEWAY NATIONAL RECREATION AREA

BAY

JAMAICA

CANARSIE POL

FOR ADJOINING AREA SEE MAP NO. 35

17

NESTEPOL

MARSH

BIG CHANNEL

Basin

ISLAND CHANNEL

© Hagstrom Map
Company, Inc.

H

J

51

BATH BEACH

14

SHORE PARKWAY

CROPSEY

BAY

U.S. Pierhead Line

GRAVESEND

BAY

BENSONHURST

LEIF ERICSON DR

CAESARE BAY S.G.

NELLIE BLY
AMUSEMENT PARK

DREIER - OFFERMAN
PARK

N

Coney Island Creek

Nortons Point

BAYVIEW AV

LEON S. KAISER
PLAY GROUND

GRAVESEND
HOUSING

NEPTUNE

MERMAID

SURF

24

CONEY

SEA GATE

NAUTILUS

ATLANTIC AV

OCEANIC AV

CONEY IS
HOUSES

RIEGELMANN

(BOARDWALK WEST)

CONEY   ISLAND

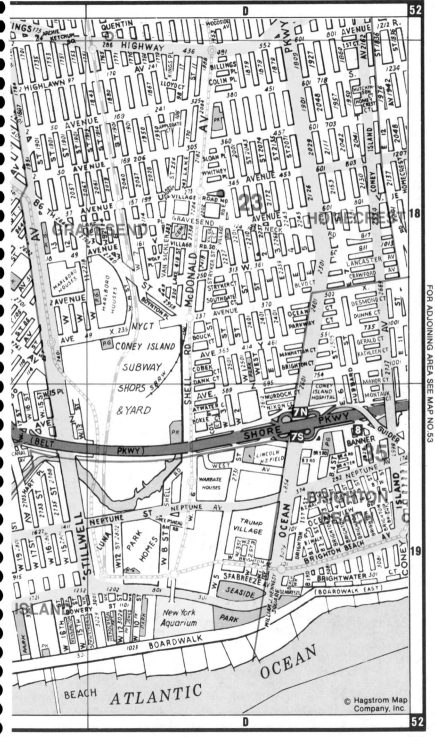

53 E

FOR ADJOINING AREA SEE MAP NO.52

MARINE PARK

AVENUE

MOORE PL

AVENUE

29

OCEAN AVENUE

BEDFORD AV

NOSTRAND AV

HARING ST

BROWN ST

BATCHELDER ST

FORD ST

COYLE ST

Avenue

HOMECREST

18

GRAVESEND AVENUE

DELAMERE PL

MANSFIELD PL

NOSTRAND AV

SHEEPSHEAD BAY

BRIGHAM ST

BRAGG ST

PARK

SEWAGE TREATMENT PLANT

AVENUE

HARING ST

BROWN ST

FORD ST

COYLE ST

35

JEROME AV

VOORHIES AVENUE

9A

SHORE PARKWAY

EMMONS AV

SHEEPSHEAD BAY

Bulkhead Line

SHORE BOULEVARD

CONEY ISLAND

BRIGHTON BEACH

OCEANVIEW

MANHATTAN BEACH

KINGSBOROUGH COMMUNITY COLLEGE

ORIENTAL BOULEVARD

MANHATTAN BEACH PARK

Board Walk Beach

ESPLANADE

U.S. Pierhead and Bulkhead Line

MANHATTAN BEACH

ORIENTAL BEACH

PARK

BRIGHTON BEACH

ATLANTIC

© Hagstrom Map Company, Inc.

53 E

F   G   53

17

MARINE

ST (8)

AVENUE

E. 64

E. 66

WHITMAN

ARKANSAS

DR

NATIONAL

34

Mill Basin

City Bulkhead Line

MARINE PARK - GOLF COURSE

FLATBUSH

AVENUE

Marine Park Creek

BURNETT ST

AV

ST

AVENUE

PLUMB

ALLEN

PLUMB

GERRITSEN

11N

SHORE

PKWY

AV

18

29

GERRITSEN BEACH

KNAPP

SEWAGE PLANT

SHELL BANK CREEK

CANAL

FLORENCE

GOTHAM

BARTLETT

LACON

PARK

9B

HARKNESS

BRAGG

BRIGHAM ST

PLUM BEACH CHANNEL

(BELT PKWY)

PLUMB BEACH
(G.N.R.A.)

DEAD HORSE INLET

(GERRITSEN INLET)

N

19

U.S. Pierhead   and   Bulkhead   Line

ENTAL
EACH

OCEAN

FOR ADJOINING AREA SEE MAP NO. 54

F   G   53

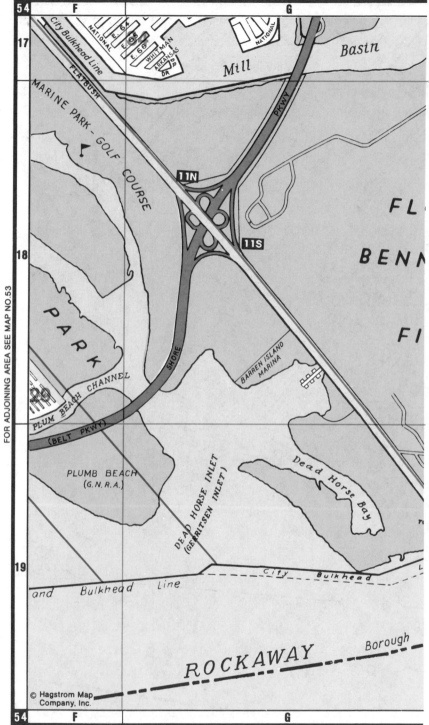

54
F
G

17

City Bulkhead Line

FLATBUSH

MARINE PARK - GOLF COURSE

NATIONAL

E. 64

E. 65

WHITMAN

ARKANSAS DR

E. 66

NATIONAL

Mill

Basin

PKWY

11N

11S

18

PARK

SHORE

FL

BENN

FI

PLUM BEACH CHANNEL

BARREN ISLAND MARINA

(BELT PKWY)

PLUMB BEACH
(G.N.R.A.)

DEAD HORSE INLET
(GERRITSEN INLET)

Dead Horse Bay

19

City Bulkhead

and Bulkhead Line

ROCKAWAY Borough

© Hagstrom Map
Company, Inc.

54
F
G

116

54

H | J

SAILS PT.
HASSOCK | 17

ISLAND CHANNEL

BIG CHANNEL

OLD SWALE
MARSH

BIG FISH KILL CHANNEL

OYD

VETT

ELD

U.S.
COAST
GUARD

N

18

J A M A I C A   B A Y

FOR ADJOINING AREA SEE MAP NO. 38

PARK HQ

UNIT HQ.

Line

U.S. NAVY
RESERVE

AVIATION RD

Bulkhead

AV

COLL

U. S.

Pierhead and

Line

MARINE

INLET

Line

Toll

PKWY. BRIDGE

19

94

© Hagstrom Map
Company, Inc.

H | J

54

55

E   F

ELIZABETH

ELIZABETH RIVER

K—I—L—L

BAYWAY STA.

278

GOETHALS BRIDGE

HOWLAND MARINE TERMI...

1

13 (TOLL)

ALLEN ST

PRIVATE (STANDARD OIL CO.) RD.

BRUNSWICK

ROCKEFELLER ST

BAY

CARRINGER RD

AMBOY

MTKLE ST

INS S

WAY

278

OLD CREEK

2

95

N.J. TURNPIKE

CONRAIL

MORSES

CONRAIL

CONRAIL

Creek

A—R—T—H—U—R

N

LINDEN

Creek

Piles Creek

3

GRASSELLI STA.

UNION CO. RICHMOND CO.

PRALL'S ISLAND BIRD SANCTUARY

PRALL'S RIVER

14

RIVER RD

CHELSEA

EDWARD

POINT

© Hagstrom Map Company, Inc.

INDUST...

BLO...

55

E   F

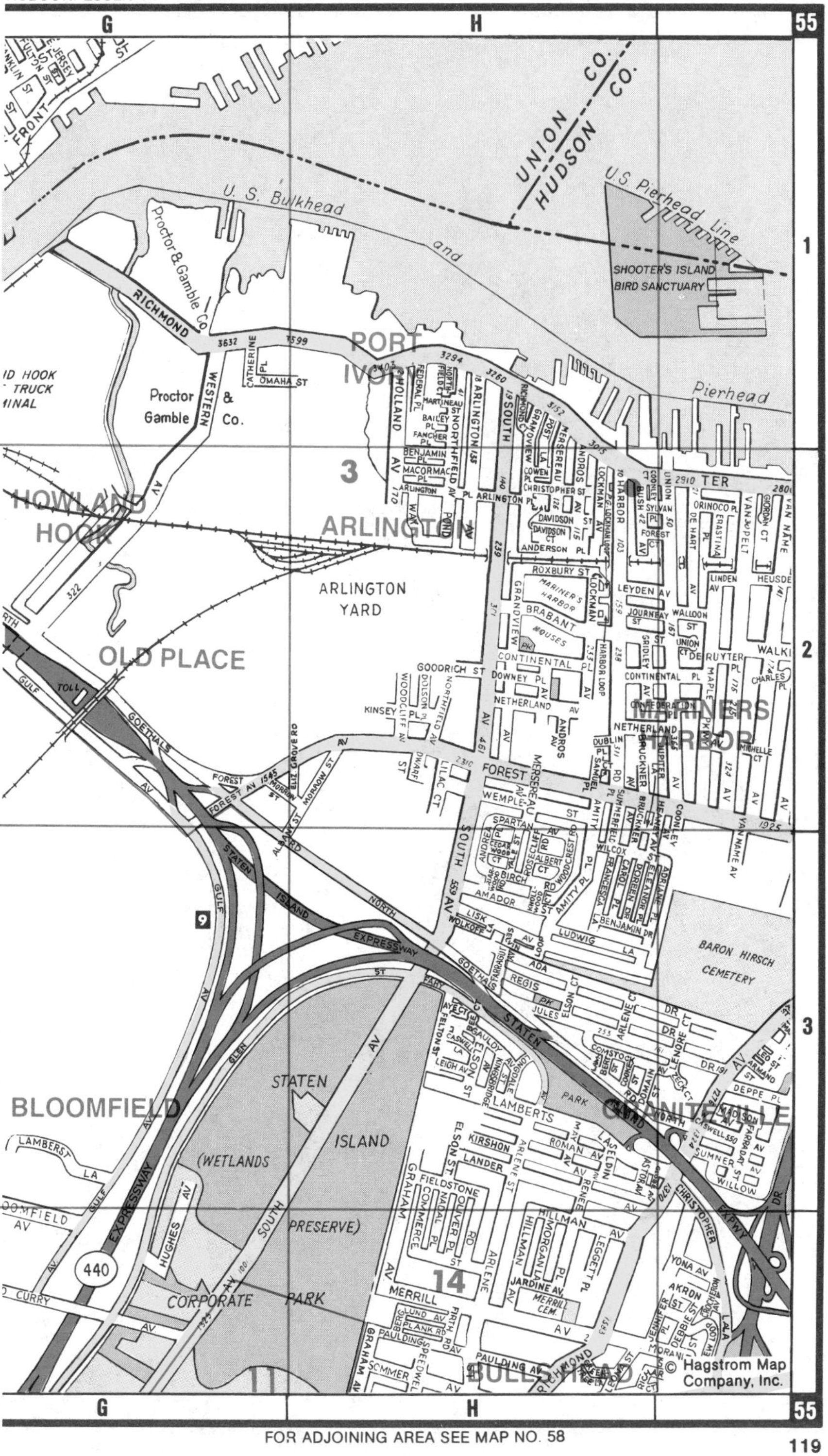

FOR ADJOINING AREA SEE MAP NO. 56

FOR ADJOINING AREA SEE MAP NO. 58

56   J   K

BAYONNE

440

NEW JERSEY
NEW YORK

U S Pierhead Line

SHOOTER'S ISLAND
BIRD SANCTUARY

K I L L

BAYONNE BRIDGE

Pierhead Line

1

RICHMOND TER

V

RICHMOND HARBOR LA

MARINERS
HARBOR

PORT
RICHMOND

CASTLETON AV

2

BARON HIRSCH
CEMETERY

440

PARK
COLLEGE

GRANITEVILLE

STATEN ISLAND EXPWY

WESTERLEIGH

VICTORY

3

© Hagstrom Map
Company, Inc.

56   J   K

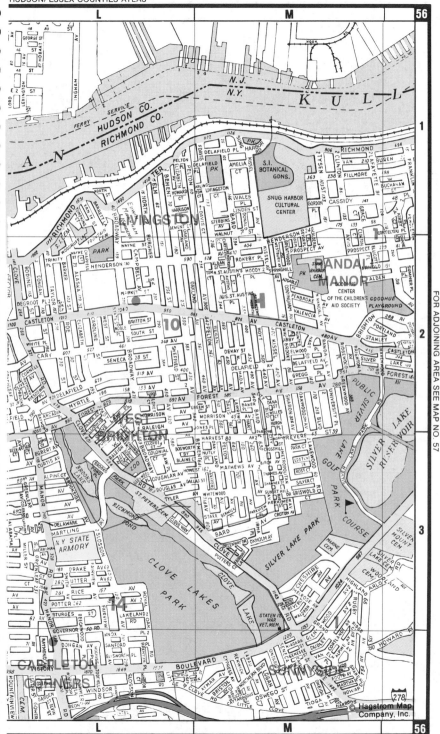

© Hagstrom Map Company, Inc.

57

M   N

KILL VAN KULL

HUDSON CO.
RICHMOND CO.

NEW BRIGHTON

S.I. BOTANICAL GDNS.

SNUG HARBOR CULTURAL CENTER

RANDALL MANOR

GOODHUE CENTER OF THE CHILDREN'S AID SOCIETY

GOODHUE PLAYGROUND

FOR ADJOINING AREA SEE MAP NO. 56

WEST BRIGHTON

SILVER LAKE RESERVOIR

SILVER LAKE PARK

PUBLIC GOLF COURSE

SILVER LAKE PARK

NOTRE DAME ACADEMY

PARK

GRYMES HILL

CLOVE LAKES PARK

STATEN IS. WAR VET. MEM.

SILVER MOUNT CEM.

SUNNYSIDE

WAGNER COLLEGE

278

PARK HILL

© Hagstrom Map Company, Inc.

57

M   N

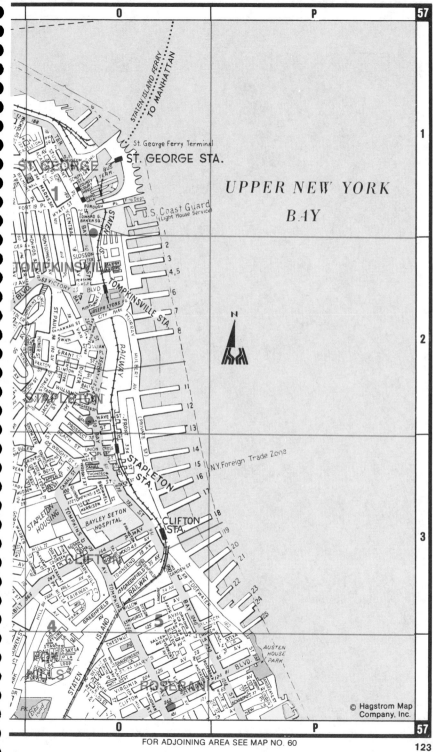

UPPER NEW YORK BAY

58

E F

UNION CO.
RICHMOND CO.

PRALL'S ISLAND
BIRD SANCTUARY

PRALL'S RIVER

POINT RD

RIVER RD

CHELSEA

BLOO

EDWARD

INDUSTRY RD

BLOOMFIELD RD

SOUTH AV

SHORE RD

4

RAHWAY

UNION MIDDLESEX

RIVER

WARNERS STA.

SPENCER 210

CHELSEA RD

SOUTH AV

MEREDITH

8

CHELSEA

N.J. N.Y. CO. CO.

U.S. Bulkhead and Pierhead Line

K—I—L—L

CONRAIL

5

BATES AV

CANNON

PARK ST

GLEN MELVIN

SYLVAN CEM

WILD

SHELLEY

BURN

ALBERTA AV

ROSWELL

SERESFORD AV

MELVIN AV

SCHM

TRAVIS

CHARLES ST
JOHN ST
LEFFERTS ST
TOMKINS ST

Consolidated Edison Co.

WEST

7

WILD

CARTERET

FITCH ST
LAFAYETTE

A—R—T—H—U—R

4R95

VICTORY

4R74

CRABS LA.

WILD

486 AV

PELCHERS LA.

14

VICTORY

6

LITTLE FRESH KILL

FRESH KILLS LANDFILL

FRESH

PARK DR

ISLAND OF MEADOW
BIRD SANCTUARY

FRESH KILLS

LANDFILL
Sewage Disposal Plant

KILLS

440

MIDDLESEX RICHMOND CO. CO.

GREAT FRESH KILL

14

© Hagstrom Map Company, Inc.

58

E F

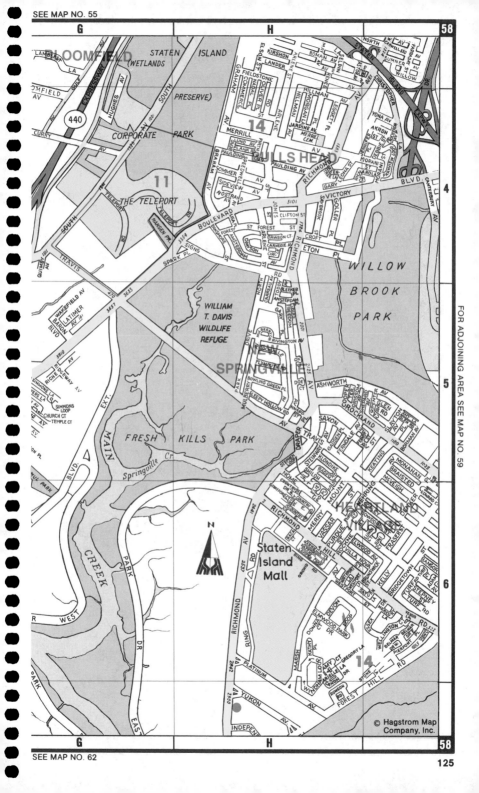

G   H   58

BLOOMFIELD   STATEN   ISLAND
STATEN (WETLANDS
PRESERVE)   PARK

440   CORPORATE

11   THE TELEPORT

BULLS HEAD   4

14

WILLIAM
T. DAVIS
WILDLIFE
REFUGE

WILLOW
BROOK
PARK

NEW
SPRINGVILLE

FRESH   KILLS   PARK   5

Staten
Island
Mall

HEARTLAND
VILLAGE

6

14

© Hagstrom Map
Company, Inc.

FOR ADJOINING AREA SEE MAP NO. 59

G   H   58

FOR ADJOINING AREA SEE MAP NO. 58

WILLOW

BROOK

PARK

COLLEGE OF
STATEN ISLAND

INSTITUTE
FOR BASIC
RESEARCH

WILLOWBROOK

STATEN ISLAND
DEVELOPMENTAL
CENTER

N.Y.C.
FARM COLONY

SEA-VIEW
HOSPITAL and HOME

ROCKLAND

PARK

La Tourette Golf Course
(PUBLIC)

LA TOURETTE

EGBERT
VILLE

LIGHTHOUSE HILL

THE TIBETAN MUSEUM

© Hagstrom Map
Company, Inc.

FOR ADJOINING AREA SEE MAP NO. 62/63

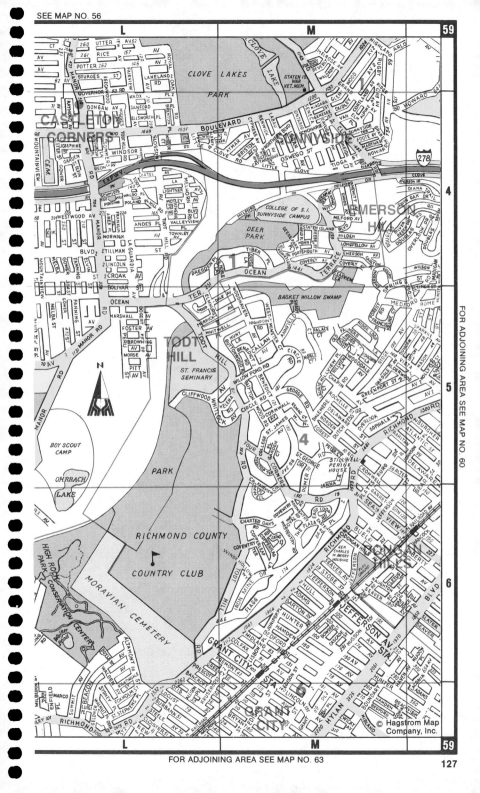

FOR ADJOINING AREA SEE MAP NO. 60

60 | M | N

14 CLOVE LAKES PARK

CLOVE LAKE

STATEN IS. WAR VET. MEM.

GRYMES HILL

WAGNER COLLEGE

SUNNYSIDE

VICTORY

278 STATEN ISLAND

PARK HILL

4

COLLEGE OF S.I. SUNNYSIDE CAMPUS

DEER PARK

EMERSON HILL

CONCORD

GRASMERE STA.

BASKET WILLOW SWAMP

TODT HILL

ST. FRANCIS SEMINARY

OLD TOWN RD. STA.

5

OLD TOWN

RICHMOND COUNTY C.C.

STILLWELL PERINE HOUSE

DONGAN HILLS STA.

DONGAN HILLS

6

BOULEVARD

STATEN ISLAND UNIVERSITY HOSPITAL (NORTH)

SO. PSYCH (N.Y.

JEFFERSON AV. STA.

GRANT CITY STA.

GRANT CITY

MIDLAND BEACH

© Hagstrom Map Company, Inc.

60 | M | N

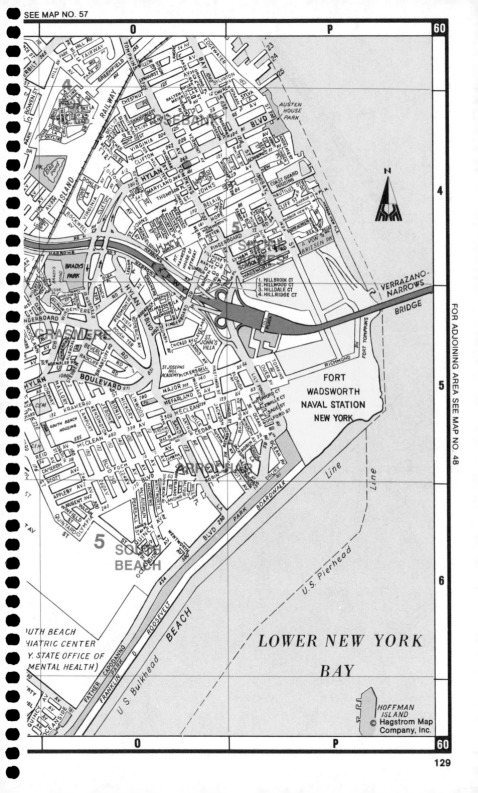

LOWER NEW YORK

BAY

FORT
WADSWORTH
NAVAL STATION
NEW YORK

VERRAZANO-
NARROWS

BRIDGE

1. HILLBROOK CT
2. HILLWOOD CT
3. HILLDALE CT
4. HILLRIDGE CT

SOUTH
BEACH

CHASMERE

HOFFMAN
ISLAND
© Hagstrom Map
Company, Inc.

UTH BEACH
HIATRIC CENTER
Y. STATE OFFICE OF
MENTAL HEALTH)

61

B

C

WOODBRIDGE

TURNPIKE

N. J.

PORT READING

WOODBRIDGE CARTERET

7

BLAIR

BLAZING STAR RD.

SCHOOL ST.

MORRIS ST.

CENTER ST. AV.

VERNON AV.

HOWELL AV.

NABENOAK

GARDEN ST.

CLIFF ST.

Smith Creek

K - I - L - L

U. S. Bulkhead and Pierhead Line

8

WEST CLIFF

CLIFF ALLEY

BROAD ST.

JOHNSON ST.

NEW JERSEY

NEW YORK

A - R - T - H - U - R

SEWAREN

WEST AV.

FERRY

OAKLAND AV.

COTTAGE ST.

SHELL AV.

9

PORT MOBIL

MOBIL OIL CORP

ELLIS RD.

ARTHUR

CLAY

STA

SHARROTTS

STORER

WINANT LA.

WINANT PL.

KRESCHER ST.

ANDROVETTE ST.

ARTHUR KILL RD.

ENGLEWOOD

LUNDSTEN

MANLEY

9

CHARLESTON

© Hagstrom Map Company, Inc.

61

B

C

D   **E**   **F**   **61**

CARTERET

ISLAND OF MEADOW
BIRD SANCTUARY

GREAT   FRESH

CO.
CO.

LEIBIG LA

ROOSEVELT
PERSHING
ATLANTIC
SALEM
LOCUST

MCKINLEY AV
PERSHING AV
UNION
WARREN
ESSEX
MERCER
BERGEN
HUDSON
CHROME AV
SOMERSET ST
PASSAIC ST
JESSIE ST

CHROME

MIDDLESEX
RICHMOND

14

7

Tufts
Pt.

WEST SERVICE RD

Smoking
Pt.

ARDEN AV

1. PRINCE LA
2. WHIRT LA
3. CANDON CT
4. PHYLLIS CT
5. ASHLEY LA
6. SANDYWOOD LA

2326 ARTHUR

WEST SHORE

KILL

4

8

ARTHUR KILL CORRECTIONAL FACILITY

CHEMICAL LA

KILL 2911

INDUSTRIAL LOOP

SHAMROCK LN

2704

BLOOMINGDALE

VETERANS

2325 2440

HERVEY ST
ZEBRA
25TH
24TH
23RD
EAST

2584 m

2694

ENGERT
POPLAR AV
BARR CT
BARRY
ROSSVILLE
KNESE
MORRIS ST

WEST

ARTHUR KILL RD

HUGUENOT RD

2000 RD

CROCKER
PETTIT
COURTNEY CT
DAILY CT
LOMBARD

GRAFF
CLINTON PL

SELKIRK

CITY PARK

SUSSEX
GREEN
SUSSEX

CHARLESTON
WINANT
LAWTON
ORDER PL
WOOD
PERRY
BALSAM
GERVIL
LOCUST CT

3

LUCILLE
WIRT AV
WIRT AV
WOODS

9

BALSAM
PL

SOUTH
SHORE
GOLF
COURSE
(PUBLIC)

AVON GREEN
CELBRA PL

LORRAINE

MALVINE AV

CORRELL

MAGUIRE

HEMLOCK ST

MALLOW ST

ALVERSON

POWELL
DAILY
AVON

PIT PONDS

SHIEL

RADIGAN

BOMBAY ST

MASON

CATHAM
PL

SPAR

ALVERSON LOOP

POWELL

12

9

ATE PARK
PRESERVE

RD

HARRIS
CRABTREE AV
TURNER ST

McBAINE

KRAMER
1530 WOODROW

McBAINE AV

GLENEVAR

BL

WOODROW RD
VERNON

W CASTOR PL
COVENTRY
LOOP

RAMAPO
STAFFORD

SINCLAIR
SMELDON 772
RENSSELAER
RATHBUN
RAMONA
LAMONT

ELLSWORTH
NANCY
DESMOND
SINCLAIR

356

WEST
EXPRESSWAY
GLADWIN

CLAY PIT RD

WOODROW

1276

ELKS

WIELAND
141

WIELAND

VERNON
RD

WOODROW

1114

3

SHARROTTS RD

ROBIN

BLOOMINGDALE RD

MARISA CIR

ALYSIA CT

FERNWOOD LOOP
MALLARD LA
MARVIN
SHARON LA
HELENE CT

CONVENT AV
MAGUIRE

STAFFORD
AV

SHELBON
RENSSELAER
RATHBUN
RAMONA 581
LAMONT
IONIA

RATHBUN
RAMONA
LAMONT
806

440

VETERANS

PARK

RAMONA

PARK

© Hagstrom Map
Company, Inc.

D   **E**   **F**   **61**

FOR ADJOINING AREA SEE MAP NO. 62

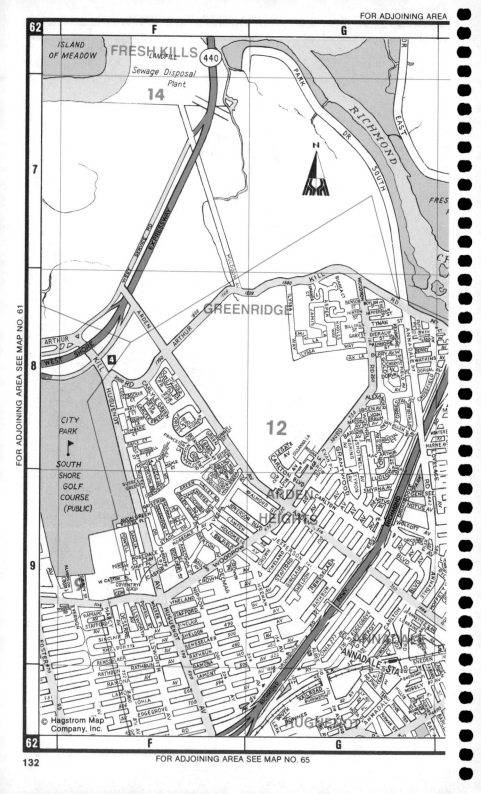

FOR ADJOINING AREA SEE MAP NO. 61

FOR ADJOINING AREA SEE MAP NO. 65

© Hagstrom Map Company, Inc.

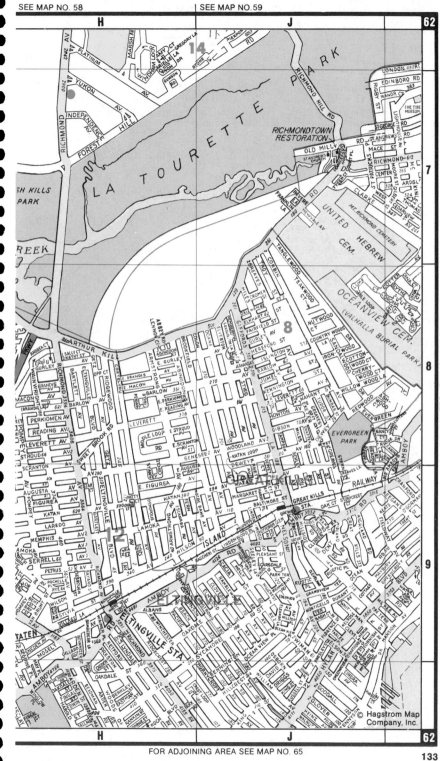

63

K L

EGBERTVILLE CEM.

LIGHTHOUSE HILL

RICHMOND-AMBOY RD

NEW DORP STA.

7

PIGTOWN

NEW DORP

OAKWOOD HTS. STA.

6

RAILWAY

GUYON AV

OAKWOOD

OCEANVIEW CEM. (VALHALLA BURIAL PARK)

1. PECK CT
2. ELISE CT
3. ELK CT
4. HART LOOP

DOUGLAS FREEK MEMORIAL PARK CEMETERY

8

BAY TERRACE STA.

STATEN

BOULEVARD

DUGDALE

OAKWOOD BEACH SEWAGE TREATMENT PLANT

NEW DORP TERRACE

9

HYLAN

GREAT

KILLS

GATEWAY NATIONAL RECREATION AREA

PARK

PARKING FIELD

GREAT KILLS YACHT CLUB

RICHMOND COUNTY YACHT CLUB

GREAT KILLS HARBOR

U.S. Pierhead & Bulkhead Line

© Hagstrom Map Company, Inc.

63

K L

M N 63

GRANT CITY STA.

SOUTH BEACH PSYCHIATRIC CENTER (N.Y. STATE OFFICE OF MENTAL HEALTH)

DONGAN HILLS

LIBERTY BUEL AV

GRANT CITY

MIDLAND BEACH

5

PK

BOARDWALK

PUBLIC BEACH

7

MILLER FIELD (U.S. GOVERNMENT)

GATEWAY NATIONAL RECREATION AREA

FATHER CAPODANNO

PARK

Line

NEWDORP BEACH

BRITTON HOUSE

8

OAKWOOD BEACH

PARK

CEDAR GROVE BEACH

GREAT KILLS YACHT CLUB

RICHMOND COUNTY YACHT CLUB

K

GREAT KILLS HARBOR

Line

U.S. Pierhead & Bulkhead Line

9

U.S. Bulkhead

PARK

N

GREAT KILLS BEACH

10

CROOKES POINT

10

K

© Hagstrom Map Company, Inc.

M N 63

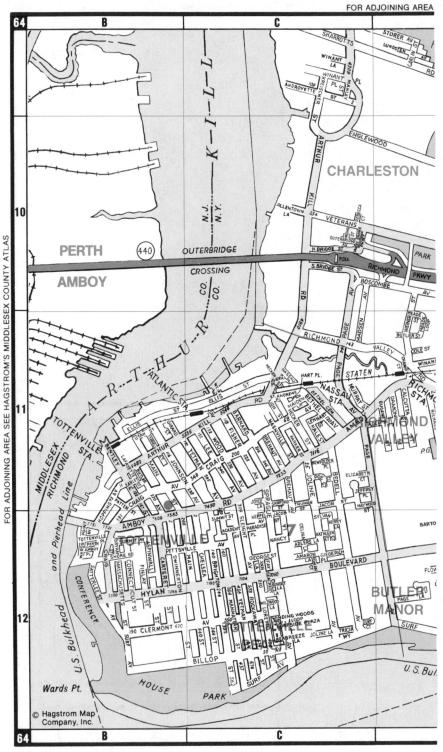

© Hagstrom Map Company, Inc.

64

9

CLAY PIT PONDS
STATE PARK
PRESERVE

WOODROW

KRAMER AV

W CASTOR

COVENTRY
LOOP

1530 WOODROW

SPAR AV

GILROY ST

RD

CLAY PIT RD

WIELAND

WIELAND

RAMPO

RD 356

CONVENT

RAMAPO

STAFFORD

DESERT

ELLSWORTH

MARIO
CIR

MAGUIRE

STAFFORD

SINCLAIR

SHELDON 773

SHARROTTS

RD

ALYSIA CT

STAFFORD

SINCLAIR

RENSSELAER

RATHBUN

ROBIN

SHELDON

RAMONA

440

MARVIN

SHARON
LA

RENSSELAER

LAMONT

PARK

PEMBROOK
LOOP

RATHBUN

RAMONA

RAMONA 581

VERNON

9

ENGLEWOOD
AV

IONIA

LAMONT AV

EDGEGROVE

RD

HERRICK AV

PARK

DARLINGTON

WEST

PKWY.

10

PITNEY AV

CARLTON

CHUCHILL AV

DRUMGOOLE

EAST
AV

VERNON

RICHMOND

RD

PRINCES

DRUMGOOLE

BRADFORD

BRADFORD

ASHLAND

MAGUIRE

GOFF

FONDAI

ASHLAND

VALDEMAR
RD

PLEASANT

OUTERBRIDGE

ALBOURNE

UNCAS

WHEELING

AMBOY

PLAINS

IDAHO

UNCAS

PRINCE'S BAY STA.

2

GAYNOR ST

PLEASANT PLAINS AV

AMBOY 6291

ATLANTIC

HERBERT
ST

STATION

29 AV

UTICA ST

WATERBURY

ISLAND

RAILWAY

BAYVIEW

RichmondValley
RD

WEIR AV

PLEASANT PLAIN STA.

GEORGE

FICARELLA

WOODVALE

FLORENCE
PL

PERCIVAL

OSWALD

ELIZABETH
PL

KNOX ST

McGREGOR

AMBOY

101 BEDELL

LATOURETTE

SHADYSIDE AV.

SHARROTT

SOUTH

LATOURETTE

EXCELSIOR

JOHANNA

11

EVERETT

GOFF

FINLAY

TRENTON

FIRENZO CT

CEMETERY

KENNETH

ELDER

BURTON

EVERETT

9

HANOVER

SEGUINE

N

STEVENSON

PRESTON

VAIL

CAROL CT

INEZ ST

TRENTON

KINGSLAND

MISSION OF THE
IMMACULATE VIRGIN
CHILDREN'S HOME

VAIL
AV

SHERWOOD
AV

WOODVALE
LOOP

LEMON

HANK ST

PARK

MELVILLE

WILBU

CEM.

BOULEVARD

JOHNSTON

MARSCHER

PURDY

MOUNT
LORETTO

MARINE
PARK

FLAGSHIP CIR

JOHNSTON
TER

HYLAN

6225

PRINCESSBAY
BOATSMENS ASSN.

RICHARD

BUTLER

PRINCE'S

OWER

CLERMONT
BLVD

BAY

AV

Line

Line

Line

12

U.S. Pierhead

lkhead

RARITAN   BAY

© Hagstrom Map
Company, Inc.

D

E

64

65 | F | G

WOODROW AV

ANNADALE STA

HUGUENOT

BLUE POND

PRINCE'S BAY

WOLFE'S POND PARK

HUGUENOT BEACH

St JOSEPH'S BY THE SEA H.S.

Arbutus Lake

9

LEMON PARK

PRINCE'S BAY

Seguine Pt.

U.S. Bulkhead

U.S. Pierhead

ATLAN

HYLAN BLVD

© Hagstrom Map Company, Inc.

65 | F | G

65

H   J

ELTINGVILLE

ELTINGVILLE STA

AM BOY RD

HYLAN BOULEVARD

BOULEVARD

HERON POND PARK

SYCAMORE ST

OAKDALE ST

WAKEFIELD RD

OCEAN DRIVEWAY

BAYVIEW

GREAT KILLS BEACH

10

U. S. Bulkhead

U. S. Pierhead

N

Line

Line

Line

11

O C E A N

12

A T L A N T I C

© Hagstrom Map Company, Inc.

H   J   65

New York City has played a significant role in the historical development of America. It was the home of the Stamp Act Congress in 1765, as well as the site of several important battles and an unsuccessful, but symbolic peace conference in 1776. As the nation's first capitol, New York was the scene of Washington's first inaugural and the session of Congress that passed the Bill of Rights in 1789.

Traces of New York City's Revolutionary heritage still remain and will be of interest to both residents and tourists. The following suggestions just give a flavor of the variety of historic relics which still exist throughout the city. Visitors are invited to take a walk through history.

Manhattan: Lower Manhattan below City Hall (Map 1 D-22) is a treasure trove of early New York. Some of Lower Manhattan's sites include: the Statue of Liberty and the American Museum of Immigration, Battery Park and Castle Clinton, Seamen's Church Institute, the Custom House, Fraunces Tavern, Federal Hall National Memorial and the South Street Seaport Museum. At the other end of Manhattan is the Morris Jumel Mansion (Map 3 C-10, W. 160th St. and Edgecomb Ave.) which was Washington's headquarters during the "Battle of Harlem Heights."

The Bronx: The Valentine-Varian House (Map 6 E-5, 3266 Bainbridge Ave.), built in 1756, houses the Museum of Bronx History. Van Cortlandt Park (Map 7 C-4) was the scene of considerable Revolutionary action and the Van Cortlandt Manor was built prior to 1750. Of course, the Bronx Zoo/International Wildlife Park and the New York Botanical Garden (Map 6 E-6,7) and the Hall of Fame (Map 6 C-7) are important Bronx sites.

Queens: Downtown Flushing (Map 21 K-9) has a group of structures called the "Flushing Freedom Mile." Three of these are: the Browne House (37-01 Bowne St.), built in 1661, Kingsland Homestead (in Weeping Beech Park), built in 1774, and the Friends Meeting House (137-16 Northern Blvd.), built in the late 1600s. Downtown Jamaica (Map 26 L-12), which for centuries has served as a regional commercial and transportation center, also contains early sites: King Mansion (in King Park), built in 1730, and two old cemeteries, The Grace Episcopal Church graveyard (155-03 Jamaica Ave.) and Prospect Cemetery (159th St. and Beaver Rd.)

Brooklyn: Elegant Brooklyn Heights (Map 41) was the scene of much action in the "Battle of Long Island." The Long Island Historical Society (128 Pierrepont St.) houses Brooklyn's outstanding collection of books and artifacts. Nearby, at the foot of Fulton St. (Map 41 C-12) is the site of Washington's ingenious evacuation from Long Island to Manhattan. The Brooklyn Museum contains many early artifacts and even part of an old house originally built in the early town of Flatlands. The Pieter Claesen Wycoff House (Map 46 F-15, Ralph Ave. and Clarendon Rd.) is considered the oldest house in New York State. A number of other structures from Brooklyn's early towns still exist, for example, in Flatbush (Map 29) and Gravesend (Map 52).

Staten Island: Richmondtown Restoration (Map 63 K-7) is a remarkable group of structures from every era of Staten Island's past. It is the home of the Staten Island Historical Society. At the very southern tip of the island is Conference House (Map 64 B-12), on Hylan Blvd., at which Benjamin Franklin, John Adams and Edward Rutledge met with Admiral Lord Richard Howe in an unsuccessful attempt to negotiate a settlement of the War for Independence.

1524 Givovanni de Verrazano discovers the island of Manhattan while in the service of Francis I, King of France.

1609 Henry Hudson, an English mariner in the employ of a Holland trading company, lands at the lower end of Manhattan.

1624 Dutch settlers arrive and settle throughout the island.

1625 1st permanent settlement established at Manhattan. It is named Nieuw Amsterdam (New Amsterdam).

1626 Peter Minuit purchases the island from the Indians for beads, buttons, and trinkets valued at $24.00.

1639 Johannes Bronck settles in the area north of the Harlem River, now known as the Bronx.

1643 1st permanent settlement in Queens established at Flushing.

1653 The West India Company incorporates Manhattan as a city — New Amsterdam. A protective wall is erected along the present site of Wall Street.

1654 1st permanent Jewish settlement in North America established in New Amsterdam.

1664 New Amsterdam surrenders to the English who rename it New York after the Duke of York, brother of Charles II, King of England.

1673 The Dutch recapture New York and rename it New Orange.

1674 The English again in possession of the island, name reverts to New York.

1754 Kings College (now Columbia University) opens.

1783 The British evacuate the city according to terms of the Treaty of Paris.

1789 George Washington takes oath of office as 1st President of the U.S. at Federal Hall.

1812 War with England. New York fortified. City Hall completed.

1834 City of Brooklyn incorporated.

1850 Population over 500,000.

1853 World's Fair at the Crystal Palace.

1858 Central Park is begun, but not officially completed until 1876.

1868 Experimental elevated railway opens in lower Manhattan (The El).

1883 Opening of the Brooklyn Bridge.

1886 Dedication of the Statue of Liberty, a gift from France.

1898 The City of New York established and incorporated into 5 boroughs: Manhattan, Brooklyn, Queens, Bronx, and Staten Island. Includes area of 300 sq. miles and a population of some 3,000,000.

1904 1st underground subway opens.

1913 Armory Show, international art exposition introduces modern art to America.

1929 Financial panic on Wall Street in October. Beginning of the Great Depression.

1931 Completion of the Empire State Building (then the tallest building in the world).

1939 New York's World Fair opens at Flushing Meadows.

1952 General Assembly of the United Nations meets at new headquarters along the East River.

1964 New York's World Fair opens at Flushing Meadows.

1973 Opening of the World Trade Center.

1983 Centennial of the Brooklyn Bridge, the world's first long span suspension bridge.

1986 Centennial of the Statue of Liberty National Monument.

1990 Ellis Island National Monument opens, celebrating the history of immigration to the United States.

Selected Points of Interest

Point of Interest	Map No.	Grid

Colleges & Universities

Barnard College, M	4	B13
Baruch College (CUNY), M	2	D19
Bronx Community College (CUNY), Bx	6	C 7
Brooklyn College (CUNY), Bk	50	E16
City College of New York (CUNY), M	4	C11
College of Aeronautics, Q	16	H 9
College of Mount St. Vincent, Bx	7	A 3
College of Staten Island (CUNY), SI	59	J 5
Columbia University, M	4	B13
Cooper Union, M	2	D19
CUNY Graduate Center, M	2	D17
Fashion Institute of Technology, M	2	C18
Fordham University, Bx	6	E 6
Fordham University, M	3	C16
Herbert H Lehman College (CUNY), Bx	6	D 6
Hostos Community College (CUNY), Bx	4	D11
Hunter College (CUNY), M	3	D16
John Jay College of Criminal Justice (CUNY), M	3	C16
Kingsborough Community College (CUNY), Bk	53	F19
Long Island University, Bk	41	C13
Manhattan College, Bx	7	B 4
Manhattan Community College (CUNY), M	1	C21
Medgar Evars Community College, Bk	46	E14
New School for Social Research, M	2	D19
New York City Technical College	41	C13
New York University, M	1	D20
Pace University, M	1	D21
* Parsons School of Design, M	2	D19
Polytechnic University, Bk	41	C13
Pratt Institute, Bk	42	D13
Queens College (CUNY), Q	21	K10
Queensborough Community College (CUNY), Q	22	N 9
Rockefeller University, M	3	E16
St. John's University, Q	27	M11
SUNY Health Science Center (Downstate), Bk	46	E15
SUNY Maritime College, Bx	13	N 7
Teacher's College, M	4	B12
Wagner College, SI	57	N 3
Yeshiva University, M	5	C 8
York College (CUNY), Q	27	L12

Hospitals

Bayley Seton, SI	57	O 3
Bellevue, M	2	E18
Beth Israel Hospital North, M	3	E15
Beth Israel Medical Center, M	2	E19
Bird S Coler Memorial, M	3	F15
Bronx-Lebanon, Bx	5	E 9
Bronx Municipal Hospital Center, Bx	9	H 5
Bronx Psychiatric Center, Bx	9	J 5
Brooklyn Hospital Center, Bk	41	D13
Columbia-Presbyterian Medical Center, M	5	B 9
Coney Island, Bk	52	D19
Elmhurst Hospital Center, Q	20	H10
Goldwater Memorial, M	2	F17
Harlem, M	4	D11
Interfaith Medical Center, Bk	42	D14
Kings County, Bk	46	E15
Kingsborough Psychiatric Center, Bk	46	E15
Kingsbrook Jewish Medical Center, Bk	46	E15
Lenox Hill, M	3	D15
Lincoln Medical Center, Bx	4	E11
Long Island Jewish-Hillside Medical Center, Q	23	P 9
Manhattan Children's Psychiatric Center, M	4	F13
Manhattan Eye, Ear and Throat, M	3	E16
Manhattan Psychiatric Center, M	4	F13
Memorial Sloan-Kettering Cancer Center, M	3	E16
Metropolitan, M	3	E14
Montefiore Hospital and Medical Center, Bx	7	D 4
Mount Sinai Medical Center, M	3	D14
New York Eye and Ear Infirmary, M	2	E19
New York Hospital-Cornell Medical Center, M	3	E16
New York Hospital Medical Center of Queens, Q	21	K10
New York University Medical Center, M	2	E18
North Central Bronx, Bx	7	D 4
North General, M	4	D12
Queens Children's, Q	23	O10
Queens Childrens Psychiatric Center, Q	23	O10
Queens Hospital Center, Q	26	L11
St. Albans Veterans Administration Extended Care Center, Q	31	N13
St. Barnabas Hospital for Chronic Diseases, Bx	6	E 7
St. Luke's Hospital Center, M	4	B13
St. Luke's Roosevelt Hospital Center, M	3	C16
St. Vincent's, M	2	C19
South Beach Psychiatric Center, SI	60	N 6
Staten Island University North	60	N 6
Staten Island University South	65	F11
US Veterans, Bx	6	C 6
US Veterans, M	2	E18
Veterans Administration, Bk	48	B17
Woodhull Medical and Mental Health Center, Bk	42	E12

Museums & Libraries

* African-American Institute 833 United Nations Plaza, M	2	E17
* American Academy of Arts and Letters Broadway & 155th St, M	5	B10
* American Craft Museum 40 W 53rd St, M	2	D17
* American Museum of Immigration Liberty Island, New York Bay		
American Museum of Natural History Central Park W & 79th St, M	3	C15
* American Museum of the Moving Image 36-01 35th Av, Q	19	F 9
* Bronx Museum of the Arts 165th St & Grand Concourse, Bx	5	D 9
* Brooklyn Children's Museum 145 Brooklyn Av, Bk	42	E14
* Brooklyn Historical Society 128 Pierrepont St, Bk	41	C13
Brooklyn Museum 200 Eastern Pkwy, Bk	45	E14
Brooklyn Public Library - Central Branch Grand Army Plz at Flatbush Av & Eastern Pkwy, Bk	45	E14
* City Island Historical Nautical Museum 190 Fordham St, Bx	12	M 4

Point of Interest	Map No.	Grid
The Cloisters - Metropolitan Museum of Art Fort Tryon Park, Washington Heights, M	6	B 7
* Cooper-Hewitt National Design Museum - Smithsonian Institution Fifth Av & 91st St, M	3	D14
* Dyckman House Broadway & 204th St, M	6	B 7
* Ellis Island Immigration Museum Ellis Island, New York Bay		
* Fordham Library Center 2556 Bainbridge Av, Bx	6	D 6
Fort Wadsworth Military Museum, SI	60	P 5
* Frick Collection and Museum 1 E 70th St, M	3	D16
* Guggenheim, Solomon R. Museum 1071 Fifth Av, M	3	D15
Hayden Planetarium Central Park W & 81st St, M	3	C15
Hispanic Society of America Broadway & 155th St, M	5	B10
* International Center of Photography 1130 Fifth Av, M	3	D14
1133 Sixth Av, M	2	D17
Intrepid Sea-Air-Space Museum 12th Av & W 46th St (Pier 86), M	2	B17
* Jamaica Arts Center 161-04 Jamaica Av, Q	27	L12
* Jefferson Market Library Av of the Americas & 10th St, M	2	D19
* Jewish Museum Fifth Av & 92nd St, M	3	D14
Leffert's Homestead Prospect Park, Bk	45	D14
* Library of the Blind and Physically Handicapped 166 Av of the Americas, M	1	D20
* Lower East Side Tenement Museum 97 Orchard St, M	1	E20
Metropolitan Museum of Art Fifth Av & 82nd St, M	3	D15
El Museo del Barrio 1230 Fifth Av, M	3	D14
* Museum of Archeology 631 Howard Av, SI	59	M 4
* Museum of Bronx History Bainbridge Av & E 208th St, Bx	6	E 5
* Museum of Chinese in the Americas 70 Mulberrry St, M	1	D21
* Museum of Modern Art 11 W 53rd St, M	2	D17
* Museum of Television and Radio 25 W 52nd St, M	2	D17
Museum of the City of New York 1220 Fifth Av, M	3	D14
National Museum of the American Indian - Smithsonian Institution - Alexander Hamilton U.S. Custom House 1 Bowling Green, M	1	D22
New York Aquarium for Wildlife Conservation Surf Av & W 8th St, Bk	52	D19
* New York City Police Museum 235 E 20th St, M	2	E19
* New York City Fire Museum 278 Spring St, M	1	C20

Point of Interest	Map No.	Grid
New York Hall of Science Flushing Meadows-Corona Pk, Q	21	J10
* New York Historical Society Central Park W & 77th St, M	3	C15
New York Public Library Central Research Library 5th Av & 42nd St, M	2	D18
* Donnell Library Center 20 W 53rd St, M	2	D17
* Jefferson Market Library 450 Sixth Av, M	2	C19
* Library of the Performing Arts at Lincoln Center 111 Amsterdam Av, M	3	C19
* Schomburg Center for Research in Black Culture 515 Lenox Av, M	4	C11
* Science, Industry, & Business Library 188 Madison Av, M	2	D18
* New York Transit Museum Boerum Pl & Schermerhorn St, Bk	41	C13
* Pierpont Morgan Library 29 E 36th St, M	2	D18
Queens Museum of Art Flushing Meadows-Corona Park, Q	21	J10
The Studio Museum 14 W 125th St, M	4	C12
* Whitney Museum of American Art 945 Madison Av, M	3	D15

Parks and Recreation

Beaches

	Map No.	Grid
Brighton, Bk	53	E19
Coney Island, Bk	52	C19
Far Rockaway, Q	36	N18
Great Kills, SI	63	K10
Huguenot, SI	65	G11
Jacob Riis Park, Q	38	H20
Manhattan, Bk	53	E19
Midland, SI	63	N 7
New Dorp, SI	63	N 8
Oakwood, SI	63	M 9
Orchard, Bx	12	L 3
Oriental, Bk	53	F19
Plumb, Bk	53	F19
Rockaway, Q	39	K19
South, SI	60	P 6
Tottenville, SI	64	C12
Wolf's Pond Park, SI	65	F11

Parks

	Map No.	Grid
Alley, Q	22	N 9
Alley Pond, Q	22	N 9
Astoria, Q	15	F 8
Baisley Pond, Q	30	M14
Battery, M	1	D22
Blue Heron Pond, SI	65	G10
Botanical Gardens, Bk	45	D14
Bronx, Bx	9	F 6
The Bronx Zoo, Bx	9	F 7
Brookville, Q	31	O14
Canarsie Beach, Bk	51	G16
Carl Schurz, M	3	E15
Central, M	3	C15
City Hall, M	1	D21
Claremont, Bx	5	D 8
Clay Pits Pond, SI	61	D 9
Clearview, Q	17	M 8

Selected Points of Interest

Point of Interest	Map No.	Grid
(Parks and Recreation continued)		
Clove Lakes, SI	56	L 3
Crocheron, Q	18	N 8
Crotona, Bx	5	E 8
Cunningham, Q	22	M10
Douglaston, Q	23	O 9
Dreier-Offerman, Bk	52	C19
Dyker Beach, Bk	48	B18
East River, M	1	F20
Ferry Point, Bx	13	L 7
Flushing Meadows-Corona, Q	21	J10
Forest, Q	25	J12
Fort Greene, Bk	41	D13
Fort Tryon, M	5	B 8
Fort Washington, M	5	A 8
Frank M Charles Memorial, Q	32	K15
Gateway National Recreation Area, Bk, Q, SI	35, 51, 63	
Great Kills, SI	63	K 9
High Rock, SI	59	L 6
Highbridge, M	5	C 9
Highland, Bk-Q	43	G13
Inwood Hill, M	6	B 7
Isham, M	6	B 7
Jackie Robinson, M	4	C11
Jacob Riis, Q	38	H20
Juniper Valley, Q	25	H11
Kissena, Q	21	L10
La Tourette, SI	59	J 6
Macombs Dam (John Mullaly), Bx	5	D 9
Marcus Garvey, M	4	D12
Marine, Bk	53	F18
Morningside, M	4	C13
New York Botanical Gardens, Bx	6	E 5
Owl's Head, Bk	44	A16
Parade Grounds, Bk	45	D15
Pelham Bay, Bx	8	J 2
Prospect, Bk	45	D14
Queens Botanical Gardens, Q	21	K 9
Randall's Island, M	11	F12
Richmond County, SI	59	L 5
Riverbank State, M	4	B11
Riverdale, Bx	6	A 5
Riverside, M	3	B15
Roberto Clemente State, Bx	5	C 8
Roy Wilkins-Southern Queens, Q	31	N13
Saint Mary's, Bx	11	F11
Seaside-Asser Levy Park & Aquarium, Bk	52	D19
Seton Falls, Bx	8	G 3
Silver Lake, SI	57	N 3
Sound View, Bx	10	H 9
Springfield, Q	31	N14
Sunset, Bk	44	B15
Van Cortlandt, Bx	7	C 3
Wards Island, M	3	F14
Wave Hill, Bx	7	A 4
Willow Brook, SI	58	H 4
Wolfes Pond, SI	65	F11
Sports Facilities		
Aqueduct Race Track, Q	29	K14
Baker Field, M	6	B 6
Belmont Park Race Track, Nassau County	28	P11
Chelsea Piers Sports & Entertainment Complex, M	2	B19
Downing Stadium, M	4	F13

Point of Interest	Map No.	Grid
Forest Hills Stadium, Q	26	J11
Madison Square Garden, M	2	C18
Rockefeller Center Skating Rink, M	2	D17
Shea Stadium, Q	21	J 9
USTA National Tennis Center, Q	21	J 9
Wollman Memorial Skating Rink, M	3	D16
Yankee Stadium, Bx	5	D10

Theaters & Concert Halls*

Point of Interest	Map No.	Grid
Alice Tully Hall Lincoln Center, Broadway & W 65th St, M	3	C16
Alvin Alley Dance Theater 1515 Broadway & 44th St, M	2	C17
Ambassador Theater 215 W 49th St, M	2	C17
Avery Fisher Hall Lincoln Center, Broadway & W 65th St, M	3	C16
Barrymore Theater 243 W 47th St, M	2	C17
Belasco Theater 111 W 44th St, M	2	C17
Biltmore Theater 261 W 47th St, M	2	C17
Booth Theater 222 W 45th St, M	2	C17
Broadhurst Theater 235 W 44th St, M	2	C17
Broadway Theater 1681 Broadway, M	2	C17
Brooklyn Academy of Music 30 Lafayette St, Bk	41	D13
Brooklyn Center for the Performing Arts (Brooklyn College) Nostrand Av & Av H, Bk	50	E16
Brooks Atkinson 256 W 47th St, M	2	C17
Carnegie Hall 881 7th Av, M	2	C17
City Center Theater 131 W 55th St, M	2	C17
Colden Center Queens College, Q	21	L10
Douglas Fairbanks Theater 432 W 42nd St, M	2	C17
Eugene O'Neill Theater 230 W 49th St, M	2	C17
Folksbiene Theater 123 E 55th St, M	2	C17
45th Street Theater 354 W 45th St, M	2	C17
Gershwin Theater 222 W 51st St, M	2	C17
Golden Theater 255 W 45th St, M	2	C17
Harmony Theater 161 W 22nd St, M	2	C19
Harold Clurman Theater 412 W 42nd St, M	2	C17
Helen Hayes Theater 240 W 44th St, M	2	C17
Imperial Theater 249 W 45th St, M	2	C17
Intar 420 W 42nd St, M	2	C17
Judith Anderson Theater 422 W 42nd St, M	2	C17

Point of Interest	Map No.	Grid
Julliard Theater 144 W 66th St, M	3	C16
Longacre Theater 220 W 48th St, M	2	C17
Lunt-Fontanne Theater 205 W 46th St, M	2	C17
Lyceum Theater 149 W 45th St, M	2	C17
Madison Square Garden 32nd & 33rd Sts bet 7th & 8th Av, M	2	C18
Majestic Theater 245 W 44th St, M	2	C17
Mark Hellinger Theater 237 W 51st St, M	2	C17
Martin Beck Theater 302 W 45th St, M	2	C17
Metropolitan Opera House Lincoln Center, Broadway & W 64th St, M	3	C16
Minskoff Theater Broadway & W 45th St, M	2	C17
Mintzi E Newhouse Theater Lincoln Center, 150 W 65th St, M	3	C16
Music Box Theater 239 W 45th St, M	2	C17
Neil Simon Theater 250 W 52nd St, M	2	C17
New Amsterdam Theater 214 W 42nd St	2	C18
New Victory Theater 209 W 42nd St, M	2	C17
New York Experience Theater 1221 Av of the Americas, M	2	C17
Queens Theatre in the Park Flushing Meadows-Corona Pk, Q	21	J 10
Palace Theater 1564 Broadway, M	2	C17
The Paramount Madison Square Garden, M	2	C18
Playhouse Theater 1 and 2 359 W 48th St, M	2	C17
Playwrights Horizon Theater 416 W 42nd St, M	2	C17
Plymouth Theaters 236 W 45th St, M	2	C17
Radio City Music Hall 1260 Av of the Americas, M	2	D17
The Ritz 260 W 54th St, M	2	C17
Royale Theater 242 W 45th St, M	2	C17
Saint James Theater 246 W 44th St, M	2	C17
Samuel Beckett Theater 410 W 42nd St, M	2	C17
Shubert Theater 225 W 44th St, M	2	C17
South Street Theater 424 W 42nd St, M	2	C17
The Supper Club 240 W 47th St, M	2	C17
Town Hall 123 W 43rd St, M	2	C17
Virginia Theater 245 W 52nd St, M	2	C17
Vivian Beaumont Theater Lincoln Center, 150 W 65th St, M	3	C16
West Side Arts Theater 407 W 43rd St, M	2	C17

Point of Interest	Map No.	Grid
Winter Garden Theater 1634 Broadway, M	2	C17

Transportation Facilities

Point of Interest	Map No.	Grid
Air Pegasus VIP Heliport Twelfth Av & W 30th St, M	2	B18
* Circle Line Sightseeing Yachts Pier 83 at W 42nd St, M	2	B17
Downtown Manhattan Heliport Pier 6 & East River, M	1	E22
East 60th Street Metroport E 60th St & Franklin D Roosevelt Dr, M	3	E16
Ellis Island Ferry (Circle Line) Battery Park, M	1	D22
Flushing Airport, Q	16	K 8
George Washington Bridge Bus Terminal 178th St & Broadway, M	5	B 9
Grand Central Terminal (MTA Metro-North Railroad) Lexington Av & 42nd St, M	2	D17
* Hudson River Day Line (to Bear Mt, West Point, Poughkeepsie) Pier 81 at W 41st St, M	2	B18
Island Helicopter Sightseeing 34th St & East River Dr, M	2	E18
John F Kennedy International Airport, Q	33	M15
La Guardia Airport Jackson Heights, Q	16	H 8
New York Waterway Ferries W 38th St, M	2	B18
World Financial Center, M	1	C22
South Ferry - Battery, M	1	D22
Battery Maritime Building, M	1	D22
Wall Street - Pier 11, M	1	E22
E 34th St, M	2	E18
Passenger Ship Terminal 47th-52nd Sts & Twelfth Av, M	2	B17
PATH (Port Authority Trans-Hudson Railway) World Trade Center, M	1	D22
Av of the Americas/33rd St, M	2	D18
Pennsylvania Station (Amtrak - MTA Long Island Rail Road - NJ Transit) Seventh Av & 33rd St, M	2	C18
Port Authority Bus Terminal Eighth Av & 41st St, M	2	C18
Seaplane Terminal 23rd St & East River, M	2	E19
Staten Island Ferry Terminal Battery Park, S Ferry, M	1	D22
Staten Island Railway St. George, SI	57	O 1
Statue of Liberty Ferry (Circle Line) Battery Park, M	1	D22
Wall Street Heliport Pier 6 & East River, M	1	E22

NOTE: * Not indicated on map due to scale.

Key to Borough Name Abbreviations

M	Manhattan
Bx	The Bronx
Q	Queens
Bk	Brooklyn
SI	Staten Island

Neighborhood	Map No.	Grid
MANHATTAN		
BATTERY PARK CITY	1	C 22
BOWERY	1	E 20
CARNEGIE HILL	3	D 14
CHELSEA	2	C 19
CHINATOWN	1	D 21
CIVIC CENTER	1	D 21
CLINTON	2	B 17
EAST HARLEM	4	D 12
EAST VILLAGE	1	E 20
FASHION CENTER	2	C 18
FINANCIAL DISTRICT	1	D 22
FLATIRON	2	D 19
FORT GEORGE	5	B 8
GRAMERCY PARK	2	D 19
GREENWICH VILLAGE	1	D 20
HAMILTON HEIGHTS	4	B 11
HARLEM	4	C 12
INWOOD	6	B 7
KIPS BAY	2	D 18
LENOX HILL	3	D 16
LINCOLN SQUARE	3	B 16
LITTLE ITALY	1	D 20
LOWER EAST SIDE	1	E 20
MANHATTAN VALLEY	3	B 14
MANHATTANVILLE	4	B 12
MARBLE HILL	6	B 6
MIDTOWN	2	C 17
MIDTOWN SOUTH	2	C 18
MORNINGSIDE		
HEIGHTS	4	B 13
MURRAY HILL	2	D 18
NOHO	1	D 20
RANDALLS ISLAND	4	F 12
ROOSEVELT ISLAND	3	F 16
SHERMAN CREEK	6	B 7
SOHO	1	D 20
SPANISH HARLEM	4	D 13
THEATER DISTRICT	2	C 17
TIMES SQUARE	2	C 17
TRIBECA	1	D 21
TURTLE BAY	2	D 17
TWO BRIDGES	1	E 21
UNION SQUARE	2	D 19
UPPER EAST SIDE	3	D 15
UPPER WEST SIDE	3	B 15
WASHINGTON		
HEIGHTS	5	B 9
WEST VILLAGE	1	C 20
YORKVILLE	3	E 15
THE BRONX		
ALLERTON	9	G 5
BATHGATE	5	E 8
BAYCHESTER	8	H 4
BEDFORD PARK	6	E 6
BELMONT	6	E 6
BRONX PARK SOUTH	9	F 7
BRONX RIVER	10	G 8
BRONXDALE	9	F 5
BRUCKNER	10	H 8
CASTLE HILL	10	J 8
CITY ISLAND	12	M 4
CLAREMONT VILLAGE	5	E 9
CLASONS POINT	14	J 9
CO-OP CITY	8	H 3
CONCOURSE	5	D 9
CONCOURSE VILLAGE	5	D 10
COUNTRY CLUB	13	K 6
CROTONA PARK		
EAST	10	F 8
EAST TREMONT	6	E 7
EASTCHESTER	8	G 2
EASTCHESTER BAY	13	L 6
EDENWALD	8	G 3
EDGEWATER PARK	13	M 6
FIELDSTON	7	B 4
FORDHAM	6	D 6
HARDING PARK	10	J 8
HART ISLAND	12	N 3
HIGHBRIDGE	5	C 9
THE HUB	4	E 10
HUNTS POINT	10	G 10
KINGSBRIDGE	6	B 5
KINGSBRIDGE		
HEIGHTS	6	C 6
LONGWOOD	10	F 10
MELROSE	5	E 10
MIDDLETOWN	13	J 6
MORRIS HEIGHTS	5	C 8
MORRIS PARK	9	H 6
MORRISANIA	5	E 9
MOTT HAVEN	4	E 12
MOUNT EDEN	5	D 8
MOUNT HOPE	5	E 8
NORTH RIVERDALE	7	A 3
NORWOOD	6	E 5
OLINVILLE	8	F 4
PARKCHESTER	9	H 7
PELHAM BAY	9	J 5
PELHAM GARDENS	9	H 5
PELHAM PARKWAY	9	G 6
PORT MORRIS	11	F 11
RIVERDALE	6	A 5
SCHUYLERVILLE	13	K 6
SOUNDVIEW	10	H 9
SOUTH RIVERDALE	6	A 5
SPENCER ESTATES	13	K 5
SPUYTEN DUYVIL	6	B 6
THROGS NECK	13	L 7
TREMONT	6	D 7
UNIONPORT	9	J 7
UNIVERSITY HEIGHTS	6	C 7
VAN CORTLANDT		
VILLAGE	6	C 5
VAN NEST	9	G 6
WAKEFIELD	8	F 2
WEST FARMS	9	G 7
WESTCHESTER		
SQUARE	9	J 6
WILLIAMSBRIDGE	8	F 4
WOODLAWN	7	D 3
QUEENS		
ARVERNE	35	M 18
ASTORIA	19	F 9
AUBURNDALE	22	M 9
BAY TERRACE	17	M 8
BAYSIDE	22	M 9
BAYSWATER	36	N 17
BEECHHURST	17	L 7
BELLAIRE	28	N 11
BELLE HARBOR	38	J 19
BELLEROSE	28	O 11
BLISSVILLE	19	E 10
BREEZY POINT	37	F 20
BRIARWOOD	26	L 12
BROAD CHANNEL	35	L 17
BROOKVILLE	31	N 14
CAMBRIA HEIGHTS	31	O 13
COLLEGE POINT	16	J 8
CORONA	20	J 10
DITMARS	15	F 8
DOUGLAS MANOR	18	N 8
DOUGLASTON	23	N 9
DUTCH KILLS	19	E 10
EAST ELMHURST	20	H 9
EDGEMERE	36	N 18
ELMHURST	20	H 10
FAR ROCKAWAY	36	N 17
FLORAL PARK	23	P 10
FLUSHING	21	K 9
FOREST HILLS	26	J 11
FRESH MEADOWS	22	M 10
GLEN OAKS	23	P 9
GLENDALE	22	H 12
HAMMELS	39	L 18
HILLCREST	27	L 11
HOLLIS	27	N 12
HOLLIS HILL	22	N 10
HOLLISWOOD	27	N 11
HOWARD BEACH	32	K 15
HUNTERS POINT	19	E 10
JACKSON HEIGHTS	20	H 9
JAMAICA	26	L 12
JAMAICA ESTATES	27	M 11
JAMAICA HILLS	27	L 11
KEW GARDENS	26	K 12
KEW GARDENS HILLS	26	K 11
LAURELTON	31	O 14
LINDEN HILL	17	K 8
LINDENWOOD	29	J 14
LITTLE NECK	18	O 8
LONG ISLAND CITY	19	E 10
MALBA	16	K 7
MASPETH	24	G 11
MIDDLE VILLAGE	25	H 11
MURRAY HILL	21	L 9
NEPONSIT	38	J 19
OAKLAND GARDENS	22	N 10
OZONE PARK	29	K 13
POMONOK	21	L 10
QUEENS VILLAGE	28	O 11
QUEENSBORO HILL	21	K 10
QUEENSBRIDGE	19	E 9
RAVENSWOOD	19	E 9
REGO PARK	25	J 11
RICHMOND HILL	26	K 12
RIDGEWOOD	24	G 12
ROCKAWAY PARK	39	K 19
ROSEDALE	31	O 14
ROXBURY	38	H 20
ST. ALBANS	31	N 13
SEASIDE	39	K 19
SOMERVILLE	35	M 18
SOUTH JAMAICA	30	L 13
SOUTH OZONE PARK	30	L 14
SPRINGFIELD		
GARDENS	31	N 14
STEINWAY	15	G 8
SUNNYSIDE	19	F 10

Neighborhood	Map No.	Grid	Neighborhood	Map No.	Grid	Neighborhood	Map No.	Grid
WAVECREST	36	N 18	MAPLETON	49	C 17	ELTINGVILLE	62	H 9
WEST MASPETH	24	F 11	MARINE PARK	50	E 17	EMERSON HILL	60	M 4
WHITESTONE	17	K 7	MIDWOOD	50	E 17	FOX HILLS	60	O 4
WOODHAVEN	29	J 13	MILL BASIN	51	G 17	FRESH KILLS	58	F 6
WOODSIDE	20	G 10	MILL ISLAND	51	G 17	GRANITEVILLE	56	J 3
			NEW LOTS	47	H 14	GRANT CITY	63	M 7
BROOKLYN			NEW UTRECHT	49	C 17	GRASMERE	60	O 5
BATH BEACH	52	B 18	NORTHSIDE	40	D 11	GREAT KILLS	62	J 9
BAY RIDGE	48	A 16	OCEAN HILL	42	F 13	GREENRIDGE	62	F 8
BEDFORD-			OCEAN PARKWAY	49	D 17	GRYMES HILL	57	N 3
STUYVESANT	42	E 13	PAERDEGAT BASIN	51	G 16	HEARTLAND VILLAGE	59	J 6
BENSONHURST	49	C 17	PARK SLOPE	45	C 14	HOWLAND HOOK	55	G 2
BERGEN BEACH	51	G 17	PARKVILLE	49	D 16	HUGUENOT	65	G 10
BOERUM HILL	41	C 13	PROSPECT - LEFFERTS			HUGUENOT BEACH	65	G 11
BOROUGH PARK	49	C 16	GARDENS	45	D 15	LIGHTHOUSE HILL	63	K 7
BRIGHTON BEACH	52	D 19	PROSPECT HEIGHTS	41	D 13	LIVINGSTON	56	L 1
BROADWAY			PROSPECT PARK			MARINERS HARBOR	56	J 2
JUNCTION	43	G 13	SOUTH	45	D 15	MIDLAND BEACH	63	N 7
BROOKLYN HEIGHTS	41	C 12	RED HOOK	41	B 14	MOUNT LORETTO	64	D 11
BROWNSVILLE	47	G 14	REMSEN VILLAGE	46	F 15	NEW BRIGHTON	57	N 1
BUSHWICK	42	F 12	RUGBY	46	E 15	NEW DORP	63	L 7
CANARSIE	47	G 15	SEA GATE	52	B 19	NEW DORP BEACH	63	M 8
CARROLL GARDENS	41	C 13	SHEEPSHEAD BAY	53	E 18	NEW SPRINGVILLE	58	H 5
CITY LINE	43	H 14	SOUTHSIDE	40	D 12	OAKWOOD	63	L 8
CLINTON HILL	42	D 13	SPRING CREEK	47	H 15	OAKWOOD BEACH	63	M 8
COBBLE HILL	41	C 13	STARRETT CITY	47	H 15	OLD PLACE	55	G 2
CONEY ISLAND	52	C 19	STUYVESANT			OLD TOWN	60	N 5
CROWN HEIGHTS	46	E 14	HEIGHTS	42	E 13	PARK HILL	60	N 4
CYPRESS HILLS	43	H 13	SUNSET PARK	44	B 16	PLEASANT PLAINS	64	E 10
DITMAS PARK	49	D 16	VINEGAR HILL	41	C 12	PORT IVORY	55	H 1
DOWNTOWN			WEEKSVILLE	42	F 14	PORT MOBIL	61	C 9
BROOKLYN	41	C 13	WILLIAMSBURG	40	D 12	PORT RICHMOND	56	K 2
DYKER HEIGHTS	48	B 17	WINDSOR TERRACE	45	D 15	PRINCE'S BAY	65	F 10
EAST FLATBUSH	50	F 16	WINGATE	46	E 14	RANDALL MANOR	57	M 2
EAST NEW YORK	47	H 14				RICHMOND VALLEY	64	D 11
EAST WILLIAMSBURG	40	E 12	**STATEN ISLAND**			RICHMONDTOWN	63	K 7
FARRAGUT	46	E 16	ANNADALE	62	G 9	ROSEBANK	60	O 4
FLATBUSH	50	E 16	ARDEN HEIGHTS	62	G 9	ROSSVILLE	61	E 8
FLATLANDS	50	F 17	ARLINGTON	55	H 2	ST. GEORGE	57	O 1
FORT GREENE	41	D 13	ARROCHAR	60	O 5	SHORE ACRES	60	P 4
FORT HAMILTON	48	A 17	BAY TERRACE	63	K 9	SOUTH BEACH	60	O 6
FULTON FERRY	41	C 12	BLOOMFIELD	55	G 3	STAPLETON	57	O 2
GEORGETOWN	51	G 16	BULLS HEAD	58	H 4	SUNNYSIDE	60	M 4
GERRITSEN BEACH	53	F 18	BUTLER MANOR	64	D 12	TODT HILL	59	L 5
GOWANUS	41	C 14	CASTLETON			TOMPKINSVILLE	57	O 2
GRAVESEND	52	C 18	CORNERS	59	L 4	TOTTENVILLE	64	B 12
GREENPOINT	40	E 11	CHARLESTON	64	C 10	TOTTENVILLE BEACH	64	C 12
GREENWOOD			CHELSEA	58	G 5	TRAVIS	58	G 5
HEIGHTS	45	C 15	CLIFTON	57	O 3	WEST BRIGHTON	56	L 2
HIGHLAND PARK	43	H 13	CONCORD	60	N 4	WESTERLEIGH	56	K 3
HOMECREST	53	D 18	DONGAN HILLS	60	M 6	WILLOWBROOK	59	J 4
KENSINGTON	45	D 16	EGBERTVILLE	59	K 6	WOODROW	61	E 9
MANHATTAN BEACH	53	E 19	ELM PARK	56	K 3			

New York City Statistics

New York City population (1990 census)
All Five Boroughs ... 7,322,564
Manhattan 1,487,536
The Bronx 1,203,789
Queens 1,951,598
Brooklyn 2,300,664
Staten Island 378,977

New York City area (in square miles)
All Five Boroughs 307
Manhattan 24
The Bronx 43
Queens 109
Brooklyn 72
Staten Island 59

.....and did you know New York City has
6,400 miles of streets
230 miles of subway lines
57 bridges
578 miles of waterfront
14.3 miles of beaches
1,543 parks and playgrounds
comprising 26,000+ acres

Quick Building Number Guide

FIRST AVENUE

Number	Location
84	5 St.
182	11 St.
236	14 St.
326	19 St.
394	23 St.
446	26 St.
576	33 St.
600	34 St.
628	36 St.
646	37 St.
742	42 St.
786	44 St.
804	45 St.
860	48 St.
876	49 St.
984	54 St.
1046	57 St.
1130	62 St.
1204	65 St.
1286	69 St.
1344	72 St.
1462	76 St.
1514	79 St.
1560	81 St.
1652	86 St.
1858	96 St.
2018	104 St.
2258	116 St.

SECOND AVENUE

Number	Location
85	5 St.
101	6 St.
173	11 St.
227	14 St.
327	19 St.
399	23 St.
561	31 St.
621	34 St.
661	36 St.
745	40 St.
823	44 St.
841	45 St.
899	48 St.
921	49 St.
1027	54 St.
1079	57 St.
1121	59 St.
1141	60 St.
1175	62 St.
1239	65 St.
1309	69 St.
1559	81 St.
1637	85 St.
1657	86 St.
1863	96 St.
2061	106 St.
2259	116 St.
2479	127 St.

THIRD AVENUE

Number	Location
125	14 St.
301	23 St.
359	26 St.
451	31 St.
507	34 St.
543	36 St.
661	42 St.
703	44 St.
795	49 St.
897	54 St.
953	57 St.
991	59 St.
1011	60 St.
1049	62 St.
1111	65 St.
1187	69 St.
1251	72 St.
1329	76 St.
1391	79 St.
1435	81 St.
1509	85 St.
1527	86 St.
1645	92 St.
1711	96 St.
1745	97 St.
1883	104 St.
1925	106 St.
2125	116 St.
2303	125 St.
2341	127 St.

LEXINGTON AVENUE

Number	Location
18	23 St.
78	26 St.
178	31 St.
236	34 St.
274	36 St.
292	37 St.
350	40 St.
392	42 St.
436	44 St.
458	45 St.
514	48 St.
536	49 St.
574	51 St.
634	54 St.
676	56 St.
698	57 St.
740	59 St.
762	60 St.
866	65 St.
942	69 St.
998	72 St.
1140	79 St.
1188	81 St.
1260	85 St.
1278	86 St.
1398	92 St.
1486	96 St.
1502	97 St.
1648	104 St.

FOURTH AVENUE

Number	Location
55	9 St.
103	11 St.
113	12 St.
159	14 St.

PARK AVENUE

Number	Location
5	34 St.
39	36 St.
49	37 St.
285	48 St.
301	49 St.
403	54 St.
439	56 St.
459	57 St.
519	60 St.
621	65 St.
701	69 St.
759	72 St.
821	76 St.
883	79 St.
921	81 St.
999	85 St.
1019	86 St.
1139	92 St.
1221	96 St.
1241	97 St.
1401	104 St.
1861	127 St.

MADISON AVENUE

Number	Location
1	23 St.
45	26 St.
133	31 St.
169	33 St.
185	34 St.
217	36 St.
233	37 St.
317	42 St.
341	44 St.
357	45 St.
411	48 St.
426	49 St.
513	53 St.
533	54 St.
571	56 St.
595	57 St.
691	62 St.
753	65 St.
829	69 St.
877	72 St.
1075	81 St.
1295	92 St.
1381	96 St.
1399	97 St.
1531	104 St.
1571	106 St.
1767	116 St.
1953	125 St.
1993	127 St.
2055	130 St.

FIFTH AVENUE

Number	Location
82	14 St.
140	19 St.
188	23 St.
216	26 St.
336	33 St.
350	34 St.
390	36 St.
406	37 St.
544	45 St.
608	49 St.
638	51 St.
670	53 St.
688	54 St.
718	56 St.
740	57 St.
839	65 St.
877	69 St.
947	76 St.
997	81 St.
1037	85 St.
1047	86 St.
1107	92 St.
1145	96 St.
1159	97 St.
1227	104 St.
1418	116 St.
2020	125 St.
2058	127 St.

SIXTH AVENUE

Number	Location
400	W.8 St.
462	11 St.
528	14 St.
634	19 St.
716	23 St.
902	34 St.
980	36 St.
1000	37 St.
1100	42 St.
1160	45 St.
1240	49 St.
1280	51 St.
1320	53 St.
1380	56 St.
1400	57 St.

SEVENTH AVENUE

Number	Location
62	14 St.
148	19 St.
222	23 St.
278	26 St.
398	32 St.
416	33 St.
438	34 St.
480	36 St.
498	37 St.
558	40 St.
598	42 St.
740	49 St.
782	51 St.
840	54 St.
884	56 St.
900	57 St.

BROADWAY

Number	Location
91	Wall St.
207	Fulton St.
271	Chambers St.
303	Duane St.
417	Canal St.
487	Broome St.
567	Prince St.
855	14 St.
887	19 St.
957	23 St.
1139	26 St.
1291	33 St.
1351	36 St.
1371	37 St.

1472	42 St.	790	48 St.	518	85 St.	1021	110 St.
1514	44 St.	810	49 St.	538	86 St.	1337	125 St.
1532	45 St.	846	51 St.	734	96 St.	1517	135 St.
1612	49 St.	910	54 St.	758	97 St.	1579	138 St.
1652	51 St.	948	56 St.	936	106 St.	1637	141 St.
1706	54 St.	968	57 St.	1017	110 St.	1721	145 St.
1752	56 St.					1919	155 St.
1774	57 St.					2119	165 St.

CENTRAL PARK WEST

Number	Location
24	62 St.
52	65 St.
90	69 St.
120	72 St.
164	76 St.
250	85 St.
262	86 St.
322	92 St.
442	104 St.
456	106 St.

TENTH AVENUE

Number	Location
58	14 St.
146	19 St.
222	23 St.
368	31 St.
404	33 St.
426	34 St.
466	36 St.
484	37 St.
538	40 St.
576	42 St.
614	44 St.
636	45 St.
686	48 St.
708	49 St.
750	51 St.
812	54 St.
852	56 St.
872	57 St.

WEST END AVENUE

Number	Location
518	85 St.
536	86 St.
656	92 St.
740	96 St.
938	106 St.

Manhattan building numbers:

1882	62 St.
2020	69 St.
2082	72 St.
2220	79 St.
2260	81 St.
2342	85 St.
2356	86 St.
2478	92 St.
2560	96 St.
2718	104 St.
2760	106 St.
2836	110 St.
3194	125 St.
3336	135 St.
3396	138 St.
3458	141 St.
3722	155 St.
4240	181 St.

NINTH AVENUE

Number	Location
45	14 St.
147	19 St.
211	23 St.
367	31 St.
431	34 St.
483	37 St.
581	42 St.
621	44 St.
719	49 St.
757	51 St.
815	54 St.
861	56 St.
875	57 St.

AMSTERDAM AVE

Number	Location
121	65 St.
259	72 St.
341	76 St.
441	81 St.
521	85 St.
539	86 St.
659	92 St.
741	96 St.
761	97 St.
901	104 St.
939	106 St.

RIVERSIDE DRIVE

Number	Location
2	72 St.
40	76 St.
90	81 St.
130	85 St.
140	86 St.
198	92 St.
248	97 St.
320	104 St.
338	106 St.
378	Cathedral St.
576	135 St.
680	145 St.

EIGHTH AVENUE

Number	Location
80	14 St.
178	19 St.
258	23 St.
322	26 St.
458	33 St.
478	34 St.
518	36 St.
538	37 St.
620	40 St.
660	42 St.
698	44 St.
724	45 St.

COLUMBUS AVENUE

Number	Location
54	62 St.
258	72 St.

BOWERY

Number	Location
77	Canal St.
95	Hester St.
129	Grand St.
155	Broome St.
215	Rivington St.
247	Stanton St.
345	3 St.

Zip Codes
New York City Post Office Areas

For complete five-digit zip codes add the appropriate numbers below to the red zone numbers shown on the maps.

MANHATTAN: add 10 before three digit zone numbers, 100 before two digit numbers, and 1000 before single digit numbers.

THE BRONX: add 104 before two digit zone numbers.

QUEENS:
    Long Island City: add 1110 before zone numbers 1-6.
    Jamaica: add 114 before zone numbers 11-36, 39, 46.
    Flushing: add 113 before zone numbers 51-85.
    Far Rockaway: add 116 before zone numbers 91-97.
    Floral Park: add 1100 before zone numbers 1-4.

BROOKLYN: add 112 before two digit zone numbers and 1120 before single digit zone numbers.

STATEN ISLAND: add 103 before two digit zone numbers and 1030 before single digit zone numbers.

USING THE "BLUE LINE" GRID SQUARE LOCATION SYSTEM

Blue lines are drawn horizontally and vertically on the map, forming grid squares. These squares can be identified by letters and numbers appearing in the map margins. Streets and roads are listed alphabetically in the index by borough. The letters and numbers after the name give the map number and grid square in which the street appears.

For example, to locate Wall St. in Manhattan, find the heading for Manhattan in the index. The 1 D22 after the street name shows that Wall St. can be located on map 1 within grid square D22, as shown to the right.

NOTES: Numbered streets are indexed after the alphabetical listing.
"*" indicates that street name is not shown on map due to lack of space.

	A	B	C	D
18				
19				
20				
21				
22				X

ABBREVIATIONS USED ON HAGSTROM MAPS

Al	Alley	N	North
Av	Avenue	Pk	Park
Blvd	Boulevard	Pkwy	Parkway
Boro	Borough	Pl	Place
Cem	Cemetery	PLGD/PG	Playground
Cir	Circle	Plz	Plaza
CO	County	Rd	Road
Cr	Creek	Riv	River
Cres	Crescent	RR	Railroad
Ct	Court	S	South
Dr	Drive	Sq	Square
E	East	St	Saint
Expwy	Expressway	St	Street
Ft	Fort	Sta	Station
GC	Golf Club	Ter	Terrace
Hts	Heights	Term	Terminal
Hwy	Highway	Tpk	Turnpike
Isl, I	Island	Tr	Trail
La	Lane	Twp	Township
Mt	Mount	W	West
		Wk	Walk

STREET	MAP	GRID

A

A Philip
Randolph Sq .... 4 C 13
Abingdon Sq .... 2 C 19
Abraham Kazan
St .... 1 F 20
Academy St .... 6 B 7
Adam Clayton
Powell Jr Blvd .. 4 C 13
Adm George
Dewey ....
Promenade ..... 1 D 22
Adrian Av .... 6 B 6
African Sq .... 4 C 12
Albany St .... 5 D 22
Alex Rose Pl .... 5 B 8
Alexander
Hamilton Sq .... 4 B 11
Allard K
Lowenstein Plz
*(West side of
United
Nations Plz at
E 45th St) .... 2 E 17
Allen St .... 1 E 21
American Express
Plz *(125
Broad St) .... 1 D 22
Amsterdam Av ... 3 B 16
Ann St .... 1 D 21
Archbishop Fulton
J Sheen Pl .... 2 D 17
Arden St .... 6 B 7
Asser Levy Pl ..... 2 E 19
Astor Pl .... 1 D 20
Astor Plz (1515
Broadway) .... 2 C 17
Attorney St .... 1 E 20
Audubon Av .... 5 B 9
Avenue A .... 2 E 19
Avenue B .... 2 E 19
Avenue C .... 2 E 19
Avenue D .... 2 F 19
Avenue of the
Americas
(6th Av) .... 1 D 20
Avenue of the
Finest .... 1 E 21

B

Bache Plz .... 1 D 21
Bank St .... 1 C 20
Banker Trust Plz
*(130 Liberty
St) .... 1 D 22
Barclay St .... 1 D 21
Barrow St .... 1 C 20
Baruch Dr .... 1 F 20
Baruch Pl .... 1 F 20
Battery Park Plz
*(Pearl & State
Sts) .... 1 D 22
Battery Pl .... 1 D 22
Baxter St .... 1 D 21
Bayard St .... 1 D 21
Beach St .... 1 C 21
Beak St .... 6 B 7
Beaver St .... 1 D 22
Bedford St .... 1 C 20
Beekman Pl .... 2 E 17
Beekman St .... 1 D 21
Bennett Av .... 5 B 8

Benson St .... 1 D 21
Bethune St .... 1 C 20
Bialystoker Pl ...... 1 F 20
Bleecker St .... 1 D 20
Bloomfield St .... 2 B 19
Bogardus Pl .... 5 B 8
Bond St .... 1 D 20
Bowery .... 1 E 21
Bowling Green ..... 1 D 22
Bradhurst Av .... 4 C 11
Bridge St .... 1 D 22
Broad St .... 1 D 22
Broadway .... 1 D 22
Broadway Alley
*(From E 26th St
to E 27th St
between 2nd
and 3rd Av) ...... 2 D 18
Broadway Pl
*(West 46th St
& Broadway) .... 2 C 17
Broadway Ter ...... 5 B 8
Broome St .... 1 D 20
Burling Slip .... 1 E 22

C

Cabrini Blvd .... 5 B 9
Canal St .... 1 C 20
Cannon St .... 1 F 20
Cardinal Hayes
Pl .... 1 D 21
Cardinal Stepinac
Pl .... 2 B 18
Carlisle St .... 1 D 22
Carmine St .... 1 C 20
Cathedral Pkwy ... 4 B 13
Catherine La .... 1 D 21
Catherine Slip ...... 1 E 21
Catherine St .... 1 E 21
Cedar St .... 1 D 22
Central Park N ..... 4 D 13
Central Park S
(Olmsted
Way) .... 3 C 16
Central Park W .... 3 C 16
Centre Market
Pl .... 1 D 20
Centre St .... 1 D 21
Chambers Ct .... 1 C 21
Chambers St .... 1 C 21
Charles La .... 1 C 20
Charles St .... 1 C 20
Charlton St .... 1 C 20
Chase Manhattan
Plz .... 1 D 22
Chatham Sq .... 1 E 21
Chelsea Sq .... 2 C 19
Cherokee Pl .... 3 E 15
Cherry St .... 1 E 21
Chisum Pl .... 4 D 11
Chittenden Av ...... 5 B 8
Christopher St ..... 1 C 20
Chrystie St .... 1 E 21
Church St .... 1 D 22
Circle Line Plz
*(west end of
42nd St &
12th Ave) .... 2 B 17
City Hall .... 1 D 21
Claremont Av ...... 4 B 13
Clarkson St .... 1 C 20
Cleveland Pl .... 1 D 20
Cliff St .... 1 D 22

Clinton St .... 1 E 21
Coenties Alley ..... 1 D 22
Coenties Slip .... 1 D 22
Collister St .... 1 C 21
Col Charles Young
Triangle .... 5 C 10
Col Robert
Magaw Pl .... 5 B 8
Columbia St .... 1 F 20
Columbus Av .... 3 C 15
Columbus Cir ...... 3 C 16
Commerce St ...... 1 C 20
Confucius Plz ...... 1 E 21
Convent Av .... 4 C 12
Convent Hill .... 4 C 12
Cooper Sq .... 1 D 20
Cooper St .... 6 B 7
Cornelia St .... 1 C 20
Cortlandt Alley .... 1 D 21
Cortlandt St .... 1 D 22
Crosby St .... 1 D 20
Cumming St .... 6 B 7

D

Dag Hammarskjold
Plz (305-311
East 47th St) ... 2 E 17
David B Friedland
Sq *(Broadway,
St Nicolas &
W 170th St) ..... 5 B 9
David Ben-Gurion
Pl *(E 43rd St,
bet Fifth &
Vanderbilt
Aves) .... 2 D 17
Delancey St .... 1 E 20
Delancey St S ...... 1 E 20
Depew Pl .... 2 D 17
Desbrosses St ..... 1 C 21
Dey St .... 1 D 22
Diamond &
Jewelry Way
*(W 47th St, bet
Fifth Av & Av of
the Americas) .. 2 D 17
Division St .... 1 E 21
Dominick St .... 1 C 20
Dongan Pl .... 6 B 7
Donnellon Sq ...... 5 C 10
Dorrence Brook
Sq *(W 136th St,
St Nicolas &
Edgecomb
Aves) .... 4 C 11
Douglas MacArthur
Plz .... 2 E 17
Dover St .... 1 E 21
Downing St .... 1 C 20
Doyers St .... 1 E 21
Duane St .... 1 D 21
Duffy Sq .... 2 C 17
Duke Ellington
Blvd
(W 106th St) .... 4 B 13
Dutch St .... 1 D 22
Dyckman St .... 6 B 7
Dyer Av .... 2 C 18

E

East Broadway .... 1 E 21
East End Av .... 3 E 15

East Houston
St .... 1 D 20
East River Dr (see
Franklin D
Roosevelt Dr) ... 4 E 13
East River Piers .. 1 D 22
East Rd
(Roosevelt
Island) .... 2 F 17
East Side Express
Hwy (South St
Viaduct) .... 1 E 22
East Tower Dr .... 3 B 16
East 1st St .... 1 E 20
East 2nd St .... 1 E 20
East 3rd St .... 1 E 20
East 4th St .... 1 E 20
East 5th St .... 1 E 20
East 6th St .... 1 E 20
East 7th St .... 1 E 20
East 8th St .... 2 D 19
East 9th St .... 2 D 19
East 10th St .... 2 D 19
East 11th St .... 2 D 19
East 12th St .... 2 D 19
East 13th St .... 2 D 19
East 14th St .... 2 D 19
East 15th St .... 2 D 19
East 16th St .... 2 D 19
East 17th St .... 2 D 19
East 18th St .... 2 D 19
East 19th St .... 2 D 19
East 20th St .... 2 D 19
East 21st St .... 2 D 19
East 22nd St ...... 2 D 19
East 23rd St .... 2 D 19
East 24th St .... 2 D 18
East 25th St .... 2 D 18
East 26th St .... 2 D 18
East 27th St .... 2 D 18
East 28th St .... 2 D 18
East 29th St .... 2 D 18
East 30th St .... 2 D 18
East 31st St .... 2 D 18
East 32nd St ...... 2 D 18
East 33rd St .... 2 D 18
East 34th St .... 2 D 18
East 35th St .... 2 D 18
East 36th St .... 2 D 18
East 37th St .... 2 D 18
East 38th St .... 2 D 18
East 39th St .... 2 D 18
East 40th St .... 2 D 18
East 41st St .... 2 D 18
East 42nd St ...... 2 D 17
East 43rd St .... 2 D 17
East 44th St .... 2 D 17
East 45th St .... 2 D 17
East 46th St .... 2 D 17
East 47th St .... 2 D 17
East 48th St .... 2 D 17
East 49th St .... 2 D 17
East 50th St .... 2 D 17
East 51st St .... 2 D 17
East 52nd St ...... 2 D 17
East 53rd St .... 2 D 17
East 54th St .... 2 D 17
East 55th St .... 2 D 17
East 56th St .... 2 D 17
East 57th St .... 2 D 17
East 58th St .... 2 D 17
East 59th St .... 3 D 16
East 60th St .... 3 D 16
East 61st St .... 3 D 16

STREET	MAP	GRID
East 62nd St	3	D 16
East 63rd St	3	D 16
East 64th St	3	D 16
East 65th St	3	D 16
East 66th St	3	D 16
East 67th St	3	D 16
East 68th St	3	D 16
East 69th St	3	D 16
East 70th St	3	D 16
East 71st St	3	D 16
East 72nd St	3	D 16
East 73rd St	3	D 16
East 74th St	3	D 15
East 75th St	3	D 15
East 76th St	3	D 15
East 77th St	3	D 15
East 78th St	3	D 15
East 79th St	3	D 15
East 80th St	3	D 15
East 81st St	3	D 15
East 82nd St	3	D 15
East 83rd St	3	D 15
East 84th St	3	D 15
East 85th St	3	D 15
East 86th St	3	D 15
East 87th St	3	D 15
East 88th St	3	D 15
East 89th St	3	D 15
East 90th St	3	D 14
East 91st St	3	D 14
East 92nd St	3	D 14
East 93rd St	3	D 14
East 94th St	3	D 14
East 95th St	3	D 14
East 96th St	3	D 14
East 97th St	3	D 14
East 98th St	3	D 14
East 99th St	3	D 14
East 100th St	3	D 14
East 101st St	3	D 14
East 102nd St	3	D 14
East 103rd St	3	D 14
East 104th St	3	D 14
East 105th St	4	D 13
East 106th St	4	D 13
East 107th St	4	D 13
East 108th St	4	D 13
East 109th St	4	D 13
East 110th St	4	D 13
East 111th St	4	D 13
East 112th St	4	D 13
East 113th St	4	E 13
East 114th St	4	E 13
East 115th St	4	D 13
East 116th St	4	D 13
East 117th St	4	D 13
East 118th St	4	D 13
East 119th St	4	D 13
East 120th St	4	D 12
East 121st St	4	D 12
East 122nd St	4	D 12
East 123rd St	4	D 12
East 124th St	4	D 12
East 125th St	4	D 12
East 126th St	4	D 12
East 127th St	4	D 12
East 128th St	4	D 12
East 129th St	4	D 12
East 130th St	4	D 12
East 131st St	4	D 12
East 132nd St	4	D 12
East 135th St	4	D 11
East 138th St	4	D 11
East 139th St	4	D 11

STREET	MAP	GRID
Edgar Allan Poe St	3	B 15
Edgar St	1	D 22
Edgecombe Av	4	C 11
Edward L Morgan Pl	5	B 10
Eighth Av	2	C 19
Eldridge St	1	E 21
Eleventh Av	2	B 18
Elizabeth St	1	E 21
Elk St	1	D 21
Ellwood St	6	B 7
Emerson St	6	B 7
Ericsson Pl	1	D 21
Esplanade Gardens Plz *(Lenox Av bet 147th and 145th Sts)	4	C 10
Essex St	1	E 21
Exchange Alley	1	D 22
Exchange Pl	1	D 22
Exchange Plz *(Broadway, Trinity Pl & Exchange Al)	1	D 22
Exterior St	6	C 7
Extra Pl	1	E 20
Fairview Av	5	B 8
Fashion Av (7th Av)	2	C 18
Father Demo Sq	1	C 20
Father Fagan Sq	1	D 20
Federal Plz	1	D 21
Federal Reserve Plz *(Liberty & Nassau Sts & Maiden La)	1	D 22
Fifth Av	2	D 18
Finn Sq	1	D 21
First Av	1	E 20
First Pl	1	D 22
Fletcher St	1	D 22
Foley Sq	1	D 21
Forsyth St	1	E 21
Fort Charles Pl	6	C 6
Fort George Av	5	B 8
Fort George Hill	5	B 8
Fort Washington Av	5	B 8
Fourth Av	1	D 20
Frank D'Amico Plz *(bet Hester St & Canal St at Forsyth St)	1	E 21
Frankfort St	1	D 21
Franklin D Roosevelt Dr	4	E 19
Franklin Pl	1	D 21
Franklin Sq*	1	D 21
Franklin St	1	D 21
Frawley Cir	4	D 13
Frederick Douglass Blvd	4	C 13
Frederick Douglass Cir	4	C 13
Freedom Pl	3	B 16
Freeman Alley	1	E 20
Front St	1	E 22

STREET	MAP	GRID
Fulton Market	1	E 22
Fulton St	1	D 21
Gansevoort St	2	C 19
Gateway Plz	1	C 22
Gay St	1	C 20
Gold St	1	D 22
Gouverneur La	1	D 22
Gouverneur Slip E	1	F 21
Gouverneur Slip W	1	F 21
Gouverneur St	1	F 21
Gracie Sq	3	E 15
Gracie Ter	3	E 15
Gramercy Park	2	D 19
Gramercy Park E	2	D 19
Gramercy Park W	2	D 19
Grand Army Plz	3	D 16
Grand St	1	E 20
Great Jones Alley	1	D 20
Great Jones St	1	D 20
Greeley Sq	2	C 18
Greene St	1	D 21
Greenwich Av	2	C 19
Greenwich St	1	C 21
Grove Pl	1	C 20
Grove St	1	C 20
Gustave Hartman Sq	1	E 20
Gustave Levy Pl *(between 5th Av & Madison Av from 98th St to 102nd St)	3	D 14
Hamill Pl * (at Foley Sq between Centre St and Worth St)	1	D 21
Hamilton Pl	4	B 11
Hamilton Ter	4	C 11
Hancock Pl	4	C 12
Hancock Sq	4	C 12
Hanover Plz *(Bounded by Beaver, Hanover & Pear Sts)	1	D 22
Hanover Sq	1	D 22
Hanover St	1	D 22
Harkness Plz *(W 62nd St, bet Columbus Av & Broadway)	3	C 16
Harlem River Dr	5	C 10
Harlem River Driveway	5	C 9
Harrison St	1	C 21
Harry Blumenstein Plz *(Broome & Pitt Sts)	1	E 20
Harry Delancey Plz	1	E 20
Harry Howard Sq	1	D 21
Haven Av	5	B 9

STREET	MAP	GRID
Haven Plz *(bet Szold Pl & Av C, at East 12th St)	2	E 19
Henderson Pl	3	E 15
Henry Hudson Pkwy	6	B 7
Henry Hudson Pkwy	3	B 15
Henry J Browne Blvd	3	C 14
Henry Phipps Plz *(East 26th to 29th Sts, bet First and Second Aves)	2	E 18
Henry St	1	E 21
Henshaw St	6	B 7
Herald Sq	2	D 18
Hester St	1	D 21
Hillside Av	5	B 8
Hogan Pl	1	D 21
Holland Tunnel Plz *(Varick St, bet Laight & Vestry Sts)	1	D 21
Holy Rosary Sq *(Pleasant Av & East 119th St)	4	E 13
Horatio St	2	C 19
Houston St (see East or West Houston Sts)		
Howard Sq	1	D 21
Howard St	1	D 21
Hubert St	1	C 21
Hudson River Piers (see North River Piers)		
Hudson St	1	D 20
Independence Plz	1	C 21
Independence Plz N	1	C 21
Independence Plz S	1	C 21
Indian Rd	6	B 6
Insurance Plz *(101 Murray St)	1	C 21
Inwood Plz	6	B 7
Irving Pl	2	D 19
Isham St	6	B 7
Jackson Sq	2	C 19
Jackson St	1	F 20
Jacobus Pl	6	B 6
James St	1	E 21
Jane St	2	C 19
Jay St	1	C 21
Jefferson St	1	E 21
Jersey St	1	D 20
Joe Louis Plz *(W 31st to 33rd Sts, bet Seventh & Eighth Aves)	2	C 18

STREET	MAP	GRID

John Delury Sr. Plz *(triangular area at intersection of Fulton St and Gold St) .... 1　D 22
John P Ladson Pl *(Lenox Av, Central Park North to West 11th St) .... 4　D 13
John St .... 1　D 22
Jones Alley .... 1　D 20
Jones St .... 1　C 20
J P Ward St .... 1　D 22
Jumel Pl .... 5　C 9
Jumel Ter .... 5　C 10

K

Kenmare St .... 1　D 20
Kent Pl *(connects Pearl St with Cardinal Hayes Pl) .... 1　D 21
King St .... 1　C 20

L

La Guardia Pl ...... 1　D 20
La Salle St .... 4　B 12
Lafayette Plz .... 5　B 8
Lafayette St .... 1　D 21
Laight St .... 1　C 21
Langston Hughes Pl .... 4　D 12
Laurel Hill Ter ...... 5　C 8
Legion Mem Sq ... 1　D 22
Lenox Av (Malcolm X Blvd) .... 4　D 13
Lenox Ter .... 4　D 11
Leonard St .... 1　D 21
Leroy St .... 1　C 20
Lewis St .... 1　F 20
Lexington Av .... 2　D 18
Liberty Pl .... 1　D 22
Liberty Plz *(77-79 Liberty St) .... 1　D 22
Liberty St .... 1　D 22
Lieut William Tighe Triangle (Dyckman St & Broadway) .... 6　B 7
Lillian Wald Dr *(LillianWald Houses) .... 1　F 20
Lincoln Pl *(East 113th St West of 3rd Av) .... 4　D 13
Lincoln Sq .... 3　C 16
Lispenard St .... 1　D 21
Little West 12th St .... 2　B 19
Livingston Pl *(see Nathan D Perlman Plz) ... 2　E 19
Louise Nevelson Plz *(William St, bet Maiden La & Liberty St) .... 1　D 22
Ludlow St .... 1　E 21
Luis Muñoz Marin Blvd .... 4　D 13

M

MacDougal Alley .... 1　D 20
MacDougal St ...... 1　D 20
Machito Sq *(Third Av & E 111th St) .... 4　E 13
Macombs Pl .... 5　C 10
Madison Av .... 2　D 18
Madison Sq Plz ... 2　D 18
Madison St .... 1　E 21
Magaw Pl .... 5　B 8
Maher Cir .... 5　C 10
Maiden La .... 1　D 22
Main St (Roosevelt Island) .... 3　F 16
Mangin St .... 1　F 20
Manhattan Alley *(connects Reade St with .... *Republican Al) .... 1　D 21
Manhattan Av ...... 3　C 14
Manhattan Pl .... 1　D 21
Manhattan Plz *(W 42nd & 43rd Sts, bet Ninth & Tenth Aves) ..... 2　B 17
Marble Hill Av ...... 6　C 6
Marble Hill La ...... 6　C 6
Margaret Corbin Dr .... 6　B 7
Margaret Corbin Plz .... 5　B 8
Market Slip .... 1　E 21
Market St .... 1　E 21
Marketfield St ...... 1　D 22
Martin Luther King Jr Blvd E .... 4　D 12
Martin Luther King Jr Blvd W ..... 4　B 12
Martin R. Celic Plz *(SW corner of Pitt St and Delancey St) .... 1　E 20
Martin Sq .... 6　B 7
McKenna Sq .... 5　B 9
McNally Plz .... 5　C 8
Mercer St .... 1　D 21
Mill La .... 1　D 22
Mill Rock Plz *(1797-1811 First Av) .... 3　E 14
Milligan Pl .... 2　C 19
Minetta La .... 1　D 20
Minetta Pl .... 1　D 20
Minetta St .... 1　D 20
Mitchell Pl .... 2　E 17
Mitchell Sq .... 5　B 9
Monroe St .... 1　E 21
Mgr Francis J Kett Plz *(Tenth Av, bet West 204th & West 205th Sts) .... 6　B 7
Montefiore Sq ..... 4　B 11
Montgomery St ... 1　F 21
Moore St .... 1　D 22
Morningside Av .... 4　C 13
Morningside Dr .... 4　C 13
Morris St .... 1　D 22
Morton St .... 1　C 20
Mosco St .... 1　E 21

Motorgate Plz (Roosevelt Island) .... 3　F 16
Mott St .... 1　E 21
Mount Carmel Sq *(Pleasant Av & East 116th St) .... 4　E 13
Mount Morris Park Av .... 4　D 12
Mount Morris Park W .... 4　D 12
Mulberry St .... 1　D 21
Mulry Sq .... 2　C 19
Murray St .... 1　C 21
Museum Mile (Fifth Av) .... 3　D 15

N

Nagle Av .... 5　B 8
Nassau St .... 1　D 22
Nathan Cummings Plz *(E 100th St bet Park & Madison Aves) .... 3　D 14
Nathan D Perlman Pl .... 2　E 19
Nelson & Winnie Mandela Corner *(E 42nd St & Second Avenue, SE Corner) ..... 2　E 18
Nevada Plz *(W 69th & 70th Sts, bet Broadway & Amsterdam Av) .... 3　B 16
New St .... 1　D 22
New York Plz ...... 1　D 22
Ninth Av .... 2　C 19
Norfolk St .... 1　E 20
North End Av ...... 1　C 21
North Moore St ... 1　C 21
North River Piers .... 1　C 21

O

Odell M Clark Pl *(W 138th St, bet Lenox Av & Adam Clayton Powell Jr Blvd) .... 4　C 11
Old Broadway ..... 4　B 12
Old Slip .... 1　D 22
Oliver St .... 1　E 21
Orchard St .... 1　E 21
Overlook Ter .... 5　B 8

P

Pace Plz .... 1　D 21
Paladino Av .... 4　E 12
Paramount Plz *(1633 Broadway) .... 2　C 17
Park Av .... 3　D 15
Park Av Plz *(55 East 52nd St) ... 2　D 17
Park Av South ..... 2　D 19
Park Pl .... 1　D 21

Park Row .... 1　D 21
Park St .... 1　D 21
Park Ter E .... 6　B 6
Park Ter W .... 6　B 6
Patchin Pl .... 2　C 19
Payson Av .... 6　B 7
Pearl St .... 1　D 22
Peck Slip .... 1　E 21
Pell St .... 1　E 21
Pennsylvania Plz .... 2　C 18
Peretz Sq .... 1　E 20
Perry St .... 1　C 20
Pershing Sq .... 2　D 17
Peter Cooper Rd .... 2　E 19
Peter Minuit Plz ... 1　D 22
Pike Slip .... 1　E 21
Pike St .... 1　E 21
Pine St .... 1　D 22
Pinehurst Av North .... 5　B 9
Pinehurst Av South .... 5　B 9
Pitt St .... 1　E 20
Platt St .... 1　D 22
Plaza Lafayette ... 5　B 9
Pleasant Av .... 4　E 13
Police Plz .... 1　D 21
PomanderWalk ... 3　B 14
Post Av .... 6　B 7
Prince St .... 1　D 20
Printing House Sq *(Park Row & Nassau St) .... 1　D 21

Q

Queensboro Bridge Plz *(East 58th & 59th Sts and Second Av) ...... 3　E 16

R

RaoulWallenberg Walk *(W side United Nations Plz, E 42nd to 47th Sts) .... 2　E 17
Reade St .... 1　D 21
Rector Pl .... 1　C 22
Rector St .... 1　D 22
Reinhold Niebuhr Pl .... 4　B 12
Renwick St .... 1　C 20
Republican Alley *(connects Elk St with *Manhattan Al) .... 1　D 21
Ridge St .... 1　E 20
River Rd .... 3　F 16
River Ter .... 1　C 21
Riverside Dr .... 3　B 16
Riverside Dr E .... 4　B 12
Riverside Dr W ... 4　B 12
Riverview Ter ...... 3　E 16
Rivington St .... 1　E 20
Robert F Wagner Sr Pl .... 1　E 21
Rockefeller Plz .... 2　D 17
Ronald E McNair Pl .... 4　E 12

STREET	MAP	GRID
Roosevelt Sq 4	C 12	
Rose St *(connects		
Frankfort St with		
Av of the		
Finest) 1	D 21	
Ruppert Plz		
*(1751-1763		
Second Av) 3	E 14	
Rutgers Slip 1	E 21	
Rutgers St 1	E 21	
Rutherford Pl 2	E 19	
Ryders Alley 1	D 21	

S

Saint Andrew's		
Plz 1	D 21	
Saint Clair Pl 4	B 12	
Saint James Pl 1	E 21	
Saint Johns La 1	D 21	
Saint Lukes Pl 1	C 20	
Saint Marks Pl 2	E 19	
Saint Nicholas		
Av 4	C 13	
Saint Nicholas		
Pl 5	C 10	
Saint Nicholas		
Ter 4	C 12	
Saint Paul's Pl		
*(E 117th St, bet		
Park & Lexington		
Aves) 4	D 13	
Sakharov Bonner		
Corner *(Third		
Av & 67th St,		
SW corner) 3	D 16	
Samuel A Spiegel		
Sq 1	F 20	
Samuel Dickstein		
Plz 1	E 20	
Samuel Marx		
Triangle *(Adam		
Clayton Powell Jr		
Blvd, St Nicolas		
Av & W 115th		
St) 4	C 13	
Schomberg Plz		
*(E 110th to		
111th Sts, bet		
Fifth & Madison		
Ave) 4	D 13	
Scott Sq 6	B 7	
Seaman Av 6	B 7	
Seaport Plz *(199		
Water St) 1	D 22	
Second Av 1	E 20	
Second Av 1	D 22	
Seminary Rd		
*(W 122nd St, bet		
Claremont Av &		
Amsterdam		
Av) 4	B 12	
Seventh Av 2	C 19	
Seventh Av S 1	C 20	
Sheridan Sq 1	C 20	
Sheriff St 1	F 20	
Sherman Av 6	B 7	
Sherman Plz		
*(2039-2049		
Broadway) 2	B 17	
Sherman Sq 3	B 16	
Shinbone Alley 1	D 20	
Sickles St 6	B 7	
Sixth Av (see		
Avenue of the		

Americas) 2	D 19	
Sniffen Ct 2	D 18	
South End Av 1	C 22	
South Ferry 1	D 22	
South Ferry Plz ... 1	D 22	
South Pinehurst		
Av 5	B 9	
South St 1	D 22	
South Street		
Seaport 1	E 22	
South Street		
Viaduct 1	E 21	
South William		
St 1	D 22	
Spring St 1	C 20	
Spruce St 1	D 21	
Staff St 6	B 7	
Stanton St 1	E 20	
Staple St 1	D 21	
State St 1	D 22	
State St Plz *(1-6		
State St) 1	D 22	
Steve Flanders Sq		
*(West side of		
Broadway &		
Murray St) 1	D 21	
Stevens Plz *(1181		
Av of the		
Americas) 2	C 17	
Stone St 1	D 22	
Straus Sq 1	E 21	
Stuyvesant		
Oval 2	E 19	
Stuyvesant Sq 2	E 19	
Stuyvesant St 2	D 19	
Suffolk St 1	E 20	
Sullivan St 1	D 20	
Sunken Plz		
*(Rockefeller		
Center) 2	D 17	
Sutton Place 3	E 17	
Sutton Place S 2	E 17	
Sutton Sq 2	E 16	
Sylvan Ct 4	D 12	
Sylvan Pl 4	D 12	
Sylvan Ter 5	C 10	
Szold Pl 2	F 19	

T

Taras Shevchenko		
Pl 1	E 20	
Temple St 1	D 22	
Tenth Av 2	B 19	
Terrace View Av ... 6	B 6	
Teunisson Pl 6	B 6	
Thames St 1	D 22	
Thayer St 6	B 7	
Theatre Alley 1	D 21	
Thelonius Sphere		
Monk Cir		
*(W 63rd St, off		
West End Av) 3	B 16	
Third Av 2	D 18	
Third Pl 1	D 22	
Thomas St 1	D 21	
Thompson St 1	D 20	
Tiemann Pl 4	B 12	
Times Sq 2	C 17	
Times Sq Plz		
*(1475		
Broadway) 2	C 17	
Trans-Manhattan		
Expwy 5	B 9	

Trimble Pl 1	D 21	
Trinity Pl 1	D 22	
Tudor City Pl 2	E 18	
Tunnel Entrance		
St 2	E 18	
Tunnel Exit St 2	E 18	
Twelfth Av 2	B 17	

U

Union Sq 2	D 19	
Union Sq E 2	D 19	
Union Sq W 2	D 19	
United Nations		
Headquarters .. 2	E 17	
United Nations		
Plz 2	E 17	
University Pl 2	D 19	
University Plz		
*(110-118		
Bleecker St) 1	D 20	

V

Van Corlear Pl 6	B 6	
Vandam St 1	C 20	
Vanderbilt Av 2	D 17	
Vanderbilt		
Concourse		
*(Grand Central		
Station) 2	D 17	
Varick St 1	D 21	
Verdi Sq 3	B 16	
Vermilyea Av 6	B 7	
Vesey St 1	D 21	
Vestry St 1	C 21	
VietnamVeterans'		
Plz 1	D 22	
Village Sq 2	D 19	
Vincent F Albano		
Sq *(Tudor City		
Pl & East 41st		
St) 2	E 18	

W

Wadsworth Av 5	B 9	
Wadsworth Ter 5	B 8	
Walker St 1	D 21	
Wall St 1	D 22	
Wall St Plz *(88		
Pine St) 1	D 22	
Wanamaker Pl 2	D 19	
Warren St 1	C 21	
Washington		
Mews 1	D 20	
Washington Pl 1	D 20	
Washington Sq		
E 1	D 20	
Washington Sq		
N 1	D 20	
Washington Sq		
S 1	D 20	
Washington Sq		
W 1	D 20	
Washington St 1	D 20	
Washington Ter ... 5	B 8	
Water St 1	D 22	
Waterside Plz 2	E 18	
Watts St 1	C 21	
Waverly Pl 1	D 20	
W. C. Handy's Pl .. 2	C 17	
Weehawken St 1	C 20	

Wesley Williams Pl		
*(W 135th St, bet		
Lenox Av & Adam		
Clayton Powell Jr		
Blvd) 4	C 11	
West Broadway ... 1	D 20	
West End Av 3	B 16	
West Houston		
St 1	C 20	
West Rd		
(Roosevelt		
Island) 2	E 17	
West St 1	D 22	
West Thames		
St 1	C 22	
West 3rd St 1	D 20	
West 4th St 1	D 20	
West 8th St 2	D 19	
West 9th St 2	D 19	
West 10th St 1	C 20	
West 11th St 1	C 20	
West 12th St 1	C 20	
West 13th St 2	C 19	
West 14th St 2	C 19	
West 15th St 2	B 19	
West 16th St 2	B 19	
West 17th St 2	B 19	
West 18th St 2	B 19	
West 19th St 2	B 19	
West 20th St 2	B 19	
West 21st St 2	B 19	
West 22nd St 2	B 19	
West 23rd St 2	B 19	
West 24th St 2	B 19	
West 25th St 2	B 18	
West 26th St 2	B 18	
West 27th St 2	B 18	
West 28th St 2	B 18	
West 29th St 2	B 18	
West 30th St 2	B 18	
West 31st St 2	C 18	
West 32nd St 2	B 18	
West 33rd St 2	B 18	
West 34th St 2	B 18	
West 35th St 2	B 18	
West 36th St 2	B 18	
West 37th St 2	B 18	
West 38th St 2	C 18	
West 39th St 2	C 18	
West 40th St 2	B 18	
West 41st St 2	B 18	
West 42nd St 2	B 17	
West 43rd St 2	B 17	
West 44th St 2	B 17	
West 45th St 2	B 17	
West 46th St 2	B 17	
West 47th St 2	B 17	
West 48th St 2	B 17	
West 49th St 2	B 17	
West 50th St 2	B 17	
West 51st St 2	B 17	
West 52nd St 2	B 17	
West 53rd St 2	B 17	
West 54th St 2	B 17	
West 55th St 2	B 17	
West 56th St 2	B 17	
West 57th St 2	B 17	
West 58th St 2	B 17	
West 59th St 3	B 16	
West 60th St 3	B 16	
West 61st St 3	B 16	
West 62nd St 3	B 16	
West 63rd St 3	B 16	
West 64th St 3	B 16	

STREET INDEX MANHATTAN

STREET	MAP	GRID	STREET	MAP	GRID	STREET	MAP	GRID	STREET	MAP	GRID
West 65th St	3	B 16	West 107th St	4	B 13	West 148th St	4	B 11	West 190th St	5	B 8
West 66th St	3	B 16	West 108th St	4	B 13	West 149th St	5	B 10	West 191st St	5	B 8
West 67th St	3	B 16	West 109th St	4	B 13	West 150th St	5	B 10	West 192nd St	5	B 8
West 68th St	3	B 16	West 110th St (see			West 151st St	5	B 10	West 193rd St	5	B 8
West 69th St	3	B 16	Cathedral Pkwy)			West 152nd St	5	B 10	West 196th St	5	B 8
West 70th St	3	B 16	West 111th St	4	B 13	West 153rd St	5	B 10	West 201st St	6	C 7
West 71st St	3	B 16	West 112th St	4	B 13	West 154th St	5	C 10	West 202nd St	6	C 7
West 72nd St	3	B 16	West 113th St	4	B 13	West 155th St	5	B 10	West 203rd St	6	C 7
West 73rd St	3	B 16	West 114th St	4	B 13	West 156th St	5	B 10	West 204th St	6	B 7
West 74th St	3	B 15	West 115th St	4	B 13	West 157th St	5	B 10	West 205th St	6	C 7
West 75th St	3	B 15	West 116th St	4	B 13	West 158th St	5	B 10	West 206th St	6	C 7
West 76th St	3	B 15	West 117th St	4	D 13	West 159th St	5	B 10	West 207th St	6	B 7
West 77th St	3	B 15	West 118th St	4	D 13	West 160th St	5	B 10	West 208th St	6	C 7
West 78th St	3	B 15	West 119th St	4	D 13	West 161st St	5	B 10	West 211th St	6	B 7
West 79th St	3	B 15	West 120th St	4	B 12	West 162nd St	5	B 10	West 212th St	6	B 7
West 80th St	3	B 15	West 121st St	4	B 12	West 163rd St	5	B 10	West 213th St	6	B 7
West 81st St	3	B 15	West 122nd St	4	B 12	West 164th St	5	B 9	West 214th St	6	B 6
West 82nd St	3	B 15	West 123rd St	4	B 12	West 165th St	5	B 9	West 215th St	6	B 6
West 83rd St	3	B 15	West 124th St	4	D 12	West 166th St	5	B 9	West 216th St	6	C 6
West 84th St	3	B 15	West 125th St	4	C 12	West 167th St	5	B 9	West 217th St	6	B 6
West 85th St	3	B 15	West 126th St	4	B 12	West 168th St	5	B 9	West 218th St	6	C 6
West 86th St	3	B 15	West 127th St	4	C 12	West 169th St	5	B 9	West 219th St	6	C 6
West 87th St	3	B 15	West 128th St	4	C 12	West 170th St	5	B 9	West 220th St	6	C 6
West 88th St	3	B 15	West 129th St	4	B 12	West 171st St	5	B 9	West 225th St	6	C 6
West 89th St	3	B 15	West 130th St	4	B 12	West 172nd St	5	B 9	West 227th St	6	B 6
West 90th St	3	B 14	West 131st St	4	B 12	West 173rd St	5	B 9	West 228th St	6	C 6
West 91st St	3	B 14	West 132nd St	4	B 12	West 174th St	5	B 9	White St	1	D 21
West 92nd St	3	B 14	West 133rd St	4	B 12	West 175th St	5	B 9	Whitehall St	1	D 22
West 93rd St	3	B 14	West 134th St	4	B 12	West 176th St	5	B 9	Willett St	1	F 20
West 94th St	3	B 14	West 135th St	4	B 11	West 177th St	5	B 9	William St	1	D 22
West 95th St	3	B 14	West 136th St	4	B 11	West 178th St	5	B 9	Wooster St	1	D 21
West 96th St	3	B 14	West 137th St	4	B 11	West 179th St	5	B 9	World Financial		
West 97th St	3	B 14	West 138th St	4	B 11	West 180th St	5	B 8	Center	1	C 22
West 98th St	3	B 14	West 139th St	4	B 11	West 181st St	5	B 8	World Trade		
West 99th St	3	B 14	West 140th St	4	B 11	West 182nd St	5	B 8	Center	1	D 22
West 100th St	3	B 14	West 141st St	4	B 11	West 183rd St	5	B 8	Worth St	1	D 21
West 101st St	3	B 14	West 142nd St	4	B 11	West 184th St	5	B 8			
West 102nd St	3	B 14	West 143rd St	4	B 11	West 185th St	5	B 8	**Y**		
West 103rd St	3	B 14	West 144th St	4	B 11	West 186th St	5	B 8			
West 104th St	3	B 14	West 145th St	4	B 11	West 187th St	5	B 8	York Av	3	E 16
West 105th St	4	B 13	West 146th St	4	B 11	West 188th St	5	B 8	York St	1	D 21
West 106th St	4	B 13	West 147th St	4	B 11	West 189th St	5	B 8			

STREET INDEX THE BRONX

STREET	MAP	GRID	STREET	MAP	GRID	STREET	MAP	GRID	STREET	MAP	GRID
A			Amundson Av	8	G 2	Austin Pl	11	F 11	Barker Av	9	F 5
			Anderson Av	5	D 9	Avenue Saint			Barkley Av	13	K 7
Abbot St	7	E 2	Andrews Av	5	C 8	John	10	F 10	Barn Hill Sq	6	D 6
Acorn Pl	13	M 7	Andrews Av N	6	C 7				Barnes Av	8	F 2
Adams Pl	6	E 7	Andrews Av S	6	C 7	**B**			Barnett Pl *(off		
Adams St	9	G 7	Anthony Av	5	D 8				Barnes Av		
Adee Av	13	M 6	Anthony J Griffin			B St * (off Baisley			between		
Adee Av	9	F 5	Pl	4	D 11	Av between			Rhinelander Av		
Adler Pl	8	H 3	Antin Pl	9	G 6	Crosby Av and			and Morris Park		
Admiral La	14	K 9	Appleton Av	9	J 5	Hobart Av)	13	K 6	Av)	9	G 6
Agar Pl	13	L 5	Aqueduct Av E	6	D 7	Babe Ruth Plz	5	D 10	Barrett Av	10	J 8
Alan Pl	13	N 7	Aqueduct Av W	6	D 6	Bagley St *(off			Barrett Pl	13	N 7
Albany Cres	6	C 5	Archer Rd	9	H 7	Hutchinson			Barretto St	10	G 9
Alcott Pl	8	H 3	Archer St	9	H 7	River Pkwy)	14	K 8	Barry St	10	G 10
Alden Pl	6	E 7	Arlington Av	7	A 4	Bailey Av	6	C 6	Bartholdi St	8	E 7
Alderbrook Rd	7	A 4	Armand Pl	6	C 5	Bailey Pl	6	C 5	Bartow Av	8	H 4
Aldrich St	8	H 4	Arnow Av	9	F 5	Bainbridge Av	7	D 4	Bassett Av	9	H 5
Aldus St	10	G 9	Arnow Pl	9	J 5	Baisley Av	13	K 6	Bassford Av	6	E 7
Alexander Av	4	E 11	Arthur Av	6	E 7	Baker Av	9	G 7	Bathgate Av	5	E 8
Allen Pl	8	H 3	Arthur H Murphy			Balcom Av	9	J 6	Bay St	12	M 4
Allerton Av	9	F 5	Sq	6	E 7	Baldwin St	7	E 2	Baychester Av	8	H 4
Amethyst St	9	G 7	Asch Loop	8	H 3	Balsam Av	13	M 7	Baychester Av	8	F 2
Ampere Av	13	K 5	Aster Pl	13	M 7	Bantam Pl	8	H 4	Bayshore Av	13	K 5
			Astor Av	9	G 5	Banyer Pl	10	H 8	Bayview Av	13	K 5

155

STREET	MAP	GRID
Beach Av 10	H	8
Beach St 12	M	4
Beaumont Av 6	E	7
Beck St 10	F	10
Bedford Park		
Blvd 6	D	5
Bedford Park		
Blvd W 6	D	5
Beech Pl 13	M	7
Beech Ter 11	F	11
Beech Tree La 8	J	2
Beekman Av 11	F	11
Belden St 12	M	4
Bell Av 8	G	2
Bellamy Loop 8	H	3
Belmont Av 6	E	7
Belmont St 5	E	8
Benchley Pl 8	H	3
Benedict Av 9	H	7
Benson St 9	J	6
Bergen Av 4	E	11
Bernard S		
Deutsch Plz 5	C	8
Betts Av 14	K	9
Bevy Pl 13	N	7
Billingsley Ter 5	C	8
Birchall Av 9	G	6
Bissel St 8	F	2
Bivona St 8	G	3
Blackrock Av 9	J	7
Blackstone Av 6	B	5
Blackstone Pl 6	B	5
Blair Av 13	M	6
Blondell Av 9	J	6
Bogart Av 9	G	6
Boller Av 8	G	2
Bolton Av 10	J	8
Bolton St 9	G	6
Bonner Pl 5	D	9
Boone Av 10	G	8
Boscobel Pl 5	C	8
Boston Close 8	G	3
Boston Rd 9	F	5
Botanical Sq 6	E	6
Bouck Av 8	G	4
Bowne St 12	M	4
Boyd Av 8	F	2
Boynton Av 10	G	8
Bradford Av 13	K	6
Bradley St 7	E	2
Bradley Ter 6	B	6
Brady Av 9	G	6
Brandt Pl 5	C	8
Bridge St 12	L	3
Briggs Av 6	D	6
Brinsmade Av 13	K	7
Bristow St 10	F	8
Britton St 9	F	5
Broadway 7	B	3
Bronx and Pelham		
Pkwy 9	G	6
Bronx and Pelham		
Pkwy 9	H	5
Bronx Blvd 7	E	2
Bronx Park Av 9	G	7
Bronx Park E 9	F	5
Bronx Park S 9	F	7
Bronx River Av .. 10	G	9
Bronx River		
Pkwy 10	G	8
Bronx River		
Pkwy 9	F	5
Bronx St 9	F	7
Bronxdale Av 9	G	6

STREET	MAP	GRID
Bronxwood Av 8	F	3
Brook Av 5	E	8
Broun Pl 8	H	3
Brown Pl 4	E	12
Bruckner Blvd 10	F	10
Bruckner		
Expwy 9	J	5
Bruner Av 8	F	2
Brush Av 13	K	7
Bryant Av 10	F	8
Buchanan Pl 6	D	7
Buck St 9	H	6
Buckley St 12	M	4
Buhre Av 9	J	5
Bullard Av 7	E	2
Burke Av 9	F	5
Burnett Pl 10	G	10
Burnside Av E 6	D	7
Burnside Av W 6	C	7
Burr Av 9	J	5
Bush St 6	D	7
Bushnell Av 8	H	4
Bussing Av 8	F	3
Bussing Pl 8	F	2
Butler Av 9	J	6
Buttrick Av 13	L	7
Byron Av 7	E	2

C

STREET	MAP	GRID
Caesar Pl 10	J	8
Calhoun Av 13	K	6
Cambreleng Av 6	E	7
Cambridge Av 6	B	5
Cameron Pl 6	D	7
Camp St 8	F	2
Campbell Dr 13	K	5
Canal Pl 4	E	11
Canal St W 4	D	11
Cannon Pl 6	C	5
Capuchin Way 8	F	4
Carlisle Pl 8	F	4
Carpenter Av 7	E	2
Carroll Pl 5	D	9
Carroll St 12	M	4
Carter Av 5	E	8
Carver Loop 8	H	3
Casals Pl 8	H	3
Casanova St 10	G	10
Casler Pl 13	N	7
Castle Hill Av 9	J	7
Catalpa Pl 13	M	7
Cauldwell Av 10	F	10
Cayuga Av 7	B	4
Cedar Av 6	C	7
Cedar La 5	D	10
Cedar Pl 13	M	7
Centre Pl 13	M	6
Centre St 12	M	4
Chaffee Av 13	M	7
Charlotte St 10	F	8
Chatterton Av 9	J	7
Chesbrough Av 9	J	6
Chester St 8	G	3
Chestnut Dr 9	F	5
Chestnut St 8	F	4
Chisholm St 10	F	9
Choctaw Pl 9	H	5
Church Sq 9	J	7
Cicero Pl 10	J	8
Cincinnatus Av .. 14	K	8
City Island Av ... 12	M	4
City Island Rd 12	K	3
Claflin Av 6	C	6

STREET	MAP	GRID
Claremont		
Pkwy 5	E	8
Clarence Av 13	L	6
Clason Point La N		
*(Clason Point		
Gardens) 10	H	8
Clason Point La S		
*(Clason Point		
Gardens) 10	H	8
Clay Av 5	E	8
Clementine St 8	H	2
Clifford Pl 5	D	8
Clinton Av 5	E	8
Clinton Pl 6	D	7
Close Av 10	G	8
Coddington Av ... 13	K	6
Colden Av 8	F	4
Coles La 6	D	6
Colgate Av 10	G	8
College Av 5	E	9
College Rd 7	B	4
Collis Pl 13	M	7
Colonial Av 9	J	5
Columbus Sq 6	E	6
Commerce Av 9	J	6
Commonwealth		
Av 10	H	8
Compton Av 14	K	8
Concord Av 11	F	11
Concourse		
Village E 5	D	10
Concourse Village		
W 5	D	10
Connell Pl 13	K	5
Conner St 8	G	2
Continental Av 9	J	5
Co-op City Blvd ... 8	H	3
Cooper Pl 8	H	3
Corlear Av 6	B	5
Cornell Av 14	K	9
Cornell Pl 13	K	6
Cpl Irwin Fischer		
Pl 5	C	9
Cpl Walter J		
Fufidio Sq 10	G	10
Corsa Av 8	G	4
Coster St 10	G	10
Cottage Av 5	E	8
Country Club		
Rd 13	K	5
Courtlandt Av 5	E	10
Crames Sq 10	G	9
Cranford Av 8	F	2
Craven St 10	G	10
Crawford Av 8	G	3
Crescent Av 6	E	7
Creston Av 6	D	7
Crimmins Av 11	F	11
Croes Av 10	H	8
Croes Pl *(Clason		
Point		
Gardens) 10	H	8
Cromwell Av 5	D	9
Crosby Av 13	K	6
Cross Bronx		
Expwy 5	E	8
Cross St 12	M	4
Crotona Av 6	E	7
Crotona Park		
E 10	F	8
Crotona Park N ... 5	E	8
Crotona Park S ... 5	E	8
Crotona Pkwy 10	F	8

STREET	MAP	GRID
Crotona Pl 5	E	8
Cruger Av 9	F	5
Cypress Av 11	F	11
Cypress Pl 11	F	11
Cyrus Pl 6	E	6

D

STREET	MAP	GRID
Daisy Pl 13	M	7
Daly Av 10	F	8
Daniel St 9	J	5
Dare Pl 13	N	7
Dark St 8	G	2
Darrow Pl 8	H	3
Dash Pl 6	B	5
David Sheridan		
Plz 7	B	3
Davidson Av 5	D	8
Davis Av 13	L	7
Dawson St 10	F	10
Dean Av 13	L	6
Debs Pl 8	H	3
Decatur Av 6	D	6
De Foe Pl 8	H	3
De Kalb Av 7	D	4
De Kruif Pl 8	H	3
Delafield Av 7	A	4
Delafield Av 6	B	5
Delafield La 6	B	5
Delafield Pl 7	A	3
Delancey Pl 9	G	6
Delanoy Av 8	H	4
Delavall Av 8	H	3
Demeyer St 8	J	4
Depot Pl 5	C	9
De Reimer Av 8	F	2
Devanney Sq 6	D	7
Devoe Av 9	G	7
Devoe Ter 6	C	6
Dewey Av 13	L	7
DeWitt Pl 8	G	4
Deyo St 8	G	4
Dickerson Av 6	D	5
Digney Av 8	F	3
Dill Pl 13	L	7
Ditmars St 12	M	4
Dock St 13	M	6
Dodgewood Rd 6	B	5
Dogwood Dr 9	H	7
Donizetti Pl 8	H	3
D'Onofrio Sq 8	F	4
Doris St 9	J	7
Dorothea Pl 6	D	6
Dorsey St 9	H	6
Douglas Av 6	B	5
Dr. Martin Luther		
King Jr Blvd 5	C	9
Dr. Theodore		
Kazimiroff		
Blvd 6	E	5
Dr. Theodore		
Kazimiroff		
Blvd 6	E	6
Drake Park S 10	H	10
Drake St 10	G	9
Dreiser Loop 8	H	3
Dudley Av 13	K	6
Duncan St 8	F	4
Duncomb Av 6	E	5
Dupont St 10	G	10
Duryea Av 8	G	2
Dwight Pl 13	K	5
Dyre Av 8	G	2

STREET	MAP	GRID	STREET	MAP	GRID	STREET	MAP	GRID	STREET	MAP	GRID
E			East 181st St	6	D 7	Edward L Grant			Fort Schuyler		
			East 182nd St	6	D 7	Hwy	5	C 9	Rd	9	J 6
Eagle Av	5	E 10	East 183rd St	6	D 7	Edwards Av	9	J 6	Fowler Av	9	G 6
Eames Pl	6	C 6	East 184th St	6	D 7	Effingham Av	14	K 8	Fox St	10	F 10
Earhart La	8	J 4	East 185th St	6	E 7	Eger Pl	13	N 7	Fox Ter	8	G 4
Earley St	12	M 4	East 186th St	6	E 7	Einstein Loop	8	J 4	Franklin Av	5	E 9
East Av	9	H 7	East 187th St	6	E 7	Einstein Loop E	8	J 4	Freeman St	10	F 9
East Bay Av	10	H 10	East 188th St	6	D 6	Einstein Loop N	8	J 4	Frisby Av	9	J 6
East Burnside			East 189th St	6	E 6	Einstein Loop S	8	J 4	Fteley Av	10	H 8
Av	6	D 7	East 190th St	6	D 6	Elder Av	10	G 8	Fuller St	9	H 6
East Clarke Pl	5	D 9	East 191st St	6	D 6	Elgar Pl	8	J 4	Fulton Av	5	E 9
East Fordham			East 192nd St	6	D 6	Elliot Pl	5	D 9	Furman Av	8	E 2
Rd	6	E 6	East 193rd St	6	D 6	Ellis Av	9	H 7			
East Gun Hill			East 194th St	6	D 6	Ellison Av	9	J 6	**G**		
Rd	8	F 4	East 195th St	6	D 6	Ellsworth Av	13	L 6			
East Kingsbridge			East 196th St	6	D 6	Elm Dr	9	H 7	Gale Pl	6	C 5
Rd	6	D 6	East 197th St	6	D 6	Elm Pl	6	D 6	Garden Pl	8	E 2
East Mosholu			East 198th St	6	D 6	Elm Pl	13	M 7	Garden St	9	F 7
Pkwy N			East 199th St	6	D 5	Elsmere Pl	9	F 7	Garfield St	9	G 7
(odd only)	6	D 5	East 201st St	6	D 5	Elton Av	5	E 10	Garrett Pl	8	G 2
East Mosholu			East 202nd St	6	D 5	Elwood Pl	8	G 4	Garrison Av	10	G 10
Pkwy S	6	D 5	East 203rd St	6	D 5	Ely Av	8	F 2	Gates Pl	7	D 4
East Mount Eden			East 204th St	6	D 5	Emerson Av	13	L 7	Geo. Farkas Sq		
Av	5	D 8	East 205th St	6	D 5	Emmet St	6	E 6	*(intersection of		
East Tremont Av	5	D 8	East 206th St	6	D 5	Erdman Pl	8	J 4	Fordam Rd and		
East 132nd St	4	E 12	East 207th St	6	E 5	Ericson Pl	9	J 6	Grand		
East 133rd St	11	F 12	East 208th St	6	E 5	Erskine Pl	8	J 4	Concourse)	6	D 5
East 134th St	4	E 11	East 209th St	6	E 5	Esplanade	9	G 5	George St * (off		
East 135th St	4	E 11	East 210th St	6	D 5	Evelyn Pl	6	D 7	Dudley Av		
East 136th St	4	E 11	East 211th St	7	E 4	Evergreen Av	10	G 8	between		
East 137th St	4	E 11	East 212th St	7	D 4	Ewen Av	6	B 5	Mayflower Av		
East 138th St	4	D 11	East 213th St	7	D 4	Exterior St	6	C 6	and Edison		
East 139th St	4	E 11	East 214th St	8	F 4				Av)	9	J 6
East 140th St	4	D 11	East 215th St	8	F 4	**F**			Geranium Pl	13	N 7
East 141st St	4	E 11	East 216th St	8	E 4				Gerard Av	5	D 10
East 142nd St	4	E 11	East 217th St	8	F 4	Faile St	10	G 9	Gerber Pl	13	L 7
East 143rd St	4	E 11	East 218th St	8	F 4	Fairfax Av	13	K 6	Gertland Pl	8	J 2
East 144th St	4	D 11	East 219th St	8	F 4	Fairfield Av	6	B 6	Giegerich Pl	13	N 7
East 145th St	4	E 11	East 220th St	8	E 4	Fairmount Av	13	K 6	Gifford Av	13	K 7
East 146th St	4	D 11	East 221st St	8	E 4	Fairmount Pl	9	F 7	Gilbert Pl	10	G 9
East 147th St	4	E 11	East 222nd St	8	E 4	Faraday Av	7	B 3	Gildersleeve		
East 148th St	4	E 11	East 223rd St	8	E 3	Farragut St	10	J 10	Av	10	J 9
East 149th St	4	D 11	East 224th St	8	E 3	Father Zeiser Pl	6	C 7	Giles Pl	6	C 5
East 150th St	5	E 10	East 225th St	8	E 3	Fearn Pl	13	N 7	Gillespie Av	13	K 6
East 151st St	5	E 10	East 226th St	8	E 3	Featherbed La	5	C 8	Gillespie Sq	5	E 9
East 152nd St	5	E 10	East 227th St	8	E 3	Fenton Av	8	G 4	Givan Av	8	G 4
East 153rd St	5	E 10	East 228th St	8	E 3	Fern Pl	13	N 7	Givan Sq	8	H 4
East 154th St	5	E 10	East 229th St	8	E 3	Ferris Av	13	K 7	Gladstone Sq	10	F 9
East 155th St	5	E 10	East 230th St	8	E 3	Ferris Pl	9	J 6	Gleason Av	10	H 8
East 156th St	5	E 10	East 231st St	8	E 3	Field Pl	6	D 7	Glebe Av	9	J 7
East 157th St	5	D 10	East 232nd St	8	E 3	Fielding St	8	H 4	Glennon Pl	13	N 7
East 158th St	5	D 10	East 233rd St	7	D 3	Fieldston Rd	7	B 4	Glover St	9	J 7
East 159th St	5	D 10	East 234th St	7	D 3	Fieldston Ter	7	B 4	Goble Pl	5	D 8
East 160th St	5	E 10	East 235th St	7	D 3	Fillmore St	9	G 7	Godwin Ter	6	C 6
East 161st St	5	D 10	East 236th St	7	D 3	Findlay Av	5	E 9	Goodridge Av	7	B 4
East 162nd St	5	D 10	East 237th St	7	D 3	Fink Av	9	J 6	Goulden Av	6	D 6
East 163rd St	5	D 10	East 238th St	7	D 3	Fish Av	8	G 4	Gouverneur Av	6	C 5
East 164th St	5	D 9	East 239th St	7	D 3	Fleet Ct	14	K 9	Gouverneur Pl	5	E 9
East 165th St	5	D 9	East 240th St	7	D 3	Fletcher Pl	6	E 7	Grace Av	8	H 4
East 166th St	5	D 9	East 241st St	7	D 2	Flint Av	8	H 2	Graff Av	13	L 7
East 167th St	5	D 9	East 242nd St	7	D 2	Folin St	6	D 7	Graham Pl *(off		
East 168th St	5	D 9	East 243rd St	8	E 2	Food Center			Morris Park Av		
East 169th St	5	D 9	Eastburn Av	5	D 8	Dr	10	H 10	between		
East 170th St	5	D 9	Eastchester Pl	8	H 2	Ford St	6	D 7	Matthews and		
East 171st St	5	D 8	Eastchester Rd	8	G 4	Fordham Pl	12	M 4	Muliner Av)	9	G 6
East 172nd St	5	D 8	Echo Pl	6	D 7	Fordham Plz	6	D 6	Graham Sq	4	E 11
East 173rd St	5	D 8	Edenwald Av	8	F 2	Fordham Rd (see			Grand Av	6	D 7
East 174th St	5	D 8	Edgar Pl	13	N 7	E or W Fordham			Grand		
East 175th St	5	D 8	Edge St	13	M 6	Rd)			Concourse	5	D 9
East 176th St	5	D 8	Edgehill Av	6	B 6	Fordham St	12	M 4	Grandview Pl	5	D 9
East 177th St	5	D 8	Edgemere St	8	J 2	Forest Av	10	F 10	Grant Av	5	D 9
East 178th St	6	D 7	Edgewater Rd	10	G 9	Forest Rd	8	J 2	Green Av	9	J 7
East 179th St	6	D 7	Edison Av	13	K 6	Forester Av	7	B 3	Greene Pl	13	K 6
East 180th St	6	D 7	Edsall Av	6	B 6	Fort Independence			Grenada Pl	8	F 3
			Edson Av	8	G 3	St	6	C 5	Greystone Av	6	B 5

STREET	MAP	GRID
Grinnell Pl	10	G 10
Griswold Av	13	K 5
Grosvenor Av	7	B 4
Grote St	9	F 7
Guerlain St	9	G 7
Guion Pl	9	G 7
Gun Hill Rd (see E or W Gun Hill Rd)		
Gunther Av	8	F 2

H

STREET	MAP	GRID
Hadley Av	6	A 5
Haight Av	9	H 6
Hall of Fame Ter	6	C 7
Hall Pl	10	F 9
Halleck St	10	H 9
Halperin Av	9	J 6
Halsey St	9	J 6
Hammersley Av	8	H 4
Hampden Pl	6	C 7
Harding Av	14	L 8
Harper Av	8	G 2
Harrington Av	13	K 6
Harrison Av	5	D 8
Harrod Av	10	G 8
Harrod Pl	10	G 8
Hart St	14	K 8
Haskin St	13	K 6
Haswell St	9	J 6
Hatting Pl	13	M 7
Havemeyer Av	9	J 7
Haviland Av	9	J 7
Hawkins St	12	M 4
Hawkstone St	5	D 8
Hawthorne Dr	9	H 7
Hawthorne St	8	H 4
Hazel Pl	13	N 7
Heath Av	6	C 6
Heathcote Av	8	H 2
Hegney Pl	5	E 10
Hennessy Pl	6	C 7
Henry Hudson Pkwy	7	B 4
Henry Hudson Pkwy E & W	6	B 5
Henwood Pl	5	D 8
Hering Av	8	G 4
Herkimer Pl	7	D 3
Hermany Av	10	J 8
Herschell St	9	J 6
Hewitt Pl	10	F 10
Hicks St	8	G 4
High Island	12	M 3
Highbridge St (now Cpl Irwin Fischer Pl)	5	D 9
Hill Av	8	F 2
Hillman Av	6	C 5
Hobart Av	9	J 5
Hoe Av	10	F 8
Hoffman St	6	E 7
Holland Av	9	F 5
Hollers Av	8	H 2
Holly Pl	13	M 7
Hollywood Av	13	L 6
Holt Pl	6	E 5
Home St	10	F 9
Homer Av	10	J 8
Hone Av	9	G 6
Honeywell Av	9	F 7
Hornaday Pl	9	F 7
Horton St	12	M 4

STREET	MAP	GRID
Hosmer Av	14	L 8
Houghton Av	10	J 8
Howe Av	14	K 8
Hoxie St	8	F 2
Hubbell St	9	H 6
Hudson Manor Ter	6	B 5
Hudson River Rd	7	A 4
Hugh J Grant Cir	9	H 7
Hughes Av	6	E 7
Huguenot Av	8	H 2
Hull Av	6	E 5
Hunt Av	9	G 6
Hunter Av	8	G 3
Hunter Close	8	G 3
Huntington Av	13	K 7
Hunts Point Av	10	G 9
Husson Av	14	K 9
Hutchinson Av	8	H 2
Hutchinson River Pkwy	8	H 2
Hutchinson River Pkwy E	9	J 5
Hutchinson River Pkwy W	8	J 4
Hutton Sq	6	E 7
Huxley Av	7	B 3

I

STREET	MAP	GRID
Independence Av	6	B 5
Indian Rd	7	B 4
Indian Ter	13	M 7
Industrial St	9	J 6
Interstate Hwy 87 (see Major Deegan Expwy)	7	C 4
Interstate Hwy 95	9	J 5
Interstate Hwy 95	10	F 8
Interstate Hwy 295	13	K 7
Interstate Hwy 678	14	L 8
Interstate Hwy 695	13	L 6
Intervale Av	10	F 9
Inwood Av	5	D 9
Irvine St	10	G 9
Irwin Av	6	B 5
Iselin Av	7	B 4
Ittner Pl	5	E 8
Ives St	9	H 6
Ivy Pl	13	N 7

J

STREET	MAP	GRID
Jackson Av	10	F 10
Jarrett Pl	9	H 6
Jarvis Av	9	J 5
Jasamine Pl	13	N 7
Jay Pl	14	K 8
Jay St	14	K 8
Jefferson Pl	5	E 9
Jennings St	10	F 8
Jerome Av	6	D 5
Jesup Av	5	D 8
Jesup Pl	5	C 8
Johnson Av	6	B 5

K

STREET	MAP	GRID
Kappock St	6	B 6
Katonah Av	7	D 3
Kearney Av	13	K 5
Kearney Av	13	M 7
Kelly St	10	F 9
Kennelworth Pl	13	K 5
Kepler Av	7	D 3
Kilroe St	12	L 3
Kimberly Pl	6	C 6
King Av	12	L 3
Kings College Pl	7	E 4
Kingsbridge Av	6	C 6
Kingsbridge Rd E	6	D 6
Kingsbridge Rd W	6	C 6
Kingsbridge Ter	6	C 6
Kingsland Av	8	H 4
Kingsland Pl	5	D 8
Kinnear Pl	9	J 7
Kinsella St	9	H 6
Kirby St	12	M 4
Knapp St	8	G 4
Knolls Crescent	6	B 6
Knox Pl	6	D 5
Kossuth Av	6	D 5

L

STREET	MAP	GRID
La Salle Av	13	K 6
Lacombe Av	10	J 9
Laconia Av	9	G 5
Ladd Rd	7	A 4
Lafayette Av	10	H 9
Lafontaine Av	6	E 7
Lake View Pl	7	B 4
Lakewood Pl	9	H 5
Lamport Pl	13	L 7
Landing Rd	6	C 7
Lane Av	9	J 6
Lang Av	9	J 6
Latting St	9	J 6
Laurel Dr	9	H 7
Laurie Av	9	J 5
Lawton Av	13	L 7
Layton Av	13	K 6
Lebanon St	9	G 7
Lee St	9	J 6
Leggett Av	10	F 10
Leland Av	10	H 8
Lenter St	13	M 6
Lester St	9	F 5
Libby Pl	9	J 6
Library Av	13	K 5
Liebig Av	7	B 3
Light St	8	G 2
Lincoln Av	4	E 12
Linden Av	13	M 7
Linden Dr	9	H 7
Lisbon Pl	6	D 5
Little League Pl	9	J 6
Livingston Av	7	B 4
Locust Av	11	F 11
Lodovick Av	8	H 4
Logan Av	13	L 6
Logan Av	13	M 7
Lohengrin Pl	13	K 5
Longfellow Av	10	F 8
Longstreet Av	13	M 7
Longwood Av	10	F 10
Loomis St	9	H 5
Lorillard Pl	6	E 7

STREET	MAP	GRID
Loring Pl N	6	C 7
Loring Pl S	5	C 8
Lou Auger Sq	6	B 5
Lou Gehrig Plz	5	D 10
Louis Nine Blvd	10	F 8
Lowell St	10	G 9
Lowerre Pl	7	E 3
Lucerne St	13	K 5
Lurting Av	9	H 6
Lustre St	8	G 2
Lydig Av	9	G 6
Lyman Pl	10	F 9
Lyon Av	9	J 7
Lyvere St	9	H 6

M

STREET	MAP	GRID
Mable Wayne Pl*	5	D 10
Mac Donough Pl	13	K 5
Mace Av	9	F 5
Maclay Av	9	H 6
Macombs Rd	5	D 8
Macy Pl	10	F 10
Magenta St	6	E 5
Magnolia Pl	13	M 7
Mahan Av	9	J 5
Main St	13	M 6
Maitland Av	9	J 6
Major Deegan Expwy	5	C 8
Major Deegan Expwy	4	D 11
Major Deegan Expwy	6	C 5
Manhattan College Pkwy	6	B 5
Manida St	10	G 10
Manning St	9	H 7
Manor Av	10	G 8
Mansion St	9	G 7
Mapes Av	9	F 7
Maple Av *(off Chaffee Av)	13	M 7
Maple Dr	9	H 7
Maran Pl	9	G 6
Marcy Pl	5	D 9
Marina Dr	13	L 7
Marine St	12	M 4
Marion Av	6	D 6
Marmion Av	10	F 8
Marolla Pl	8	G 3
Martha Av	7	D 2
Marvin Pl	9	H 6
Matilda Av	7	E 2
Matthews Av	9	F 5
Matthewson Rd	5	C 8
Mayflower Av	9	J 5
Mayflower Av	9	J 6
McAlpin Av	9	J 6
McClellan St	5	D 9
McCracken Av	9	H 5
McDonald St	9	H 5
McGraw Av	9	H 7
McKinley Sq	5	E 9
McOwen Av	8	H 2
Mead St	9	G 7
Meagher Av	13	M 7
Melrose Av	5	E 10
Melville St	9	G 7
Merriam Av	5	C 9
Merrill St	9	G 7

STREET	MAP	GRID
Merritt Av	8	G 2
Merry Av	13	K 6
Metcalf Av	10	H 8
Metropolitan Av	9	H 7
Metropolitan Oval		
*(Parkchester)	9	H 7
Meyers St	13	K 6
Mickle Av	8	G 4
Mickle Av	8	H 4
Middletown Rd	9	J 6
Miles Av	13	L 7
Milton Pl	13	M 7
Minerva Pl	6	D 6
Minford Pl	10	F 8
Minnieford Av	12	M 3
Miriam St	6	D 6
Mitchell Pl	13	N 7
Mohegan Av	9	F 7
Monroe Av	5	D 8
Monsignor Halpin		
Pl	13	M 7
Monterey Av	6	E 7
Montgomery Av	5	C 8
Montgomery Pl	9	H 6
Monticello Av	8	F 2
Morgan Av	8	H 4
Morris Av	6	D 6
Morris Park Av	9	G 7
Morrison Av	10	G 8
Morton Pl	5	D 8
Mosholu Av	7	B 4
Mosholu Pkwy	7	C 3
Mosholu Pkwy	6	E 5
Mount Eden		
Pkwy	5	D 8
Mount Hope Pl	5	D 8
Mulford Av	9	J 5
Muliner Av	9	G 6
Mullan Pl	13	M 7
Mulvey Av	8	G 2
Mundy La	8	F 2
Munn Av	9	J 7
Murdock Av	8	F 2

N

Napier Av	7	D 3
Naples Ter	6	C 5
Narragansett Av	9	H 5
Needham Av	8	G 3
Neill Av	9	G 6
Nelson Av	5	C 8
Neptune Ct	14	K 9
Neptune La	14	K 9
Nereid Av	7	E 2
Netherland Av	6	B 6
Neumann Goldman		
Memorial Plz	6	E 5
New England		
Thruway	8	H 2
Newbold Av	9	H 7
Newell St	8	E 4
Newman Av	10	J 9
Newport Av	9	H 6
Noble Av	10	H 8
Noell Av	8	H 2
North Botanical		
Sq	6	E 6
North Brother		
Island	11	G 11
North Oak Dr	9	F 5
North St	6	D 7
Norton Av	14	K 8
Nuvern Av	8	G 2

O

Oak Av	13	M 7
Oak La	8	J 2
Oak Point Av	10	G 10
Oak Ter	11	F 11
Oak Tree Pl	6	E 7
Oakland Pl	6	E 7
Oakley St	8	G 4
O'Brien Av	10	J 9
O'Brien Sq	5	E 8
Odell St	9	H 7
Ogden Av	5	C 9
Ohm Av	13	K 5
Olinville Av	8	E 4
Oliver Pl	6	E 6
Olmstead Av	9	J 7
One Lighting		
Pl	10	H 10
Oneida Av	7	D 3
O'Neill Pl	8	H 4
Orloff Av	6	C 5
Osborne Pl	6	C 7
Osgood St	7	E 2
Osman Pl	8	F 2
Otis Av	13	K 6
Outlook Av	13	K 5
Overing St	9	H 6
Oxford Av	6	B 5

P

Paine St	13	K 6
Palisade Av	6	A 5
Palisade Pl	5	C 8
Palmer Av	8	G 3
Park Av	4	D 11
Park Dr	8	J 2
Park Dr	12	K 3
Parkchester Rd	9	H 7
Parker St	9	H 7
Parkside Pl	6	E 5
Parkview Av	9	J 5
Parkview Ter	6	D 6
Parsifal Pl	13	K 5
Patterson Av	10	J 9
Paul Av	6	D 5
Paulding Av	8	F 3
Paulis Pl	12	M 4
Pawnee Pl	9	H 5
Pearsall Av	8	G 4
Peartree Av	8	H 2
Pelham Bay Park		
W	8	H 2
Pelham Bridge		
Rd	12	K 3
Pelham Parkway		
N	9	G 6
Pelham Parkway		
S	9	G 6
Pell Pl	12	M 4
Penfield St	8	E 2
Pennyfield Av	13	M 7
Perot St	6	C 5
Perry Av	6	E 5
Peters Pl	7	E 3
Phelan Pl	5	C 8
Philip Av	13	L 7
Pierce Av	9	H 6
Pilgrim Av	9	J 5
Pilot St	12	M 4
Pinchot Pl	9	H 5
Pine Dr	9	H 7
Pinkney Av	8	H 2

Pitman Av	8	F 2
Plimpton Av	5	C 9
Ploughman's		
Bush	6	A 5
Plymouth Av	9	J 6
Poe Pl *(off Coles		
La)	6	D 6
Polo Pl	13	K 5
Pond Pl	6	D 6
Pontiac Pl	10	F 10
Ponton Av	9	J 6
Popham Av	5	C 8
Poplar Av	13	M 7
Poplar St	9	H 6
Post Rd	7	B 4
Powell Av	9	J 7
Powers Av	11	F 11
Pratt Av	8	G 2
Prentiss Av	13	M 6
Prospect Av	10	F 10
Prospect Pl	5	D 8
Provost Av	8	H 2
Public Pl	6	E 5
Pugsley Av	9	J 7
Purdy St	9	H 7
Puritan Av	13	K 6
Putnam Av W	6	C 5
Putnam Pl	7	E 4

Q

Quarry Rd	6	E 7
Quimby Av	10	J 8
Quincy Av	13	K 6
Quincy Av	13	L 7

R

Radcliff Av	9	G 6
Radio Dr	13	K 5
Rae St	5	E 10
Randall Av	10	G 10
Randolph Pl	13	K 5
Rawlins Av	13	K 6
Raymond Av	9	J 6
Red Oak Dr	9	H 7
Reed Pl	13	K 5
Reeds Mill La	8	H 3
Reeds Mill La * (at		
intersection of		
Boston Rd and		
Steenwick Av)	8	H 3
Regina Pl	8	H 2
Reiss Pl	9	F 6
Research Av	13	K 5
Reservoir Av	6	C 6
Reservoir Oval		
E	6	E 5
Reservoir Oval		
W	6	E 5
Reservoir Pl	7	E 4
Rev James A Polite		
Av (Dawson to		
Bristow)	10	F 9
Revere Av	13	K 6
Review Pl	6	C 5
Reville St	12	M 4
Reynold St	12	M 4
Reynolds Av	13	M 6
Rhinelander Av	9	G 6
Richardson Av	8	E 2
Richman Plz	5	C 8
Rider Av	4	E 11
Ridge Pl	8	J 2

Risse St	6	D 5
Ritter Pl	10	F 9
River Av	5	D 10
River Rd	6	A 5
Rivercrest Rd	7	A 4
Riverdale Av	7	A 4
Roberts Av	9	J 5
Roberts Av	9	J 6
Robertson Pl	13	K 5
Robertson St	7	E 2
Robinson Av	13	L 7
Rochambeau		
Av	7	D 4
Rochambeau		
Av	6	E 5
Rochelle St	12	M 4
Rockwood St	5	D 8
Rodman Pl	10	F 8
Roebling Av	9	J 6
Rogers Pl	10	F 9
Rohr Pl	13	K 7
Rombouts Av	8	G 2
Roosevelt Av	13	L 7
Roosevelt Pl	12	K 2
Ropes Av	8	H 2
Rosedale Av	10	H 8
Roselle St	9	H 6
Rosewood St	9	F 5
Rowe St	9	J 6
Rowland St	9	J 6
Ruppert Pl	5	D 10
Ryawa Av	10	H 10
Ryer Av	6	D 7

S

Sacket Av	9	H 6
Sagamore St	9	G 6
Saint Ann's Av	11	F 11
Saint Ann's Pl	11	F 11
Saint George's		
Crescent	6	D 5
Saint Lawrence		
Av	10	H 8
Saint Mary's		
St	11	F 11
St Mary's St	11	F 11
Saint Ouen St	7	E 2
Saint Paul Av	9	J 5
Saint Paul's Pl	5	E 8
Saint Peter's Av	9	H 6
Saint Raymond's		
Av	9	H 7
Saint Theresa		
Av	9	J 6
Sampson Av	13	L 7
Sampson Av	13	M 6
Sands Pl	9	J 5
Santo Donato		
Pl	9	J 5
Saxon Av	6	D 5
Scenic Pl	6	A 6
Schieffelin Av	8	G 3
Schieffelin Pl	8	G 3
Schley Av	14	K 8
Schofield St	12	M 4
Schorr Pl	12	M 4
Schurz Av	14	L 8
Schurz Av (Marina		
Dr (Calhoun Av		
to		
Hollywood))	13	M 7
Schuyler St	9	J 5
Schuyler Ter	13	N 7

STREET	MAP	GRID
Scott Pl	13	L 6
Screvin Av	14	K 8
Seabury Av	9	J 6
Seabury Pl	10	F 8
Secor Av	8	G 2
Seddon St	9	H 6
Sedgwick Av	6	C 5
Selwyn Av	5	D 8
Seminole Av	9	H 5
Seminole St	9	H 5
Seneca Av	10	G 9
Senger Pl	13	K 7
Seton Av	8	F 2
Seward Av	10	H 9
Sexton Pl	8	G 4
Seymour Av	8	G 4
Shakespeare Av	5	D 9
Sheridan Av	5	D 9
Sheridan Expwy	10	G 9
Sherman Av	5	D 10
Shore Dr	13	L 6
Shore Dr	13	M 6
Shore Rd (now Pelham Bridge Rd)	8	J 3
Shrady Pl	6	C 5
Siegfried Pl	13	K 5
Sigma Pl	7	A 3
Silver St	9	H 6
Silverman Pl	5	D 8
Simpson St	10	F 9
Sommer Pl	13	K 6
Soundview Av	10	H 8
Soundview Dr	13	M 6
Soundview Ter	13	N 7
South Botanical Sq	6	E 6
South Brother Island	11	H 11
South Oak Dr	9	F 5
Southern Blvd	11	F 11
Spencer Av	7	B 3
Spencer Dr	13	K 5
Spencer Pl (now Anthony J Griffin Pl)	5	D 10
Spencer Ter *(off Spencer Av)	7	B 3
Split Rock Rd	8	H 2
Spofford Av	10	G 10
Stadium Av	13	K 5
Starling Av	9	H 7
Stearns St	9	H 7
Stebbins Av	10	F 8
Stedman Pl	9	G 5
Steenwick Av	8	H 3
Stell Pl	9	G 5
Stephens Av	14	K 9
Steuben Av	7	D 4
Stevens Av	7	D 4
Stevenson Pl	6	C 5
Stickball Blvd	10	J 8
Stickney Pl	8	F 4
Stillwell Av	9	H 5
Story Av	10	G 9
Strang Av	8	G 2
Stratford Av	10	G 8
Strong St	6	D 6
Suburban Pl	10	F 8
Sullivan Pl	13	L 6
Summit Av	5	C 10
Summit Pl	6	C 5
Sunset Blvd	14	K 9
Sunset Plz	13	M 7
Sunset Tr	13	M 7

STREET	MAP	GRID
Sutherland St	12	L 3
Swinton Av	13	K 6
Sycamore Av	7	A 4
Sycamore Dr	9	H 7
Sylvan Av	7	B 4

T

Tan Pl	9	J 6
Taylor Av	9	G 7
Teller Av	5	E 9
Tenbroeck Av	8	G 4
Tenny Pl	5	C 8
Terrace Pl	8	J 2
Terrace St	12	L 3
Terrace View Av	6	B 6
Teumissin Pl	6	B 6
Theriot Av	10	H 8
Third Av	5	E 8
Throgmorton Av	13	K 6
Throgs Neck Blvd	13	L 6
Throgs Neck Expwy	13	L 6
Throop Av	8	G 4
Thwaites Pl	9	F 6
Tibbett Av	7	B 4
Tiebout Av	6	D 7
Tiemann Av	8	G 4
Tier St	12	M 4
Tierney Pl	13	N 7
Tiffany St	10	F 9
Tilden St	8	F 4
Tillotson Av	8	G 4
Tim Hendrick Pl	6	C 5
Timpson Pl	10	F 10
Tinton Av	10	F 9
Tomlinson Av	9	H 6
Topping Av	5	E 8
Torry Av	14	K 8
Townsend Av	5	D 8
Trafalgar Pl	5	E 8
Tratman Av	9	J 6
Tremont Av E	5	D 8
Tremont Av W	5	C 8
Trinity Av	10	F 10
Truxton St	10	G 10
Tryon Av	7	E 4
Tudor Pl	5	D 9
Tulfan Ter	6	B 5
Turnbull Av	10	J 8
Turneur Av	14	K 8
Tyndall Av	7	B 3

U

Undercliff Av	5	C 8
Underhill Av	10	J 8
Union Av	10	F 9
Union Pl	5	C 9
Unionport Rd	9	G 6
Unionport Rd	9	H 7
University Av (Now Dr Martin Luther King Jr Blvd)	5	C 9
Unknown Soldier Plz	5	C 8

V

Valentine Av	6	D 6
Valhalla Pl	13	K 5

STREET	MAP	GRID
Valles Av	7	B 4
Van Buren St	9	G 7
Van Corlear Pl	6	B 6
Van Cortlandt Av E	6	D 5
Van Cortlandt Av W	6	C 5
Van Cortlandt Park E	7	D 3
Van Cortlandt Park S	6	C 5
Van Hoesen Av	9	H 5
Van Nest Av	9	G 7
Vance St	8	J 4
Varian Av	8	G 3
Verveelen Pl	6	C 6
Victor St	9	G 7
Viele Av	10	H 10
Villa Av	6	D 5
Vilmont Rd *(near College of Mount Saint Vincent)	7	A 3
Vincent Av	13	L 6
Vineyard Pl	10	F 8
Vireo Av	7	E 2
Virgil Pl	10	J 8
Virginia Av	9	H 7
Vreeland Av	9	J 6
Vyse Av	10	F 8

W

Wade Sq	6	E 7
Waldo Av	7	B 4
Wales Av	11	F 11
Wallace Av	9	F 5
Walnut Av (Rose Feiss Blvd)	11	F 11
Walton Av	6	D 7
Ward Av	10	G 8
Waring Av	9	F 5
Washington Av	6	E 7
Waterbury Av	9	J 7
Waterloo Pl	10	F 8
Waters Pl	9	J 6
Watson Av	10	G 8
Watt Av	13	K 5
Wayne Av	7	E 4
Webb Av	6	C 6
Webster Av	6	E 6
Weeks Av	5	D 8
Weiher Ct	5	E 9
Wellman Av	9	J 6
Wenner Pl	13	K 7
West Av	9	H 7
West Botanical Sq	6	E 6
West Burnside Av	6	C 7
West Clarke Pl	5	D 9
West Farms Rd	10	F 9
West Fordham Rd	6	C 7
West Gun Hill Rd	7	D 4
West Kingsbridge Rd	6	C 6
West Mosholu Pkwy N (all odd numbers)	6	D 5
West Mosholu Pkwy S (all even numbers)	6	D 5

STREET	MAP	GRID
West Mount Eden Av	5	D 8
West Tremont Av	5	C 8
West 161st St	5	C 10
West 162nd St	5	C 10
West 163rd St	5	C 10
West 164th St	5	C 9
West 165th St	5	C 9
West 166th St	5	C 9
West 167th St	5	C 9
West 168th St	5	C 9
West 169th St	5	C 9
West 170th St	5	C 9
West 171st St	5	C 9
West 172nd St	5	C 8
West 173rd St	5	C 8
West 174th St	5	C 8
West 175th St	5	C 8
West 176th St	5	C 8
West 177th St	5	D 8
West 178th St	5	C 8
West 179th St	6	C 7
West 180th St	6	C 7
West 181st St	6	D 7
West 182nd St	6	D 7
West 183rd St	6	C 7
West 184th St	6	D 7
West 188th St	6	D 6
West 190th St	6	D 6
West 192nd St	6	D 6
West 193rd St	6	C 6
West 195th St	6	D 6
West 197th St	6	C 6
West 205th St	6	D 5
West 225th St	6	C 6
West 227th St	6	B 6
West 228th St	6	C 6
West 229th St	6	C 6
West 230th St	6	B 6
West 231st St	6	B 5
West 232nd St	6	B 5
West 233rd St	6	C 5
West 234th St	6	B 5
West 235th St	6	B 5
West 236th St	6	B 5
West 237th St	6	B 5
West 237th St	6	C 5
West 238th St	6	C 5
West 238th St	6	C 5
West 239th St	6	B 5
West 239th St	6	C 5
West 240th St	6	B 5
West 241st St	6	B 5
West 242nd St	6	B 5
West 243rd St	6	B 5
West 244th St	7	B 4
West 245th St	7	B 4
West 246th St	7	B 4
West 247th St	7	A 4
West 248th St	7	A 4
West 249th St	7	A 4
West 250th St	7	B 4
West 251st St	7	B 4
West 252nd St	7	A 4
West 252nd St	7	B 4
West 253rd St	7	B 4
West 254th St	7	B 4
West 255th St	7	A 4
West 256th St	7	B 3
West 256th St	7	B 3
West 259th St	7	A 3
West 260th St	7	A 3

STREET	MAP	GRID	STREET	MAP	GRID	STREET	MAP	GRID	STREET	MAP	GRID
West 261st St	7	A 3	Wilkinson Av	9	J 5	Wood Rd	9	H 7	**Z**		
West 262nd St	7	A 3	Willett Av	8	E 4	Woodhull Av	8	H 4			
West 263rd St	7	A 3	William Av	12	M 4	Woodmansten			Zerega Av	9	J 7
Westchester Av	5	E 10	William Pl	9	J 6	Pl	9	G 6	Zulette Av	9	J 6
Westchester Sq	9	J 6	Williamsbridge			Woodrow Wilson					
Westervelt Av	8	H 4	Rd	9	G 5	Sq	10	J 9	**Numbered**		
Whalen St	7	B 3	Williamsbridge			Woodycrest Av	5	C 9	**Streets**		
Wheeler Av	10	G 8	Sq	8	F 4	Worthen St	10	G 10			
White Plains Rd	7	E 3	Willis Av	4	E 11	Wright Av	8	H 3	1st Av	13	M 6
Whitehall Pl	8	F 2	Willow Av	11	F 11	Wyatt St	9	G 7	2nd Av	13	M 6
Whitehead Pl	13	M 6	Willow La	9	J 5	Wythe Pl	5	D 9	3rd Av	13	M 6
Whitlock Av	10	G 9	Wilson Av	8	G 4				4th Av	13	M 6
Whittemore Av	13	K 6	Windham Pl	6	C 6	**Y**			5th Av	13	M 6
Whittier St	10	G 9	Windward La	12	M 4				7th Av	13	M 6
Wickham Av	8	F 2	Winter St	12	M 4	Yates Av	9	G 5	9th Av	13	M 6
Wilcox Av	13	L 6	Wissman Av	13	M 6	Young Av	8	G 4	11th Av	13	M 6
Wilder Av	8	F 2	Wood Av	9	H 7	Yznaga Pl	14	K 8	229th Dr N	8	F 3
Wilkinson Av	9	H 5							229th Dr S	8	F 3

A

STREET	MAP	GRID
Abbott Rd	17	M 7
Aberdeen Rd	27	M 11
Abigail Adams Av	27	M 11
Abingdon Rd	26	K 12
Acme Ter	35	K 17
Adair St	31	N 13
Adams Ct *(off Beach 39th St)	36	N 18
Adelaide Rd	30	M 13
Adirondack Blvd	38	J 19
Admiral Av	24	G 12
Aguilar Av	26	L 11
Alameda Av	23	O 9
Albany Ct *(off Beach 109th St)	39	K 19
Albert Rd	29	K 14
Albion Av	20	H 10
Alderton St	25	H 11
Alecia Av	31	N 14
Alice Ct *(off Saint Marks Av)	39	K 19
Alison St	23	O 9
Allen St *(off Beach 88th St)	35	L 18
Allendale St	26	L 12
Almeda Av	35	L 18
Almeda Ct *(off Beach 107th St)	39	K 19
Almont Rd	36	O 17
Alonzo Rd	36	O 17
Alston Pl	18	N 8
Alstyne Av	20	H 10
Alwick Rd	30	L 14
Amber St	29	J 14
Amboy La	28	O 11
Amboy Pl	28	O 11
Amelia Rd	31	N 13
Amory Ct	24	G 12
Amstel Blvd	35	L 18
Anchor Dr	36	N 17
Anderson Rd	31	N 13
Andrews Av	24	G 11
Ankener Av	20	H 10

STREET	MAP	GRID
Ann Ct *(off Beach 49th St)	35	M 18
Annandale La	18	O 8
Annapolis Rd	36	O 17
Anthony Ct *(off Seagirt Av near Beach 7th St)	36	O 18
Apex Pl	20	J 10
Arcade Av	27	M 12
Arcadia Walk	37	G 20
Arch St	19	E 10
Archer Av	27	M 12
Archway Pl	25	J 11
Ardsley Rd	18	N 8
Arion Rd	29	J 14
Arleigh Rd	18	N 8
Arlene Ct *(off Beach 116th St)	39	K 19
Arlington Ter	30	L 13
Arnold Av	24	G 11
Arnold Ct *(off Beach 28th St)	36	N 18
Arthur St	31	N 14
Arverne Blvd	36	M 18
Ascan Av	26	K 12
Ash Av	21	K 9
Ashby Av	22	M 9
Ashford St	28	O 11
Aske St	20	H 10
Aspen Pl	27	M 11
Asquith Cres	25	J 11
Astor Ct *(off Beach 107th St)	39	K 19
Astoria Blvd	15	F 8
Astoria Blvd N	19	F 9
Astoria Blvd S	19	F 9
Astoria Pk S	15	F 8
Astoria Sq	15	F 8
Atlantic Av	29	J 13
Atlantic Ct *(off Beach 107th St)	39	K 19
Atlantic Walk	37	G 20
Aubrey Av	25	J 11
Auburndale La	21	L 9
Audley St	26	K 12

STREET	MAP	GRID
Auer's Pier *(off Beach 95th St)	35	L 18
Augusta Ct	30	M 13
Augustina Av	36	O 17
Austell Pl	19	E 10
Austin St	25	H 11
Ava Pl	27	M 11
Avery Av	21	K 9
Avon Rd	27	M 11
Avon St	27	M 11
Aztec Pl	36	N 18

B

STREET	MAP	GRID
Babbage St	26	K 12
Babylon Av	27	N 12
Bagley Av	22	M 9
Bailey Ct	36	N 17
Baisley Blvd	30	M 14
Baker's Ct *(off Beach 101st St near RR)	39	L 19
Baldwin Av	25	J 11
Balsam Ct *(off Sage St)	36	O 17
Barbadoes Dr	35	L 18
Barclay Av	21	K 9
Bardwell Av	28	O 12
Barnett Av	19	F 10
Barnwell Av	20	H 10
Barrington St	27	M 11
Barron St	30	M 13
Barrows Ct	23	O 9
Barton Av	21	L 9
Bascom Av	30	M 14
Bates Rd	18	O 8
Bath Walk	37	F 20
Battery Rd	36	N 17
Baxter Av	20	H 10
Bay Club Dr	17	M 8
Bay Ct *(off Beach 101st St)	39	L 19
Bay Ct	36	N 17
Bay Park Pl	36	N 17
Bay St	18	N 8
Bay Ter	37	F 20
Bay 24th St	36	N 17
Bay 25th St	36	N 17

STREET	MAP	GRID
Bay 27th St	36	N 17
Bay 28th St	36	N 17
Bay 30th St	36	N 18
Bay 31st St	36	N 18
Bay 32nd St	36	N 18
Bayfield Av	35	M 18
Bayport Pl	36	O 17
Bayside Av	17	K 8
Bayside Av	37	G 20
Bayside Dock *(off Beach 94th St)	35	L 18
Bayside Dr	37	G 20
Bayside La	17	L 8
Bayside St	17	M 7
Bayside St	37	G 20
Bayside Walk	37	G 20
Bayswater Av	36	N 17
Bayswater Ct	36	N 17
Bayview Av	18	N 8
Bayview Walk	39	L 19
Bayway Walk	37	F 20
Beach Channel Dr	39	K 19
Beach 3rd St	36	O 18
Beach 4th St	36	O 18
Beach 5th St	36	O 18
Beach 6th St	36	O 18
Beach 7th St	36	O 18
Beach 8th St	36	O 18
Beach 9th St	36	O 18
Beach 11th St	36	O 17
Beach 12th St	36	O 17
Beach 13th St	36	O 18
Beach 14th St	36	O 18
Beach 15th St	36	O 18
Beach 16th St	36	O 17
Beach 18th St	36	O 17
Beach 19th St	36	O 18
Beach 20th St	36	O 18
Beach 21st St	36	O 18
Beach 22nd St	36	N 17
Beach 24th St	36	N 17
Beach 25th St	36	N 18
Beach 26th St	36	N 18
Beach 27th St	36	N 18
Beach 28th St	36	N 17
Beach 29th St	36	N 17
Beach 30th St	36	N 18
Beach 31st St	36	N 18

STREET	MAP	GRID
Beach 32nd St ..	36	N 18
Beach 35th St ...	36	N 18
Beach 36th St ...	36	N 18
Beach 37th St ...	36	N 18
Beach 38th St ...	36	N 18
Beach 39th St ...	36	N 18
Beach 40th St ...	36	N 18
Beach 41st Pl	36	N 18
Beach 41st St ...	36	N 18
Beach 42nd St ..	36	N 18
Beach 43rd St ...	36	N 18
Beach 44th St ...	36	N 18
Beach 45th St ...	36	N 18
Beach 46th Pl	36	N 18
Beach 46th St ...	36	N 18
Beach 47th St ...	36	N 18
Beach 47th Way	36	N 18
Beach 48th St ...	36	N 18
Beach 48th Way	36	N 18
Beach 49th St ...	36	M 18
Beach 50th St	36	M 18
Beach 51st St	36	M 18
Beach 52nd St ...	35	M 18
Beach 53rd St ...	35	M 18
Beach 54th St ...	36	M 18
Beach 55th St ...	36	M 18
Beach 56th Pl	35	M 18
Beach 56th St ...	36	M 18
Beach 57th St ...	36	M 18
Beach 58th St ...	36	M 18
Beach 59th St ...	35	M 18
Beach 60th St ...	35	M 18
Beach 61st St ...	35	M 18
Beach 62nd St ...	35	M 18
Beach 63rd St ...	35	M 18
Beach 64th St ...	35	M 18
Beach 65th St ...	35	M 18
Beach 66th St ...	35	M 18
Beach 67th St ...	35	M 18
Beach 68th St ...	35	M 18
Beach 69th St ...	35	M 18
Beach 70th St	35	M 18
Beach 71st St	35	M 18
Beach 72nd St ..	35	L 18
Beach 73rd St ...	35	L 18
Beach 74th St ...	35	L 18
Beach 75th St ...	35	L 18
Beach 76th St ...	35	L 18
Beach 77th St ...	35	L 18
Beach 79th St ...	35	L 18
Beach 80th St ...	35	L 18
Beach 81st St ...	35	L 18
Beach 82nd St ...	35	L 18
Beach 83rd St ...	35	L 18
Beach 84th St ...	35	L 18
Beach 85th St ...	35	L 18
Beach 86th St ...	35	L 18
Beach 87th St ...	35	L 18
Beach 88th St ...	35	L 18
Beach 89th St ...	35	L 18
Beach 90th St ...	35	L 18
Beach 91st St ...	35	L 18
Beach 92nd St ...	35	L 18
Beach 93rd St ...	39	L 19
Beach 94th St ...	39	L 19
Beach 95th St ...	39	L 19
Beach 96th St ...	35	L 18
Beach 97th St ...	39	L 19
Beach 98th St ...	39	L 19
Beach 99th St ...	39	L 19
Beach 100th St ...	39	L 19
Beach 101st St ..	39	L 19
Beach 102nd La ...	39	K 19
Beach 102nd St	39	L 19
Beach 104th St .	39	K 19
Beach 105th St .	39	K 19
Beach 106th La .	39	K 19
Beach 106th St .	39	K 19
Beach 108th St .	39	K 19
Beach 109th St .	39	K 19
Beach 110th St .	39	K 19
Beach 111th St .	39	K 19
Beach 112th St .	39	K 19
Beach 113th St .	39	K 19
Beach 114th St .	39	K 19
Beach 115th St .	39	K 19
Beach 116th St .	39	K 19
Beach 117th St .	39	K 19
Beach 118th St .	39	K 19
Beach 119th St .	39	K 19
Beach 120th St .	39	K 19
Beach 121st St .	39	K 19
Beach 122nd St	39	K 19
Beach 123rd St .	39	K 19
Beach 124th St .	39	K 19
Beach 125th St .	38	J 19
Beach 126th St .	38	J 19
Beach 127th St .	38	J 19
Beach 128th St .	38	J 19
Beach 129th St .	38	J 19
Beach 130th St .	38	J 19
Beach 131st St .	38	J 19
Beach 132nd St	38	J 19
Beach 133rd St .	38	J 19
Beach 134th St .	38	J 19
Beach 135th St .	38	J 19
Beach 136th St .	38	J 19
Beach 137th St .	38	J 19
Beach 138th St .	38	J 19
Beach 139th St .	38	J 19
Beach 140th St .	38	J 19
Beach 141st St .	38	J 19
Beach 143rd St .	38	J 19
Beach 144th St .	38	J 19
Beach 145th St .	38	O 11
Beach 146th St .	38	J 19
Beach 147th St .	38	J 19
Beach 148th St .	38	J 19
Beach 149th St .	38	J 19
Beach 169th St .	38	H 20
Beach 193rd St .	37	G 20
Beach 201st St .	37	G 20
Beach 204th St .	37	G 20
Beach 207th St .	37	G 20
Beach 208th St .	37	G 20
Beach 209th St .	37	G 20
Beach 210th St .	37	G 20
Beach 213th St .	37	F 20
Beach 214th St .	37	F 20
Beach 215th St .	37	F 20
Beach 216th St .	37	F 20
Beach 217th St .	37	F 20
Beach 219th St .	37	F 20
Beach 220th St .	37	F 20
Beach 221st St .	37	F 20
Beach 222nd St	37	F 20
Beacon Pl	36	N 17
Beatrice Ct	36	N 17
Beaver Rd	26	L 12
Beck Rd	36	O 17
Bedell St	30	M 13
Bedford Av	37	G 20
Beech Av	21	K 9
Beech Cir	16	J 8
Beech Ct	16	J 8
Beechknoll Av ...	23	O 9
Beechknoll Pl	26	K 11
Belknap St	31	N 13
Bell Blvd	17	M 8
Bellaire Pl	27	N 11
Belmont Av	29	J 14
Belt Pkwy	32	J 15
Benham St	20	H 10
Benida Ct *(off Jarvis Ct near Beach 9th St)	36	O 18
Bennett Ct	31	N 13
Bennett St	31	N 13
Bentley Rd	34	O 15
Benton St	31	N 13
Bergen Rd	30	L 14
Berkely Ct *(off Beach 50th St)	35	M 18
Berkey Av	20	G 9
Berkley Ct *(off Beach 56th Pl)	35	M 18
Bernal Colony *(off Beach 46th St)	36	N 18
Bernard Ct *(off Beach 55th St)	35	M 18
Berrian Blvd	15	G 8
Berrian St	16	H 8
Bert Rd	35	L 17
Bessemer St	26	K 12
Bessemund Av ..	36	N 18
Betty Ct *(off Beach 109th St)	39	K 19
Beverley Rd	26	K 12
Beverley Rd	18	N 8
Beverly Ct *(off Brookhaven Av)	36	N 18
Billings St	28	O 11
Birdsall Av	36	O 17
Birmingham Pkwy	22	N 9
Blake Av	29	J 14
Bleecker St	24	G 12
Blossom Av	21	K 9
Boardwalk	35	M 18
Boelsen Cres ...	25	J 11
Boker Ct	16	J 8
Bolton Rd	36	O 17
Bonnie La	17	M 8
Boody St	20	G 9
Booth Memorial Av	21	K 10
Booth St	25	H 11
Borage Pl	26	K 11
Borden Av	19	E 10
Borkel Pl	28	O 11
Borough Pl	20	G 9
Boss St	29	K 13
Boulevard St	16	K 7
Boundary Rd	17	M 7
Bourton St	25	H 11
Bow St	25	J 11
Bowden Av	22	M 9
Bowne St	21	K 9
Boyce Av	22	M 9
Braddock Av	28	O 11
Bradley Av	19	E 10
Brant Walk	37	G 20
Brattle Av	23	O 9
Braus Ct *(off 69th St)	35	M 18
Breezy Point Blvd	37	F 20
Brefney Ct *(off Beach 108th & 109th Sts)	39	K 19
Brevoort St	26	K 12
Brewster Ct *(off Beach 109th St)	39	K 19
Brian Cres	17	M 8
Briar Pl	36	N 18
Bridge Plz N	19	E 10
Bridge Plz S	19	E 9
Bridgeton St	29	K 14
Bridgewater Av (Floral Park) ...	23	P 9
Brinkerhoff Av	27	N 12
Brisbin St	26	L 12
Bristol Av	29	K 14
Britton Av	20	H 10
Broacher Rd	31	N 13
Broadway	19	F 9
Broadway Ct *(off Sage St)	36	O 17
Brookhaven Av ..	36	N 18
Brooklyn-Queens Expwy	19	F 10
Brookside St	18	O 8
Brookville Blvd ..	31	O 14
Brown Pl	24	G 11
Brown's Blvd	37	G 20
Browvale La	18	O 8
Brunswick Av	36	O 17
Budd Pl	21	K 9
Buell St	20	J 9
Bunnecke Ct	24	G 12
Burchell Av	35	L 18
Burchell Pl *(off Rockaway Beach Blvd near 102nd St)	39	L 19
Burchell Rd	35	M 18
Burden Cres	26	L 12
Burdette Pl	26	L 12
Burling St	21	K 9
Burns St	25	J 11
Burrough Pl	20	G 10
Burton St	17	L 8
Butler Av	24	G 12
Butler St	20	J 9
Bye St	26	K 11
Byrd St	21	K 9
Byron St	30	M 14

C

STREET	MAP	GRID
Cabot Rd	24	G 13
Caffrey Av	36	O 18
Calamus Av	20	G 10
Calamus Cir	20	H 10
Caldwell Av	24	G 11
Calloway St	20	J 10
Calsing St *(off Beach 107th St)	39	K 19
Cambria Av	23	O 9
Cambridge Rd ..	27	M 11
Camden Av	27	N 12
Camp Rd	36	N 18
Caney La	31	O 14
Caney Rd	31	P 14
Capstan Ct	16	J 7
Cargo Plz	33	M 15

STREET	MAP	GRID
Cargo Service Rd	33	L 15
Carleton Pl	21	K 9
Carlton St	25	H 11
Carolina Rd	23	O 9
Carpenter Av	27	N 12
Carson St	31	N 14
Case St	20	H 10
Castlewood St (Floral Park)	23	P 10
Catalpa Av	24	G 12
Catherine Ct *(off Beach 104th St)	39	K 19
Cedar La	29	J 14
Cedarcroft Rd	27	M 12
Cedarhill Rd	36	O 18
Cedarlawn Av *(off Reads La)	36	O 17
Cedric Rd	30	L 14
Celtic Av	19	F 10
Center Cargo Rd	33	M 15
Center Cargo Rd	18	N 8
Center Dr	17	K 7
Center St	38	H 20
Centerville St	29	K 14
Central Av	25	H 12
Central Av	36	O 17
Centre St	24	G 12
Champlain Rd	35	K 17
Chandler Ct *(near 165th Av & 104th St)	32	K 15
Chandler St	36	N 17
Channel Rd	35	L 17
Channing Rd	36	O 17
Chapel Rd	17	M 7
Chapel Walk	37	G 20
Chapin Ct	26	L 11
Chapin Pkwy	26	L 11
Charlecote Ridge	27	M 11
Charlotte St	24	F 12
Charter Rd	26	L 11
Chelsea St	27	M 11
Cheney St	31	N 14
Cherry Av	21	K 9
Chester Walk	37	G 20
Chevy Chase St	27	M 11
Chicot Ct	29	K 13
Christie Av	20	J 10
Church Av	38	H 20
Church Rd	35	L 17
Cinder Rd *(off Rockaway Point Blvd)	37	G 20
Circle Rd	18	N 8
Claran Ct	24	G 12
Claremont Ter	20	H 10
Claude St	30	M 13
Clearview Expwy	17	M 8
Clinton Av	24	G 11
Clinton Pl	26	L 12
Clinton Ter	26	L 12
Clintonville St	17	L 7
Clio St	27	N 11
Clover Hill Dr	27	N 11
Clover Hill Rd	27	N 11
Clover Pl	24	G 13
Clover Pl	24	G 13
Cloverdale Blvd	22	N 9
Clyde St	25	J 11
Coast Guard Ct *(off Beach 58th St)	35	M 18
Codwise Pl	20	H 10
Cody Av	24	G 13
Cohancy St	29	K 14
Cold Spring Rd	36	N 17
Colden St	21	K 9
Coleman Sq	29	K 14
Coles La *(off Beach 9th St)	36	O 18
Colfax St	28	O 12
College Pl	16	J 7
College Point Blvd	16	J 8
Collier Av	36	N 18
Collins Pl	21	K 9
Colonial Av	21	J 10
Colonial Ct *(off Beach 107th St)	39	K 19
Columbus Sq	19	F 9
Commissary Rd	33	L 15
Commonwealth Blvd	23	O 9
Como Av	27	N 11
Compass Rd	33	M 15
Conch St	36	N 18
Concord St	18	O 8
Congressman Rosenthal Av	21	K 9
Constance Ct *(off Beach 101st St)	39	K 19
Continental Av	25	J 12
Cook Av	25	H 12
Coolidge Av	26	L 11
Coolidge Ct *(off Beach 39th St)	36	N 18
Coombs St	31	N 14
Cooper Av	25	H 12
Cooper Ter	25	H 12
Corbett Rd	22	N 9
Cornaga Av	36	N 18
Cornaga Ct *(off Reads La)	36	O 17
Cornelia St	24	G 12
Cornell La *(north from Northern Blvd east of Marathon Pkwy)	23	O 9
Cornish Av	20	H 10
Corona Av	20	H 10
Coronado Ct *(off Seagirt Av near Beach 6th St)	36	O 18
Corporal Kennedy St	17	M 8
Corporal Stone St	22	N 9
Costa Av	35	L 18
Couch Pl	20	J 9
Court Sq	19	E 10
Courtney Av	22	M 9
Courtney La	37	G 20
Cove Ct	16	J 7
Covert St	43	F 13
Cowles Ct	25	H 11
Craft Av	34	O 15
Crandall Av	31	N 14
Crane St	19	E 10
Cranford St	26	K 11
Cranston St	30	M 14
Crawford Ct *(off Beach 19th St near Cornaga Av)	36	O 18
Creekside Av	37	G 20
Crescent St (25th St)	19	E 10
Creskill Pl	26	L 12
Crest Rd *(in Wavecrest Gdns)	36	N 18
Crocheron Av	21	L 9
Crommelin St	21	K 9
Cromwell Cres	25	J 11
Cronston Av	38	J 19
Cross Bay Blvd	29	K 13
Cross Bay Pkwy	35	L 18
Cross Bay Veterans Memorial Bridge (Broad Channel)	35	L 18
Cross Island Pkwy	17	M 8
Croydon Rd	27	M 11
Crugers Rd	35	L 18
Cryders La	17	L 8
Cullman Av	23	O 9
Culloden Pl	29	J 13
Curley Ct *(off Beach 102nd St near Beach Channel Dr)	35	K 18
Curtis St	20	H 9
Curzon Rd	26	K 12
Cuthbert Rd	26	K 12
Cynthia Ct *(off Beach 101st St near RR)	39	L 19
Cypress Av	24	F 12
Cypress Hills St	24	G 12
D		
Dahlia Av	21	K 9
Daisy Pl	23	O 9
Dalny Rd	27	M 11
Dana Ct	25	H 11
Dane Pl	25	J 11
Daniels St	26	L 11
Darren Dr	17	M 8
Dartmouth St	25	J 11
Dashby Ct *(off Beach 79th St)	35	L 18
Davenport Av	28	O 11
Davenport Ct *(near 163rd Rd & 164th Av)	32	K 15
David Ct *(off Beach 55th St)	35	M 18
Davies Rd	36	O 18
Davis Ct *(off Beach 88th St)	35	L 18
Davis Ct	19	E 10
Davis St	19	E 10
Deauville Walk	37	F 20
Decatur St	24	G 12
De Costa Av	35	L 18
Deepdale Av	23	O 9
Deepdale Pl	23	O 9
Deepdene Pl	26	K 11
Deerfield Rd	36	N 18
Defoe St	31	N 13
De Kalb Av	24	F 12
Delaney Ct *(off Saint Marks Av near Beach 104th St)	39	K 19
Delaware Av	21	L 9
Delevan St	28	O 12
Delmore Ct *(off Beach 43rd St)	36	N 17
Delong St	21	K 9
Demerest Rd (Broad Channel)	35	L 18
Denis St	31	N 13
Denman St	20	H 10
De Orio Ct *(off Saint Marks Av)	39	K 19
Depew Av	18	O 8
Depot Rd	21	L 9
Desarc Rd	29	J 14
DeSota Pl *(off Beach 92nd St)	35	L 18
DeSota Rd	35	L 18
Devon Walk	37	G 20
Devonshire Rd	27	M 11
Dexter Ct	29	H 13
Diamond St	25	J 12
Diane Pl	17	M 8
Dickens St	36	N 17
Dieterle Cres	25	J 11
Digby Pl	29	J 13
Dillon St	30	M 13
Dinsmore Av	36	O 17
Ditmars Blvd	15	F 8
Division St	34	O 16
Dix Av	36	O 17
Dix Pl *(off Beach Channel Dr near Mott Av)	36	N 17
Donald Ct *(off New Haven Av near Beach 15th St)	36	O 17
Doncaster Pl	27	M 11
Dongan Av	20	H 10
Doran Av	25	J 12
Dorian Ct	36	O 18
Doris La	37	G 20
Dorman Ct *(off Beach 88th St)	35	L 18
Dormans Rd	27	N 12
Dorothy Ct *(off Rockaway Beach Blvd near Beach 106th St)	39	K 19
Dorothy Pl	15	F 8
Douglas Av	27	M 12

STREET	MAP	GRID
Douglas Rd	18	N 8
Douglaston Pkwy	22	N 9
Downing St	21	K 9
Drew St	29	J 13
Dry Harbor Rd	25	H 11
Duane Rd	17	M 7
Dumfries Pl	27	M 11
Dumont Av	29	J 14
Dunbar St	36	N 17
Dune St *(off Seagirt Blvd At Beach 25th St)	36	N 18
Dunkirk St	27	M 12
Dunlop Av	27	N 12
Dunton Av	27	N 11
Dunton St	27	N 11
Dutch Kills St	19	E 10
Dwight Av	36	N 18

E

STREET	MAP	GRID
East Dock St	34	O 16
East Dr	18	N 8
East Gate Plz	31	N 14
East Hampton Blvd	22	N 9
East Hangar Rd	33	L 15
East Loop	17	M 7
East Main Dr	25	J 12
East Williston Av (Floral Park)	23	P 10
East 1st Rd	35	L 17
East 3rd Rd	35	L 17
East 4th Rd	35	L 17
East 6th Rd	35	L 17
East 7th Rd	35	L 17
East 8th Rd	35	L 17
East 9th Rd	35	L 17
East 10th Rd	35	L 17
East 12th Rd	35	L 17
East 14th Rd	35	L 18
East 16th Rd	35	L 18
East 18th Rd	35	L 18
East 20th Rd	35	L 18
Eckford Av	29	K 14
Edgemere Av	36	M 18
Edgemere Ct *(off Beach 50th St)	35	M 18
Edgemere Rd	36	N 18
Edgemere Ter *(off Beach 33rd St)	36	N 18
Edgerton Blvd	27	M 11
Edgerton Rd	27	M 11
Edgewood Av	31	N 14
Edgewood St	34	O 15
Edmore Av	28	O 11
Edsall Av	25	H 12
Edward Ct *(off Beach 98th St)	35	L 18
Effington Av	21	L 9
Eggert Pl	36	N 17
Egmont Pl	36	N 17
Elbertson St	20	H 10
Elder Av	21	K 9
Elder La	29	J 13
Eldert St	24	G 13
Eldsea Ct *(off Rockaway Beach Blvd near Beach 106th St)	39	K 19

STREET	MAP	GRID
Eleanor Ct *(off Beach 98th St & Beach 109th St)	39	K 19
Eliot Av	24	G 11
Elizabeth Av	35	L 18
Elizabeth Rd	35	M 18
Elk Dr	36	N 18
Elkmont Av	23	P 10
Elks Rd	20	H 10
Ellwell Cres	25	J 11
Elm Av	21	L 9
Elmhurst Av	20	H 10
Elmira St	27	N 12
Elvia Ct *(off Beach 51st St)	36	O 18
Elvira Av	36	O 18
Emerald St	29	J 14
Emily Rd	17	M 8
Empire Av	36	O 17
Enfield Pl	22	N 9
Enid Ct *(off Beach 101st St)	39	L 19
Enright Rd	36	N 17
Epsom Course	27	N 11
Ericsson St	20	H 9
Essex Walk	37	G 20
Estates Dr	17	M 8
Estates La	17	M 8
Estelle Ct *(off Beach 58th St)	35	M 18
Eton St	27	M 11
Evans Rd	26	L 12
Eveleth Rd	31	N 13
Everdell Av	36	O 18
Everdell Pl	36	N 17
Everitt Pl	31	N 13
Everton St	25	H 11
Exeter St	25	J 11

F

STREET	MAP	GRID
Faber Ter	36	N 17
Failing St *(off Beach 69th St)	35	M 18
Fairbury Av	28	O 11
Fairchild Av	21	L 10
Fairfield Pl	29	J 14
Fairview Av	24	G 12
Fairway Close	26	K 11
Falcon Av	36	N 18
Fan Rose Ct *(off Beach 55th St)	35	M 18
Far Rockaway Blvd	36	N 18
Farmers Blvd	27	N 12
Farrington St	21	K 9
Fay Ct *(off Beach 40th St)	36	N 18
Federal Cir	33	L 15
Felio Ct *(off Beach 52nd St)	35	M 18
Fern Pl	27	M 12
Ferndale Av	30	L 13
Fernside Pl	36	N 18
Finnard Av	35	L 18
Finns Ct *(off Beach 102nd St)	39	K 19

STREET	MAP	GRID
Firwood Pl	27	N 12
Fitchett St	25	H 11
Fleet Ct	25	H 11
Fleet St	25	J 11
Floral Ct *(off Beach 108th St)	39	K 19
Florence Ct *(off Beach 49th St)	35	M 18
Florence Ct *(off Beach 55th St)	35	M 18
Flushing Av	24	F 11
Foam Pl	36	O 17
Foch Blvd	30	L 13
Fonda Av	27	N 12
Foothill Av	27	N 11
Forbell St	29	J 13
Forest Av	24	G 12
Forest Pkwy	25	J 12
Forest Rd	18	N 8
Forley St	20	H 10
Fowler Av	21	K 9
Frame Pl	21	K 9
Fran Wayne Ct *(off Beach 51st St)	35	M 18
Frances Ct *(off Beach 56th St)	35	M 18
Francis Lewis Blvd	17	L 8
Franklin Av	21	K 9
Franklin Ct *(off Beach 39th St)	36	N 18
Frankton St	31	P 14
Frederick Ct *(off Reads La)	36	O 17
Freedom Dr	25	J 12
Fremont St	24	G 12
Fresh Meadow La	21	L 10
Fresh Pond Rd	24	G 11
Friendly Ct *(off Beach 56th St)	35	M 18
Frisco Av	36	O 18
Fuller Pl	21	K 9
Fulton Walk	37	F 20
Furmanville Av	25	H 11

G

STREET	MAP	GRID
Galasso Pl	24	F 11
Gale Av	19	F 10
Galway Av	27	N 12
Garbe Ct *(off Beach 51st St)	35	M 18
Garden Ct *(off Beach 56th St)	35	M 18
Garden Ct *(off Beach 9th St)	36	O 17
Garden Ter *(off Beach 56th St)	35	M 18
Garfield Av	20	G 10
Garland Dr	22	N 9
Garland Ter	22	N 9
Garrett St	31	N 14
Gaskell Rd	23	O 9

STREET	MAP	GRID
Gates Av	24	G 12
Gateway Blvd	36	O 18
General R W Berry Dr	17	M 7
George Ct *(off Beach 50th St)	35	M 18
George St	24	G 12
Georgia Rd	21	L 9
Georgian Ct *(off Beach 109th St)	39	K 19
Geranium Av	21	K 9
Gerard Ct *(off Beach 57th St)	39	K 19
Gerard Ct	35	M 18
Gerard Pl	25	J 11
Gettysburg St	28	O 11
Gilmore St	20	H 9
Gipson St	36	N 17
Gladwin Av	21	L 10
Gladys Ct *(off Beach 55th St)	35	M 18
Glassboro Av	30	L 13
Gleane St	20	H 10
Glenmore Av	29	J 13
Glenn Av	26	L 12
Glenwood St	18	O 8
Goethals Av	26	L 11
Gold St	29	J 14
Goldington Ct	25	J 11
Goldsmith St	20	H 10
Goodward Rd	26	K 11
Gorsline St	20	H 10
Gotham Rd	30	L 14
Gotham Walk	37	F 20
Gothic Dr	26	L 11
Gouverneur Av	35	L 18
Grace Ct	26	L 12
Grace Ct *(off Beach 107th St)	35	K 18
Graham Ct	16	J 8
Graham Pl	37	G 20
Granada Pl	36	N 17
Grand Av	24	G 11
Grand Central Pkwy	16	H 8
Grandview Av	24	G 12
Grandview Ter *(off Caffrey Av near Mott Av)	36	O 17
Granger St	20	J 10
Grannatt Pl	30	M 14
Grassmere Ter	36	N 18
Gravett Rd	21	K 10
Gray St	25	H 11
Grayson St	31	N 13
Greene Av	24	F 12
Greenpoint Av	19	E 10
Greenway N	26	K 11
Greenway S	25	J 11
Greenway Ter	26	K 11
Grenfell St	26	K 12
Grosvenor La	26	K 12
Grosvenor Rd	26	K 12
Grosvenor St	18	N 8
Groton St	25	J 11
Grove Ct *(off Seagirt Av)	36	O 18
Grove St	24	G 12
Grover Ct *(off Beach 39th St)	36	N 18

STREET	MAP	GRID
Guilford St	25	J 12
Guinzburg Rd	26	L 12
Gull Ct	35	L 18
Guy R Brewer Blvd	27	M12
H		
Haddon St	27	M 11
Hague Pl	30	M14
Haight St	21	K 9
Hamilton Pl	24	G11
Hampton St	20	H 10
Hancock St	43	F 13
Hand Rd	23	O 9
Hanford St	23	O 9
Hannibal St	27	N 12
Hanover Ct *(off Saint Marks Av near Beach 105th St)	39	K 19
Hantz Rd	36	N 18
Harbour Ct	36	N 17
Haring St	25	H 11
Harmon St	24	F 12
Harmony Rd	38	H 20
Harold Ct *(off Beach 52nd St)	35	M 18
Harper St	20	J 9
Harriet Ct *(off Beach 56th St)	35	M 18
Harris St	36	O 17
Harrison Ct *(off Beach 39th St)	35	M 18
Harrow St	25	J 11
Harry Van Ardsley Av (see Jewel Av)	21	L 10
Hart St	24	F 12
Hartland Av	22	N 10
Hartman La *(off Cornaga Av)	36	N 18
Haspel St	20	H 10
Hassock St	36	O17
Hawthorne Av	21	L 9
Hawtree Creek Rd	30	L 13
Hawtree St	29	K 14
Haywood Rd	27	N 11
Hazen St	20	G 9
Healy Av	36	N 17
Helen Ct *(off Beach 26th St)	36	N 18
Hempstead Av	28	O 11
Henderson Av	27	M 12
Hendrickson Pl	27	M 12
Henley Rd	27	M 11
Henry Av	20	G 10
Henry Rd	36	O 17
Herrick Av	25	J 12
Hessler Av	35	M 18
Hewlett St	23	P 9
Heyson Rd	36	O 18
Hiawatha Av	27	N 11
Hicks Dr	20	G 10
Hicksville Rd	36	O 18
Higgins La	17	L 8
Higgins St	21	K 9
Highland Av	26	L 12
Highland Ct	36	N 18
Highland Pl	37	G 20
Hilburn Av	27	N 12
Hillcrest Av	18	N 8
Hillcrest Walk	37	G 20
Hillmeyer Av	35	L 18
Hillside Av	26	K 12
Hillside Av	38	H 20
Hillyer St	20	H 10
Himrod St	24	F 12
Hobart St	20	G 9
Hoffman Dr	20	H 10
Holder Pl	26	K 11
Holland Av	35	L 18
Hollis Av	27	N 12
Hollis Court Blvd	22	M10
Hollis Hills Ter	22	N 10
Holly Av	21	K 9
Hollyhurst Ct *(off Beach 101st St near RR)	35	L 18
Hollywood Av	21	L 9
Hollywood Ct *(off McBride St)	36	N 17
Hollywood Ct *(off Beach 29th St)	36	N 18
Home Lawn St	27	M 11
Homenhurst Ct *(off Beach 107th St)	39	K 19
Honeywell St	19	F 10
Hook Creek Blvd	34	P 15
Hoover Av	26	K 11
Horace Harding Blvd *(service road for Long Island Expwy)	20	J 10
Horatio Pkwy	22	N 9
Hortense Ct *(off Beach 40th St)	36	N 18
Horton Av	36	O 17
Hough Pl *(off Beach 45th St North of Beach Channel Dr)	36	N 18
Hovendon Rd	27	M 11
Hoxie Dr	22	N 9
Hoyt Av N	15	F 8
Hoyt Av S	15	F 8
Hudson Walk	37	F 20
Hull Av	24	G 11
Humphreys St	20	H 9
Hungry Harbor Rd	34	P 15
Hunter St	19	E 10
Hunters Point Av	19	E 10
Hurley Ct	36	O 18
Huron St	29	K 14
Huxley St	34	O 15
I		
Ida Ct *(off Beach 101st St near Beach Channel Dr)	36	N 18
Ide Ct	36	N 17
Ilion Av	27	N 12
Indiana Av	25	H 12
Ingram St	25	J 11
Interborough Pkwy	24	G 13
Interstate Hwy 278	15	F 8
Interstate Hwy 295	17	M 7
Interstate Hwy 495	19	E 10
Interstate Hwy 678	16	K 8
Inwood St	30	L 13
Iowa Rd	18	O 8
Ireland St	20	H 10
Irene Ct *(off Saint Marks Av near Beach 108th St)	39	K 19
Irving Av	24	F 12
Irving Ct *(off Beach 49th St)	35	M 18
Irving Walk	37	F 20
Irwin Pl	31	N 13
Ithaca St	20	H 10
Ives Ct *(off Beach Dickens Av)	36	N 17
Ivy Close	26	K 11
J		
Jack Ct *(off Beach 56th St)	35	M 18
Jackson Av	19	E 10
Jackson Mill Rd	20	H 9
Jacobus St	20	H 10
Jaegers La *(off Albert Rd)	29	K 14
Jamaica Av	29	J 13
Jamaica Walk	37	F 20
James St	30	M 13
Janet La	37	G 20
Janet Pl	21	K 9
Jarman Rd	17	M 7
Jarvis Ct	36	O 18
Jasmine Av	21	L 9
Java Pl	35	L 18
Jay Av	24	G 11
Jefferson Av	43	F 13
Jefferson Ct *(off Beach 40th St)	36	N 18
Jessie Ct *(off Beach 49th St)	36	N 18
Jessie Ct	18	O 8
Jewel Av	26	K 11
Jones Ct *(off Beach 81st St)	35	L 18
Jordan Av	27	N 12
Jordan Ct	17	M 8
Jordan Dr	17	M 8
Jordan St	17	M 8
Judell Ct *(off Beach 55th St)	35	M 18
Judge St	20	H 10
Jullius Rd	16	J 7
Junction Blvd	20	H 9
Juniper Av	21	K 9
Juniper Blvd N	25	H 11
Juniper Blvd S	25	H 11
JuniperValley Rd	25	H 11
Juno St	25	J 11
Justice Av	20	H 10
K		
Kalmia Av	21	K 10
Kathy Ct *(off Beach 56th St)	35	M18
Kearney St	20	H 9
Keel Ct	16	J 7
Keeseville Av	27	N 12
Kelp Rd	35	M 18
Kendrick Pl	27	M 11
Kenilworth Dr	22	N 9
Kenmore Rd	18	N 8
Keno Av	27	N 11
Kent St	27	M 11
Kessel St	25	J 11
Ketch Ct	16	J 7
Ketcham Pl	20	H 10
Ketcham St	20	H 10
Kew Forest La	26	K 11
Kew Gardens Rd	26	K 11
Kildare Rd	27	M 11
KildareWalk	37	F 20
Killarney St	29	K 14
King Rd	21	K 9
Kingsbury Av	22	N 10
Kingston Pl	27	M 11
Kissena Blvd	21	K 9
Kneeland Av	20	H 10
Knollwood Av	18	N 8
Kramer Ct *(off Beach 54th St)	35	M 18
Kramer Ct *(off Beach 70th St)	35	M 18
Krayer Ct *(off Beach 54th St)	35	M 18
Kruger Rd	27	M 11
L		
La Rue Av	20	J 10
Laburnum Av	21	K 10
Lafayette Ct *(off Beach 51st St)	35	M 18
Lafayette St	29	K 14
Lahn St	29	K 14
Lake Av	30	M 13
Lakeview Blvd	30	M 13
Lakeview La	30	M 13
Lakeview St	31	N 14
Lakewood Av	30	L 13
Lamont Av	20	H 10
Lanark Rd	35	L 17
Lander St	21	K 9
Lanett Av	36	O 18
Langdale St (New Hyde Park)	23	P 9
Langston Av	23	P 9
Lansing Av	31	O 14
Larkin Av	35	M 18
Larkin Ct *(off Beach 65th St)	35	M 18
Larue Av	20	J 10

STREET	MAP	GRID
Lasan Ct *(off Beach 105th St)	39	K 19
Latham La	31	N 14
Latimer Pl	21	K 9
Laurel Hill Blvd	20	G 10
Laurelton Pkwy	31	O 14
Law Rd	25	H 11
Lawrence St	21	K 10
Lax Av	16	J 7
Layton St	20	H 10
Leavitt St	21	K 9
Lee Ct	17	K 8
Lee Rd	17	M 7
Leeds Rd	23	O 9
Lefferts Blvd	26	K 12
Leggett Pl	17	L 7
Leith Pl	23	O 9
Leith Rd	23	O 9
Leslie Rd	31	N 13
Lester Ct *(off Beach 40th St)	36	N 18
Leverich St	20	G 10
Lewis Av	20	J 10
Lewiston Av	27	N 12
Lewmay Rd	36	N 18
Liberty Av	30	L 13
Liberty La	37	G 20
Lincoln Ct *(off Beach 56th Pl)	35	M 18
Lincoln St	30	L 14
Lincoln Walk	37	G 20
Linden Blvd	29	K 14
Linden Pl	16	K 8
Linden Spring Ct *(off Beach 56th St)	35	M 18
Linden St	24	G 12
Lineaus Pl	21	K 9
Lithonia Av	21	L 10
Little Bay Rd	17	M 7
Little Neck Blvd	17	M 8
Little Neck Pkwy	18	O 8
Liverpool St	26	L 12
Lloyd Rd	30	L 13
Locke Av	17	L 8
Long Island Expwy	19	E 10
Long St	30	M 13
Loop Rd	33	M 15
Loretta Rd	36	N 18
Lori Dr	17	M 8
Loubet St	25	J 11
Louise Ct *(off Beach 50th St)	35	M 18
Lovingham Pl	31	N 13
Lowe Ct	26	L 12
Lucas St	31	N 13
Ludlum Av	27	N 12
Luke Pl	22	N 9
Luther Rd	25	H 12
Lutheran Av	25	H 11
Lux St	30	L 13
Lyman St	28	O 11
Lynch Ct *(off Beach 105th St)	39	K 19

M

STREET	MAP	GRID
MacIntosh Pl	20	G 10
MacNish St	20	H 10
Madison St	24	G 12
Mador Ct *(off Cornaga Av)	36	O 17
Mae Ct *(off Beach 109th St)	39	K 19
Magnolia Pl	21	K 9
Main Av	15	F 8
Main St	21	K 9
Malba Dr	17	K 7
Mangin Av	27	N 12
Manilla St	20	H 10
Manor Rd	18	N 8
Manor Rd	23	O 10
Manse St	25	J 11
Manton St	26	L 12
Manville La	37	G 20
Maple Av	21	K 9
Marathon Pkwy	23	O 9
Marengo St	27	N 11
Margaret Pl	25	J 12
Marie Ct *(off Beach 101st St near R R)	39	K 19
Marie Jean Ct *(off Beach 56th St)	35	M 18
Marietta Ct *(off Saint Marks Av near Beach 105th St)	39	K 19
Marine Terminal Rd	20	H 9
Marinette St	18	N 8
Marion Ct *(off Beach 56th Pl)	35	M 18
Marion Walk	37	F 20
Marissa St	31	N 14
Market St	37	G 20
Markwood Pl	26	K 12
Marne Pl	30	M 13
Mars Pl	31	N 13
Marsden St	30	M 13
Marsells Ct *(off Beach 98th St)	39	L 19
Marshall Av	37	G 20
Martense Av	20	J 10
Marvin Ct *(off Beach 28th St)	35	M 18
Marvin Ct	36	N 18
Mary Morris Ct *(off Beach 98th St)	39	L 19
Maryland Rd	23	O 9
Maspeth Av	24	F 11
Mathewson Ct	31	N 13
Mathias Av	30	M 13
Maurice Av	24	G 11
May Ct *(off Saint Marks Ave near Beach 107th St)	39	K 19
Mayda Rd	31	O 14
Mayfair Rd	26	K 12
Mayfield Rd	27	M 11
Mayville St	27	N 12
Mazeau St	24	G 11

STREET	MAP	GRID
McBride St	36	N 17
McIntosh St	20	H 9
McKin Av	22	M 9
McLaughlin Av	27	M 11
Meehan Av	36	O 18
Mekin Av	22	M 9
Melbourne Av	21	K 10
Melissa Ct	17	M 8
Melrose La	18	N 8
Melvina Pl	24	G 11
Memorial Cir	39	K 19
Memorial Dr	26	K 12
Memphis Av	31	O 14
Menahan St	24	G 12
Mentone Av	31	O 14
Merrick Blvd	27	M 12
Merrill St	31	N 13
Metcalf Av	21	L 10
Metropolitan Av	25	H 12
Mexico St	31	N 13
Meyer Av	30	M 13
Michael Ct	17	M 8
Michael Pl	17	M 8
Middle May Pl	25	J 11
Midland Pkwy	27	M 11
Midtown Tunnel Plz	19	E 10
Milburn St	31	N 13
Miller St	21	K 9
Minton St	36	O 17
Mobile Rd	36	O 17
Mobray Dr	26	K 12
Moline St	28	O 11
Montauk St	31	N 13
Monterey St	28	O 12
Moran Ct *(off Beach 98th St)	39	L 19
Morden Rd	26	K 12
Morenci La	23	O 9
Morgan St	18	O 8
Morse Ct *(off Cornaga Av near Mott Av)	36	O 17
Moss Pl *(off Harris St & Empire Av)	36	O 17
Mott Av	36	N 17
Mott Pl *(off Mott Av near Cornaga Av)	36	O 17
Mount Olivet Cres	24	G 11
Muhlbach Ct *(off Beach 19th St near New Haven Av)	36	N 18
Mulberry Av	21	K 10
Murdock Av	30	M 13
Murial Ct *(off 107th St)	29	K 13
Murray Av	17	M 7
Murray La	21	L 9
Murray St	17	L 8
Musket St	23	O 10
Myrtle Av	25	J 12

N

STREET	MAP	GRID
Nancy Ct *(off Beach 100th St)	39	L 19

STREET	MAP	GRID
Nansen St	25	J 11
Nasby Pl	36	N 18
Nashville Blvd	31	N 13
Nassau Blvd	23	O 9
National St	20	J 10
Negundo Av	21	L 10
Neilson Av *(off Central Av)	36	O 17
Neilson St	36	O 17
Nellis St	31	N 13
Neponsit Av	38	J 19
Nepton St	31	N 13
Neptune Ct *(off Beach 107th St)	39	K 19
Neptune Walk	37	G 20
Nero Av	27	M 11
Nettie Ct *(off Beach 49th St)	35	M 18
New Haven Av	36	N 18
Newbold Pl	26	K 12
Newburg St	31	N 13
Newhall Av	31	O 14
Newport Av	38	J 19
Newport Walk	37	F 20
Newtown Av	19	F 9
Newtown Rd	19	F 9
Nicolls Av	20	J 10
Noel Rd	35	L 17
Normal Rd	26	L 12
Norman St	24	G 12
North Boundary Rd	30	M 14
North Conduit Av	29	J 14
North Dr	17	K 7
North Hangar Rd	33	M 15
North Loop	17	M 7
North Service Ct	33	M 15
North Service Rd	33	L 15
Northern Blvd	19	F 10
Norton Av	36	N 18
Nunly Ct *(off Beach 99th St)	35	L 18
Nurge Av	24	F 11

O

STREET	MAP	GRID
Oak Av	21	L 9
Oak Dr	36	O 18
Oak La	18	N 8
Oak Park Dr	23	O 10
Oakley Pl	18	O 8
Ocean Av	37	G 20
Ocean Crest Blvd	36	N 18
Ocean Ct *(off Beach 12th St)	36	O 18
Ocean Promenade	39	K 19
Oceania St	22	M 9
Oceanside Av	37	F 20
Oceanside Ct *(off Beach 56th St)	35	M 18
Oceanside St	37	G 20
Oceanview Av	38	H 20
O'Connell Ct	20	H 10
O'Donnell Rd	30	M 13

STREET	MAP	GRID
Officer's Dr	17	M 7
Olcott St	25	J 12
Old Rockaway Blvd	34	N 15
Old South Rd	30	L 14
Olive Pl	25	J 11
Olive Walk	37	F 20
Onderdonk Av	24	F 12
O'Neil Ct *(off Beach 52nd St)	35	M 18
Onslow Pl	26	K 12
Orchard St	19	E 10
Ordnance Rd	17	M 7
Ostend Pl *(off New Haven Av near Beach 17th St)	36	O 18
Ostend St	36	O 18
Otis Av	20	J 10
Otto Rd	24	G 12
Overbrook Pl	23	O 9
Overhill Rd	26	K 11
Overlook Rd	23	O 9
Ovid Pl	27	N 12

P

STREET	MAP	GRID
Page Pl	24	F 11
Palermo St	27	N 11
Palmer Dr	37	F 20
Palmetto St	24	G 12
Palo Alto Av	27	M 11
Palo Alto St	27	M 11
Park Av	26	L 11
Park Cres *(off 36th Rd near 164th St)	27	M 11
Park Drive E	26	K 11
Park La	26	K 12
Park La	18	N 8
Park La S	25	J 12
Park Pl	26	K 11
Parsons Blvd	17	K 8
Parvine Av	35	M 18
Pavo Rd	26	L 12
Pearl Rd	16	J 7
Pearl St *(off Enright Rd)	36	N 17
Pearson Pl	19	E 10
Pearson St	19	E 10
Peartree Av	26	K 11
Peck Av	22	M 10
Peconic St	29	K 14
Pelham Walk	37	F 20
Pell Av	20	J 9
Pembroke Av	18	O 8
Pembroke Pl	26	K 12
Penelope Av	25	H 11
Penrod St	20	J 10
Perry Av	24	G 11
Pershing Cres	26	L 12
Perth Rd	27	M 11
Petracca Pl	17	K 8
Pettit Pl	20	H 10
Phlox Pl	21	K 9
Phroane Av	30	M 13
Pidgeon Meadow Rd	21	L 9
Pilot Rd	33	M 15
Pinegrove St	30	L 13
Pineville La	31	N 13
Pinson St	36	N 17
Pinto St	27	N 11

STREET	MAP	GRID
Pitkin Av	29	J 13
Plainview Av	36	O 18
Plattwood Av	29	K 13
Pleasant Ct *(off Beach 56th Pl)	35	M 18
Pleasant View St	25	H 11
Plunkett Av	36	N 17
Point Breeze Pl	36	N 17
Point Breezy Av	37	F 20
Point Cres	17	K 7
Polhemus Av	27	M 12
Polo Pl	25	J 12
Pompeii Av	27	N 11
Pompeii La	27	N 11
Pontiac St	28	O 11
Poplar Av	21	L 10
Pople Av	21	K 9
Poppenhusen Av	16	J 7
Porter Rd	31	N 14
Powells Cove Blvd	16	J 7
Power Rd	35	L 17
Poyer St	20	H 10
Pratt Av	17	M 7
President St	36	N 18
Prince St	21	K 9
Princeton St	30	L 13
Prospect Ct	31	O 14
Puritan Av (75th Rd)	26	K 12
Purves St	19	E 10
Putnam Av	24	G 12

Q

STREET	MAP	GRID
Queen Louise Ct *(off Beach 107th St)	39	K 19
Queens Blvd	19	F 10
Queens Midtown Expwy (now Long Island Expwy)	19	E 10
Queens Plz E	19	E 10
Queens Plz N	19	E 10
Queens Plz S	19	E 9
Queens St	19	E 10
Queens Walk	37	F 20
Quencer Rd	31	N 13
Quentin St	26	K 12
Quigley Blvd	34	O 16
Quince St	21	L 10

R

STREET	MAP	GRID
Race Track Rd	29	K 14
Radar Rd	34	N 15
Radcliff Av	20	J 10
Radnor Rd	27	M 11
Radnor St	27	M 11
Railroad Av	18	O 8
Railroad Ct *(off Beach 98th St)	35	L 18
Railroad Pl	24	F 11
Raleigh St	29	K 14
Range St	23	O 10
Ransom St	28	O 11

STREET	MAP	GRID
Rau Ct *(near 163rd Av & 104th St)	32	K 15
Reads La	36	O 17
Red Cross La	17	M 7
Redding St	29	K 14
Redfern Av	36	O 17
Redfield St	23	O 9
Reeder St	20	H 10
Reeves Av	21	K 10
Regan Ct *(off Beach 49th St)	35	M 18
Regatta Pl	18	N 8
Regina Av	36	N 17
Reid Av	37	G 20
Reinhart Rd	36	N 18
Remington St	26	L 12
Remsen Pl	24	G 11
Rene Ct	24	F 12
Rentar Plz	24	G 12
Review Av	19	E 10
Rex Pl	27	M 12
Ricard St	24	G 12
Richland Av	22	N 10
Richmond Rd	18	N 8
Rico Pl	29	K 14
Ridge Rd	18	N 8
Ridgedale St	31	N 13
Riis Av	38	J 19
Ring Pl	30	M 13
Rio Dr	27	M 11
Riverside Dr	17	L 7
Riverton St	31	N 13
Robard La	28	O 12
Robert Rd	17	M 8
Robin La	17	M 8
Robinson St	21	K 9
Rockaway Beach Blvd	38	J 19
Rockaway Blvd	29	J 13
Rockaway Breezy Blvd	37	G 20
Rockaway Freeway	39	K 19
Rockaway Freeway	35	L 18
Rockaway Freeway	35	L 18
Rockaway Freeway	36	N 18
Rockaway Point Blvd	37	F 20
Rockrose Pl	26	K 12
Rocky Hill Rd	22	M 9
Roe Pl	17	M 8
Roe Rd	31	N 13
Roma Ct *(off Beach 50th St)	35	M 18
Roman Av	25	J 12
Rome Dr	31	N 13
Romeo Ct	27	N 11
Roosevelt Av	20	G 10
Roosevelt St	36	O 18
Roosevelt Walk	37	F 20
Rose Av	21	L 10
Rose Ct *(off Beach 104th St)	39	K 19
Rose Ct	36	O 17
Rose St	36	O 17

STREET	MAP	GRID
Rosewood	22	M 9
Rosita Rd	29	K 13
Roxbury Av	38	H 20
Roxbury Blvd	38	H 20
Ruby St	29	J 13
Rufus King Av	26	L 12
Ruscoe St	27	M 12
Rushmore Av	23	O 9
Rushmore Ter	23	O 9
Russell Pl	26	K 11
Russell St	32	K 15
Rust St	24	F 11
Rutland Pl *(off Beach 87th St)	35	L 18
Rutledge Av	25	J 12
Ryan Rd	31	N 14
Ryan St	17	K 8
Ryans Ct *(off Saint Marks Av near Beach 106th St)	39	K 19
Rye Pl	27	N 12

S

STREET	MAP	GRID
Sabre St	28	O 11
Sagamore Av	27	N 12
Sagamore Rd	27	N 12
Sage St	36	O 17
Saint Cloud Rd	35	L 18
Saint Felix Av	24	G 12
Saint James Av	20	H 10
Saint John's Rd	24	G 12
Saint Mark's Av	39	K 19
Saint Nicholas Av	24	F 12
Salerno Av	27	N 11
Samuel Ct *(off Beach 56th St)	35	M 18
Sancho St	27	N 11
Sanders Pl	26	L 12
Sandhill Rd	18	O 8
Sandra Gail Ct *(off Beach 50th St)	35	M 18
Sandy Road	36	N 18
Sanford St	21	K 9
Santiago St	27	M 11
Saull St	21	K 9
Saultell Av	21	J 10
Saunders St	25	H 11
Sawyer Av	27	N 11
Sayres Av	27	M 12
Schaefer St	43	G 13
Scheer St	35	L 18
Schorr Dr	16	K 7
Sea Beach Ct *(off Beach 109th St)	39	K 19
Sea Breeze Av	37	G 20
Sea Breeze Walk	37	F 20
Seabury St	20	H 10
Seafoam Ct	35	M 18
Seagirt Av	36	N 18
Seagirt Blvd	36	N 18
Seaside Av	39	K 19
Seaside Av	36	N 18

STREET	MAP	GRID
Seasongood Rd	26	K 11
Seaview Ct *(off Beach 63rd St)	35	M 18
Selfridge St	25	J 11
Selover Rd	31	N 13
Senate Ct *(off Beach 98th St)	35	L 18
Seneca Av	24	G 12
Sergeant Beers Av	17	M 7
Sergeant Beers La	17	M 7
Seward Av	23	O 10
Shad Creek Rd	35	K 17
Shaler Av	24	G 12
Shelbourne St	25	J 11
Sheridan Blvd	36	O 17
Shiloh Av	23	P 10
Shirley Ct *(off Beach 40th St)	35	M 18
Shirley Ct *(off Beach 56th Pl)	36	N 18
Shore Av	26	L 12
Shore Blvd	15	F 8
Shore Front Pkwy	39	K 19
Shore Rd	17	M 7
Shore Rd E (Douglas Rd)	18	N 8
Shore Rd E (Marinette St)	18	N 8
Shore Rd W (Bayshore Blvd)	18	N 8
Shorthill Pl	26	K 11
Shorthill Rd	26	K 12
Sidway Pl	31	N 13
Sign Test Rd	33	M 15
Sigourney Av	28	O 11
Silver St	29	K 14
Simonson St	20	H 10
Sitka St	29	K 14
Skillman Av	19	E 10
Slither Pl *(off Cedar Grove Cem)	21	K 10
Sloan St	31	N 14
Slocum Cres	25	J 11
Smart St	21	K 9
Smedley St	26	L 11
Smith Ct	36	O 17
Smith Pl *(off Mott St near Beach 19th St)	36	O 17
Smith St	30	M 13
Soho Dr	27	M 11
Solomon Ct *(off Beach 49th St)	35	M 18
Somerset St	27	M 11
Sound St	20	G 9
South Cargo Rd	33	M 15
South Conduit Av	30	L 14
South Dr	17	K 7
South Railroad Av	20	H 10
South Rd	30	L 13
South Service Ct	33	M 15
South Service Rd	33	L 15
Southern Pkwy	29	K 14
Southern Pkwy	30	M 14
Southgate Plz	31	N 14
Southgate St	31	N 14
Spa Pl	30	L 13
Spar Ct	35	M 18
Spencer Av	27	N 11
Spencito Rd	35	K 18
Spiller Rd	17	M 7
Sprague Pl *(off Beach 88th St)	35	L 18
Springer Ct *(off Beach 58th St)	35	M 18
Springfield Blvd	22	N 10
Springfield La	34	N 15
Spritz Rd	29	K 14
Spruce St	20	J 10
Stafford Av	25	J 11
Standish Pl	26	K 11
Stanhope St	24	F 12
Stanley Ct *(off Beach 40th St)	36	N 18
Stanton Ct *(off Saint Marks Av near 106th St)	39	K 19
Stark Ct *(off Beach 55th St)	35	M 18
Starr Av	19	E 10
Starr St	24	F 12
State Hwy 24	28	P 12
State Hwy 25	20	H 10
State Hwy 25A	19	E 10
State Hwy 25B	23	P 10
State Hwy 27	29	K 14
State Hwy 27A	32	J 15
State Rd	37	G 20
Station La	21	L 9
Station Sq	25	J 11
Steeplechase Ct *(off Beach 100th St near RR)	39	L 19
Steinway Pl	15	G 8
Steinway St	19	F 9
Stephen St	24	G 12
Stewart Rd	22	N 10
Stier Pl	24	G 12
Stockholm St	24	F 12
Story Av	17	M 7
Story Rd	35	M 18
Stratford St	26	K 12
Strong Av	20	J 10
Stronghurst Av	23	O 10
Suffolk St	31	N 13
Suffolk Walk	37	F 20
Sullivan Rd	31	N 13
Summer St	26	K 11
Summerfield St	24	G 12
Summit Ct	21	K 9
Summit Pl	17	K 7
Sunbury St	31	N 13
Sunnyside St	36	N 17
Sunrise Hwy	31	O 14
Surf Ct *(off Beach 107th St)	39	K 19
Surf Rd	36	N 18
Surrey Pl	27	M 11
Susan Ct *(off Beach 106th St & 109th St)	39	K 19
Sutphin Blvd	26	L 12
Sutro St	27	N 11
Sutter Av	29	J 14
Sutton Pl	26	L 11
Suydam St	24	F 12
Swan Rd *(off Beach 51st St)	35	M 18
Sybilla St	25	J 12
Sylvester La	17	M 7
Syringa Pl	21	K 9

T

STREET	MAP	GRID
Tahoe St	29	K 14
Talbot St	26	K 12
Teal Dr	36	N 18
Tennis Pl	25	J 11
Theater Rd	17	M 7
Thebes Av	23	O 9
Theresa Ct *(off Beach 51st St)	36	N 18
Theresa Pl	25	J 12
Thetford La	37	G 20
Thompson Pl *(off Cedar Grove Cem)	21	K 10
Thomson Av	19	E 10
Thornhill Av	23	O 9
Thornton Pl	25	J 11
Thursby Av	35	M 18
Thurston St	31	N 14
Tilden Walk *(off State St)	38	H 20
Tioga Dr	31	N 13
Tioga Walk	37	F 20
Tonsor St	24	G 12
Totten Av	17	M 7
Totten St	17	M 7
Traffic Av	24	G 12
Trappe Pl	27	M 12
Triborough Plz	15	F 8
Trimble Rd	20	G 10
Trist Pl	36	N 17
Troon Rd	27	M 11
Trotting Course La	25	J 12
Troutman St	24	F 12
Troutville Rd	31	N 13
Tryon Pl	27	M 11
Tuckerton St	26	L 12
Tudor Rd	27	M 11
Turin Dr	31	N 13
Turpin Ct *(off Beach 99th St)	39	L 19
Tyler Av	20	G 10

U

STREET	MAP	GRID
Underhill Av	22	M 10
Underhill Rd	17	M 7
Underwood Rd	26	K 11
Union Hall St	26	L 12
Union St	21	K 9
Union Tpk	25	J 12
Upland Rd	18	O 8
Upshaw Rd	26	K 12
Ursina Rd	31	N 13
Utica Walk	37	F 20
Utopia Pkwy	17	M 8

V

STREET	MAP	GRID
Valentine Pl	25	H 12
Van Brunt Rd	35	L 18
Van Cleef St	21	J 10
Van Dam St	19	F 10
Van Doren St	21	J 10
Van Horn St	20	H 10
Van Kleeck St	20	H 10
Van Loon St	20	H 10
Van Sicklen St	30	L 13
Van Wyck Expwy	21	K 9
Van Zandt Av	23	O 9
Vanderveer St	27	N 11
Vaux Rd	20	G 10
Vermont Av	24	G 13
Vernon Blvd	19	E 9
Victor Ct *(off Beach 55th St)	35	M 18
Victoria Dr	31	N 13
Victoria Rd	31	N 13
Vietor Av	20	H 10
Village Rd	26	L 11
Virginia St	36	O 17
Vleigh Pl	26	L 11

W

STREET	MAP	GRID
Wainwright Ct	39	K 19
Walden Av	18	O 8
Waldron St	21	J 10
Walnut St	25	J 12
Walter Reed Rd	17	M 7
Waltham St	26	L 12
Walton Rd	35	L 17
Wareham Pl	27	M 11
Warren St	20	H 9
Warwick Av	18	N 8
Warwick Cres	27	M 12
Washington Ct *(off Beach 56th St)	35	M 18
Water Edge Dr	17	M 8
Waterloo Pl	36	N 17
Waterloo Rd	36	N 17
Waterview Pl *(off Bayswater Av)	36	N 17
Waterview St	36	N 17
Watjean Ct	36	N 18
Watson Pl	27	M 12
Wavecrest La *(off Beach 21st & 22nd Sts)	36	N 18
Weaver Av	17	M 7
Webe Pl	17	L 8
Weeks La	22	M 9
Weimar St	20	H 10
Weirfield St	43	F 13
Weller Av	31	O 14

STREET	MAP	GRID
Weller La	34	O 15
Welling Ct	15	F 8
Wendover Rd	26	K 12
West Alley Rd	23	O 9
West Dr	18	N 8
West End Dr	18	O 8
West End Dr	25	H 12
West Hangar		
Rd	33	L 15
West Main Dr	25	J 12
West Market		
St	37	G 20
West Rd	35	L 17
West St	19	E 10
Westaway Rd	17	M 7
Westbourne		
Av	36	N 17
Westbourne Blvd		
*(off Mott Av)	36	N 17
Westgate St	31	N 14
Westmoreland		
Pl	18	N 8
Westmoreland		
St	18	O 8
Westside Av	21	J 10
Wetherole St	25	H 11
Wexford Ter	27	M 11
Wheatley St	36	O 17
Whistler Av	17	M 7
White Oak Ct	20	G 9
White St *(off Elk		
Ct Near Beach		
22nd St)	36	O 18
Whitehall Ter	27	N 11
Whitehouse Ct		
*(off Beach		
110th St)	39	K 19
Whitelaw St	29	K 14
Whitestone		
Expwy	16	K 8
Whitney Av	20	H 10
Whitson St	26	K 12
Wicklow Pl	27	M 11
Wilder Ct *(off		
Beach 98th		
St)	39	L 19
Willets Point		
Blvd	17	L 8
Willets St	17	M 7
William Ct	36	O 18
Williamson Av	31	N 13
Willoughby Av	24	F 12
Willow St	18	N 8
Winchester		
Blvd	23	O 10
Winter St	26	K 11
Witthoff St	28	O 12
Wood St	27	N 12
Woodbine St	24	G 12
Woodhaven		
Blvd	25	H 11
Woodhaven Ct	29	J 13
Woodhull Av	27	N 12
Woodrow Ct *(off		
Beach 56th		
St)	35	M 18
Woodside Av	20	G 10
Woodside Ct *(off		
St Marks Av		
Near Beach		
107th St)	39	K 19
Woodward Av	24	F 12
Wren Pl	27	M 12
Wyckoff Av	24	G 12

X

STREET	MAP	GRID
Xenia St	20	J 10

Y

STREET	MAP	GRID
Yates Rd	30	L 13
Yellowstone		
Blvd	25	J 11

Z

STREET	MAP	GRID
Zion St	23	O 9
Zoller Rd	31	N 13

Numbered Streets

STREET	MAP	GRID
1st Rd	35	K 17
1st St	15	E 8
1st St	32	K 15
2nd Av	17	K 7
2nd Rd	35	L 17
2nd St	15	E 8
3rd Av	17	K 7
3rd Rd	35	L 17
3rd St	15	E 8
4th Av	17	K 7
4th Av	37	F 20
4th Rd	35	L 17
4th St	15	F 8
5th Av	16	J 7
5th Av	37	F 20
5th Rd	35	L 17
5th St	19	D 10
6th Av	16	J 7
6th Av	17	L 7
7th Av	16	J 7
7th Av	37	G 20
8th Av	16	J 7
8th Av	37	G 20
8th Rd	17	L 7
8th Rd	35	L 17
8th St	15	F 8
9th Av	16	J 7
9th Av	37	G 20
9th Rd	16	J 8
9th Rd	35	L 17
9th St	19	E 9
10th Av	16	J 8
10th Av	37	G 20
10th Rd	35	L 17
10th St	19	E 9
11th Av	16	J 8
11th Rd	35	L 17
11th St	19	E 9
12th Av	16	J 8
12th Av	37	G 20
12th Rd	17	L 7
12th Rd	35	L 17
12th St	19	E 9
13th Av	16	J 8
13th Rd	17	K 8
13th Rd	35	K 17
13th St	19	E 9
14th Av	16	J 8
14th Pl	15	F 8
14th Rd	16	J 8
14th Rd	35	K 18
14th St	19	E 9
15th Av	16	J 8
15th Dr	17	K 8
15th Rd	17	K 8

STREET	MAP	GRID
15th Rd	35	L 18
16th Av	17	L 8
16th Rd	17	L 8
16th Rd	35	L 18
17th Av	17	K 8
17th Av	17	L 8
17th Rd	35	L 18
18th Av	16	J 8
18th Rd	35	L 18
18th St	15	F 8
19th Av	15	G 8
19th Dr	15	G 8
19th Rd	15	G 8
19th Rd	35	L 18
19th St	15	F 8
20th Av	15	F 8
20th Rd	35	L 18
20th St	15	F 8
21st Av	15	F 8
21st Dr	15	F 8
21st Rd	15	F 8
21st St	19	E 9
22nd Av	16	J 8
22nd Dr	15	F 8
22nd Rd	15	F 8
22nd St	19	E 9
23rd Av	15	F 8
23rd Dr	15	F 8
23rd Rd	15	F 8
23rd St	15	F 8
23rd Ter	15	F 8
24th Av	15	F 8
24th Dr	15	F 8
24th Rd	15	F 8
24th St	19	E 10
24th Ter	15	F 8
25th Av	19	F 9
25th Dr	17	K 8
25th Rd	15	F 8
25th St (Crescent		
St)	19	E 10
26th Av	15	E 8
26th Rd	15	F 8
26th St	15	F 8
27th Av	15	E 8
27th Rd	15	F 8
27th St	19	E 10
28th Av	15	F 8
28th Rd	19	F 9
28th St	19	E 10
29th Av	15	F 8
29th Rd	16	K 8
29th St	15	F 8
30th Av	19	F 9
30th Dr	19	F 9
30th Pl	19	E 10
30th Rd	15	F 8
30th St	19	E 10
31st Av	19	E 9
31st Dr	19	E 9
31st Pl	19	E 10
31st Rd	19	F 9
31st St	19	E 10
32nd Av	20	G 9
32nd Rd	17	M 8
32nd St	15	F 8
33rd Av	19	E 9
33rd Rd	19	E 9
33rd St	15	F 8
34th Av	19	E 9
34th Rd	20	H 9
34th St	19	E 10
35th Av	19	E 9

STREET	MAP	GRID
35th Rd	20	G 10
35th St	19	E 10
36th Av	19	E 9
36th Rd	21	K 9
36th St	15	F 8
37th Av	19	E 9
37th Dr	20	J 9
37th Rd	20	G 10
37th St	15	F 9
38th Av	19	E 9
38th Dr	18	N 8
38th St	19	F 9
39th Av	19	E 9
39th Dr	19	F 10
39th Pl	19	F 10
39th Rd	19	F 10
39th St	19	F 10
40th Av	19	E 9
40th Dr	20	H 10
40th Rd	19	E 10
40th St	19	F 10
41st Av	19	E 9
41st Dr	20	G 10
41st Rd	19	E 9
41st St	15	G 8
42nd Av (Sanford		
Ave)	20	H 10
42nd Pl	19	F 9
42nd Rd	19	E 10
42nd St	15	G 8
43rd Av	19	E 10
43rd Rd	19	E 10
43rd St	15	G 8
44th Av	19	E 10
44th Dr	19	E 10
44th Rd	19	E 10
44th St	19	F 9
45th Av	19	E 10
45th Dr	22	M 9
45th Rd	19	E 10
45th St	19	F 9
46th Av	19	E 10
46th Rd	19	E 10
46th St	15	G 8
47th Av	19	E 10
47th Rd	19	E 10
47th St	19	F 9
48th Av	19	D 10
48th St	19	F 9
49th Av	19	E 10
49th Rd	22	N 9
49th St	24	F 11
49th St	20	G 9
50th Av	19	E 10
50th St	20	G 9
51st Av	19	D 10
51st Dr	20	G 10
51st Rd	19	F 10
51st St	19	F 10
52nd Av	20	G 10
52nd Ct	24	G 11
52nd Dr	20	G 10
52nd Rd	20	G 10
52nd St	19	F 10
53rd Av	19	E 10
53rd Dr	24	G 11
53rd Pl	20	G 9
53rd Rd	24	G 11
53rd St	19	F 10
54th Av	19	D 10
54th Dr	24	F 11
54th Pl	24	G 11
54th Rd	24	F 11

STREET	MAP	GRID	STREET	MAP	GRID	STREET	MAP	GRID	STREET	MAP	GRID
54th St	20	G 10	68th St	20	G 9	84th Rd	26	K 12	102nd Av	29	J 13
55th Av	19	D 10	69th Av	24	G 12	84th St	20	H 9	102nd Rd	29	J 13
55th Dr	24	F 11	69th Dr	25	H 12	85th Av	25	J 12	102nd St	20	H 9
55th Rd	24	F 11	69th La	24	G 11	85th Dr	25	J 12	103rd Av	29	K 13
55th St	20	G 10	69th Pl	20	G 10	85th Rd	25	J 12	103rd Dr	29	K 13
56th Av	24	G 11	69th Rd	25	H 12	85th St	20	H 9	103rd Rd	29	K 13
56th Dr	24	F 11	69th St	20	G 9	86th Av	25	J 12	103rd St	20	J 9
56th Pl	20	G 9	70th Av	24	G 12	86th Cres	26	L 12	104th Av	30	L 13
56th Rd	24	F 11	70th Dr	25	J 12	86th Dr	25	J 12	104th Rd	27	M 12
56th St	24	F 11	70th Rd	26	K 11	86th Rd	25	J 12	104th St	20	J 9
56th Ter	24	F 11	70th St	20	G 9	86th St	20	H 9	105th Av	30	L 13
57th Av	24	F 11	71st Av	24	G 12	87th Av	29	J 13	105th Pl	29	K 13
57th Dr	24	G 11	71st Cres	22	M 10	87th Dr	27	M 11	105th St	20	J 9
57th Pl	24	F 11	71st Dr	25	J 12	87th Rd	29	J 13	106th Av	29	J 13
57th Rd	24	G 11	71st Pl	25	H 12	87th St	20	H 9	106th Rd	27	M 12
57th St	24	F 11	71st Rd	25	J 12	87th Ter			106th St	20	J 9
58th Av	24	G 11	71st St	20	G 9	(Floral Pk)	28	P 11	107th Av	29	J 13
58th La	20	G 10	72nd Av	25	J 12	88th Av	29	J 13	107th Rd	30	L 13
58th Pl	20	G 10	72nd Cres	26	K 11	88th Dr	28	P 11	107th St	20	J 9
58th Rd	24	G 11	72nd Dr	26	K 11	88th La	25	J 12	108th Av	29	J 13
58th St	24	F 11	72nd La	25	H 12	88th Pl	25	J 12	108th Dr	27	M 12
59th Av	24	G 11	72nd Pl	20	G 10	88th Rd	29	J 13	108th Pl	30	L 13
59th Dr	24	G 11	72nd Rd	26	K 11	88th St	20	H 9	108th Rd	27	M 12
59th Pl	20	G 10	72nd St	20	G 9	89th Av	29	J 13	108th St	21	J 9
59th Rd	24	G 11	73rd Av	25	J 12	89th Rd	26	L 12	109th Av	29	J 13
59th St	20	G 10	73rd Pl	20	G 10	89th St	20	H 9	109th Dr	30	M 13
60th Av	24	G 11	73rd Rd	26	K 11	90th Av	29	J 13	109th Rd	30	L 13
60th Ct	24	G 11	73rd St	20	G 9	90th Ct *	27	N 11	109th St	20	J 9
60th Dr	24	G 11	73rd Ter	26	K 11	90th Pl	20	H 9	110th Av	30	L 13
60th La	24	G 11	74th Av	25	J 12	90th Rd	29	J 13	110th Rd	30	M 13
60th Pl	20	G 9	74th Pl	29	J 13	90th St	20	H 9	110th St	20	J 9
60th Rd	24	G 11	74th St	20	G 9	91st Av	29	J 13	111th Av	29	K 13
60th St	20	G 9	75th Av	25	J 12	91st Dr	29	J 13	111th Rd	30	M 13
61st Av	24	G 11	75th Pl	25	H 11	91st Pl	20	H 10	111th St	16	J 8
61st Dr	25	H 11	75th Rd	26	K 11	91st Rd	29	J 13	112th Av	30	M 13
61st Rd	24	G 11	75th St	20	G 9	91st St	20	H 9	112th Pl	20	J 9
61st St	20	G 9	76th Av	25	J 12	92nd Av	29	J 13	112th Rd	30	M 13
62nd Av	24	G 11	76th Dr	26	K 11	92nd Rd	27	M 12	112th St	16	J 8
62nd Dr	25	H 11	76th Rd	26	K 11	92nd St	20	H 9	113th Av	30	M 13
62nd Rd	24	G 12	76th St	15	G 8	93rd Av	29	J 13	113th Dr	28	O 12
62nd St	20	G 9	77th Av	25	H 12	93rd Rd	28	O 11	113th Pl	26	K 11
63rd Av	25	H 11	77th Cres	23	O 10	93rd St	20	H 9	113th Rd	27	N 12
63rd Dr	25	J 11	77th Pl	25	H 11	94th Av	29	K 13	113th St	16	J 8
63rd Pl	24	G 11	77th Rd	25	H 12	94th Dr	28	O 11	114th Av	29	K 13
63rd Rd	25	H 11	77th St	15	G 8	94th Pl	29	K 14	114th Dr	27	N 12
63rd St	20	G 10	78th Av	24	G 12	94th Rd	27	N 11	114th Pl	29	K 14
64th Av	25	J 11	78th Cres	26	K 11	94th St	16	H 8	114th Rd	30	M 13
64th Cir	22	M 10	78th Dr	26	K 11	95th Av	29	J 13	114th St	16	J 8
64th La	24	G 12	78th Rd	25	H 12	95th Pl	29	K 14	114th Ter	28	O 12
64th Pl	24	G 12	78th St	15	G 8	95th St	20	H 9	115th Av	30	L 13
64th Rd	25	H 11	79th Av	24	G 12	96th Av	28	O 11	115th Ct	28	O 12
64th St	20	G 9	79th La	25	H 12	96th Pl	29	K 14	115th Dr	30	M 13
65th Av	25	J 11	79th Pl	25	H 11	96th Rd	28	O 11	115th Rd	30	M 13
65th Cres	22	M 10	79th St	15	G 8	96th St	20	H 9	115th St	16	J 8
65th Dr	25	H 11	80th Av	24	G 12	97th Av	29	J 13	115th Ter	28	O 12
65th La	24	G 12	80th Dr	27	M 11	97th Pl	20	J 10	116th Av	30	L 13
65th Pl	20	G 10	80th Rd	24	G 12	97th St	20	H 9	116th Dr	30	M 13
65th Rd	25	J 11	80th St	15	G 8	98th Av	28	O 11	116th Rd	30	L 13
65th St	20	G 10	81st Av	25	J 12	98th Pl	20	J 10	116th St	16	J 8
66th Av	25	J 11	81st Rd	25	J 12	98th St	20	H 9	117th Rd	30	L 14
66th Dr	25	H 12	81st St	15	G 8	99th Av	29	K 13	117th St	16	J 8
66th Pl	25	H 12	82nd Av	25	J 12	99th Pl	29	K 14	118th Av	30	M 13
66th Rd	25	H 11	82nd Dr	26	K 12	99th Rd *(off			118th Rd	30	M 13
66th St	20	G 10	82nd Pl	25	H 11	197th St)	27	N 12	118th St	16	J 8
67th Av	24	G 12	82nd Rd	25	J 12	99th St	20	H 9	119th Av	30	M 13
67th Dr	25	H 12	82nd St	20	H 9	100th Av	27	N 12	119th Dr	30	M 13
67th Pl	25	H 12	83rd Av	25	J 12	100th Dr	28	O 11	119th Rd	30	M 13
67th Rd	25	H 12	83rd Pl	25	H 11	100th Rd	28	O 11	119th St	16	J 7
67th St	20	G 10	83rd Rd	23	P 10	100th St	20	H 9	120th Av	30	L 14
68th Av	24	G 12	83rd St	20	H 9	101st Av	29	J 13	120th Rd	31	N 13
68th Dr	25	J 11	84th Av	26	K 12	101St Rd *(off			120th St	16	J 8
68th Pl	25	H 12	84th Dr	26	L 12	105th St)	29	K 13	121st Av	30	M 13
68th Rd	24	G 12	84th Pl	25	H 11	101st St	20	H 9	121st St	16	J 7
									122nd Av	30	M 13

STREET	MAP	GRID	STREET	MAP	GRID	STREET	MAP	GRID	STREET	MAP	GRID
122nd Pl	30	L 14	143rd Rd	31	N 14	161st Pl	31	M 13	194th St	22	M 9
122nd St	16	J 8	143rd St	17	K 8	161st St	17	L 7	195th La	22	M 10
123rd Av	30	M 14	144th Av	31	N 14	162nd Av	32	K 15	195th Pl	27	N 11
123rd St	16	J 8	144th Dr	30	M 14	162nd Rd *(off			195th St	22	M 9
124th Av	30	M 14	144th Pl	17	K 8	102nd St)	32	K 15	196th Pl	22	M 9
124th Pl	26	K 12	144th Rd	30	M 14	162nd St	17	L 8	196th St	22	M 9
124th St	16	J 8	144th St	17	K 7	163rd Av	32	K 15	197th St	22	M 9
125th Av	30	M 14	144th Ter	30	M 14	163rd Dr *(off			198th St	22	M 9
125th St	16	J 8	145th Av	30	M 14	102nd St)	32	K 15	199th St	22	M 9
126th Av	31	N 13	145th Dr	31	N 14	163rd Pl	21	L 9	200th St	17	M 8
126th Pl	21	J 9	145th Pl	17	K 8	163rd Rd *(off			201st Pl	31	N 13
126th St	16	J 8	145th Rd	30	M 14	102nd St)	32	K 15	201st St	17	M 8
127th Av	31	N 13	145th St	17	K 8	163rd St	17	L 8	202nd St	17	M 8
127th Pl	21	J 9	146th Av	31	N 14	164th Av	32	K 15	203rd Pl	17	M 8
127th St	16	J 8	146th Dr	31	N 14	164th Dr *(off			203rd St	17	M 8
128th Av	30	M 14	146th Pl	17	K 8	102nd St)	32	K 15	204th St	17	M 8
128th Dr	31	O 13	146th Rd	31	N 14	164th Pl	26	L 11	205th Pl	27	N 12
128th Rd	31	O 13	146th St	17	K 8	164th Rd *(off			205th St	17	M 8
128th St	16	J 8	146th Ter	31	N 14	102nd St)	32	K 15	206th St	17	M 8
129th Av	30	M 14	147th Av	31	N 14	164th St	17	L 8	207th St	17	M 8
129th Rd	31	P 13	147th Dr	34	O 15	165th Av	32	K 15	208th Pl	17	M 8
129th St	16	J 8	147th Pl	17	K 7	165th St	17	L 8	208th St	17	M 8
130th Av	30	L 14	147th Rd	34	O 15	166th Pl	31	N 14	209th Pl	17	M 8
130th Dr	31	O 13	147th St	17	K 8	166th St	17	L 8	209th St	17	M 8
130th Pl	30	L 14	148th Av	31	N 14	167th St	21	L 9	210th Pl	17	M 8
130th Rd	31	N 13	148th Dr	34	N 15	168th Pl	26	L 11	210th St	17	M 8
130th St	16	K 8	148th Pl	21	K 10	168th St	21	L 9	211th Ct *(off		
131st Av	30	L 14	148th Rd	34	N 15	169th Pl	27	M 12	104th Av)	28	O 12
131st Rd	31	P 14	148th St	17	K 7	169th St	21	L 9	211th Pl	27	N 11
131st St	16	K 8	149th Av	29	J 14	170th Pl	21	L 10	211th St	17	M 8
132nd Av	30	L 14	149th Dr	34	O 15	170th St	21	L 9	212th Pl	27	N 11
132nd Rd	31	O 13	149th Pl	17	K 7	171st Pl	21	L 9	212th St	17	M 8
132nd St	16	K 8	149th Rd	34	N 15	171st St	21	L 9	213th St	17	M 8
133rd Av	29	J 14	149th St	21	K 10	172nd St	26	L 11	214th La	22	N 9
133rd Dr	31	P 14	150th Av	30	L 14	173rd St	21	L 9	214th Pl	17	M 8
133rd Pl	16	K 8	150th Dr	34	N 15	174th Pl	31	N 13	214th St	17	M 8
133rd Rd	31	N 14	150th Pl	17	L 7	174th St	21	L 10	215th Pl	17	M 8
133rd St	16	K 8	150th Rd	29	K 14	175th Pl	22	M 10	215th St	17	M 8
134th Av	29	K 14	150th St	17	L 8	175th St	22	M 10	216th St	17	M 8
134th Pl	30	L 14	151st Av	29	J 14	176th Pl	31	N 13	217th Dr	17	M 8
134th Rd	29	K 14	151st Dr	34	N 15	176th St	27	M 11	217th La	28	O 11
134th St	21	K 10	151st Pl	17	L 7	177th Pl	31	N 13	217th Pl	28	O 11
135th Av	30	L 14	151st St	17	L 7	177th St	27	M 11	217th St	17	M 8
135th Dr	29	K 14	152nd Av	30	L 14	178th Pl	27	M 12	218th Pl	28	O 11
135th Pl	30	L 14	152nd St	17	L 7	178th St	22	M 10	218th St	18	N 8
135th Rd	29	K 14	153rd Av	29	J 14	179th Pl	27	M 12	219th St	22	N 9
135th St	21	K 10	153rd Ct	30	M 14	179th St	22	M 10	220th Pl	22	N 9
136th Av	30	M 14	153rd La	30	M 14	180th Pl	27	M 12	220th St	22	N 9
136th Rd	31	N 14	153rd Pl	17	L 8	180th St	22	M 10	221st Pl	28	O 11
136th St	16	K 8	153rd St	21	L 9	181st Pl	27	M 12	221st St	22	N 9
137th Av	30	M 14	153rd Way	30	M 14	181st St	22	M 10	222nd St	22	N 9
137th Pl	21	K 9	154th Pl	17	L 7	182nd Pl	27	M 12	223rd Pl	22	N 10
137th Rd	31	O 14	154th St	17	L 8	182nd St	22	M 10	223rd St	22	N 9
137th St	21	K 9	155th Av	29	J 14	183rd Pl	27	M 12	224th St	22	N 9
138th Av	31	N 14	155th St	17	L 8	183rd St	22	M 10	225th St	22	N 9
138th Pl	16	K 8	156th Av	29	J 14	184th Pl	27	M 12	226th St	22	N 9
138th Pl	26	L 12	156th Ct	17	L 8	184th St	22	M 10	227th St	28	O 12
138th Rd	31	N 14	156th Pl	26	L 12	185th St	22	M 10	228th St	22	N 9
138th St	16	K 8	156th St	17	L 8	186th La	22	M 10	229th St	22	N 9
139th Av	31	N 14	157th Av	29	J 14	186th St	22	M 10	230th Pl	31	O 14
139th Rd	16	K 8	157th St	17	L 8	187th Pl	27	N 11	230th St	22	N 9
139th St	16	K 8	158th Av	32	J 15	187th St	22	M 10	231st St	22	N 9
140th Av	30	M 14	158th St	17	L 7	188th St	22	M 10	232nd St	22	N 9
140th St	16	K 8	159th Av	32	J 15	189th St	22	M 9	233rd Pl	18	N 8
141st Av	31	N 14	159th Dr	32	K 15	190th La	22	M 10	233rd St	22	N 9
141st Pl	26	K 11	159th Rd	32	K 15	190th Pl	27	N 12	234th Pl	31	O 14
141st Rd	31	N 14	159th St	17	L 7	190th St	22	M 9	234th St	18	N 8
141st St	16	K 8	160th Av	32	J 15	191st St	22	M 9	235th Ct	23	O 10
142nd Av	31	N 14	160th Dr *(off			192nd St	22	M 9	235th St	18	N 8
142nd Pl	30	M 14	102nd St)	32	K 15	193rd La	22	M 10	236th St	23	O 10
142nd Rd	31	N 14	160th Rd *(off			193rd St	22	M 9	237th St	23	O 10
142nd St	16	K 8	102nd St)	32	K 15	193rd St	22	M 9	238th St	28	O 11
143rd Av	31	N 14	160th St	17	L 8	194th La	22	M 10	239th St	28	O 11
143rd Pl	17	K 8	161st Av	32	J 15						

STREET	MAP	GRID	STREET	MAP	GRID	STREET	MAP	GRID	STREET	MAP	GRID
240th Pl	23	O 9	246th St	23	O 9	255th St	23	O 9	264th St	23	P 9
240th St	22	N 9	247th St	18	O 8	256th St	23	O 9	265th St	23	P 9
241st St	23	O 9	248th St	18	O 8	257th St	23	P 10	266th St	23	P 9
242nd St	23	O 9	249th St	18	O 8	258th St	23	P 10	267th St	23	P 9
243rd St	23	O 9	250th St	18	O 8	259th St	23	P 10	268th St	23	P 9
244th St	23	O 9	251st Pl	23	O 9	260th Pl	23	P 9	269th St (New Hyde Park)	23	P 9
245th La	23	O 9	251st St	23	O 9	260th St	23	O 9	270th St (New Hyde Park)	23	P 9
245th Pl	23	O 9	252nd St	23	O 9	261st St	23	P 9	271st St (New Hyde Park)	23	P 9
245th St	23	O 9	253rd Pl	34	O 15	262nd Pl	34	P 15			
246th Cres	23	O 9	253rd St	23	O 9	262nd St	23	P 9			
246th St	23	O 9	254th St	23	O 9	263rd St	23	P 9			

STREET	MAP	GRID	STREET	MAP	GRID	STREET	MAP	GRID	STREET	MAP	GRID
A			Avenue B	46	F 15	Bay Ridge Pl	48	A 16	Beadel St	40	E 11
Abbey Ct	53	F 18	Avenue C	45	D 16	Bay St	41	B 14	Beard St	41	B 14
Aberdeen St	43	G 13	Avenue D	50	E 16	Bay View Av	52	B 19	Beaumont St	53	E 19
Academy Park Pl	41	D 13	Avenue F	49	D 16	Bay View Pl	47	G 15	Beaver St	42	E 12
Adams St	41	C 13	Avenue H	49	D 16	Bay 7th St	48	B 17	Bedell La	46	F 15
Adelphi St	41	D 13	Avenue I	49	D 16	Bay 8th St	48	B 17	Bedford Av	40	D 11
Adler Pl	43	H 13	Avenue J	49	D 16	Bay 10th St	48	B 17	Bedford Pl	42	E 13
Agate Ct	42	E 13	Avenue K	50	E 16	Bay 11th St	48	B 17	Beekman Pl	45	D 15
Ainslie St	40	E 12	Avenue L	50	E 17	Bay 13th St	48	B 17	Belmont Av	47	G 14
Aitken Pl	41	C 13	Avenue M	50	E 17	Bay 14th St	48	B 17	Belt Pkwy (see Shore Pkwy)	52	B 19
Alabama Av	47	G 14	Avenue N	50	E 17	Bay 16th St	52	B 18	Belt Pkwy (see Shore Pkwy)	54	G 18
Albany Av	42	E 13	Avenue O	49	D 17	Bay 17th St	52	B 18	Belvidere St	42	E 12
Albee Sq	41	C 13	Avenue of Puerto Rico	40	E 12	Bay 19th St	52	B 18	Bennett Ct	48	B 16
Albemarle Rd	45	D 15	Avenue P	49	D 17	Bay 20th St	52	B 18	Bennett Pl	45	C 14
Albemarle Ter	45	D 15	Avenue R	50	E 17	Bay 22nd St	52	C 18	Benson Av	48	B 17
Alben Sq	45	C 16	Avenue S	52	D 18	Bay 23rd St	52	C 18	Bergen Av	50	F 16
Alice Ct	42	E 13	Avenue T	52	D 18	Bay 25th St	52	C 18	Bergen Ct	51	G 16
Allen Av	53	F 18	Avenue U	52	D 18	Bay 26th St	52	C 18	Bergen Pl	44	A 16
Alton Pl	50	E 16	Avenue V	52	D 18	Bay 28th St	52	C 18	Bergen St	41	C 13
Amber St	47	J 14	Avenue W	52	D 18	Bay 29th St	52	C 18	Berkeley Pl	41	D 14
Amboy St	47	G 15	Avenue X	52	D 18	Bay 31st St	52	C 18	Berriman St	47	H 14
Amersfort Pl	50	E 16	Avenue Y	52	D 18	Bay 32nd St	52	C 18	Berry St	40	D 11
Ames La	46	F 15	Avenue Z	52	C 19	Bay 34th St	52	C 18	Bethel Loop	47	H 15
Amherst St	53	E 19	Aviation Rd	54	H 19	Bay 35th St	52	C 18	Beverly Rd	45	D 15
Amity St	41	C 13				Bay 37th St	52	C 18	Bevy Ct	53	F 18
Anchorage Pl *(off Plymouth St)	41	C 12	**B**			Bay 38th St	52	C 18	Bijou Av	53	F 18
Anna Ct	47	G 15	Bainbridge St	42	F 13	Bay 40th St	52	C 18	Billings Pl	52	D 18
Anthony St	40	F 11	Balfour Pl	46	E 14	Bay 41st St	52	C 18	Bills Pl	45	C 15
Apollo St	40	E 11	Baltic St	41	B 13	Bay 43rd St	52	C 18	Blake Av	46	F 14
Applegate Ct	53	E 18	Bancroft Pl	42	F 14	Bay 44th St	52	C 18	Blake Ct	52	D 19
Archie C Ketchum Sq	49	C 17	Bank St	47	G 15	Bay 46th St	52	C 18	Bleecker St	42	F 13
Ardsley Loop	47	H 15	Banker St	40	E 11	Bay 47th St	52	C 18	Bliss Ter	48	A 16
Argyle Rd	45	D 15	Banner Av	52	D 19	Bay 48th St	52	C 19	Boardwalk E	52	D 19
Arion Pl	42	E 12	Barberry Ct	43	G 13	Bay 49th St	52	C 19	Boardwalk W	52	D 19
Arkansas Dr	51	G 17	Barbey St	43	G 13	Bay 50th St	52	C 19	Boerum Pl	41	C 13
Arlington Av	43	G 13	Barlow Dr N	51	G 17	Bay 52nd St	52	C 19	Boerum St	40	E 12
Arlington Pl	42	E 13	Barlow Dr S	51	G 17	Bay 53rd St	52	C 19	Bogart St	42	F 12
Ash St	40	E 10	Bartel Pritchard Sq	45	C 14	Bay 54th St	52	C 19	Bokee Ct	52	D 19
Ashford St	47	H 14	Bartlett Pl	53	F 18	Bayard St	40	E 11	Bond St	41	C 13
Ashland Pl	41	D 13	Bartlett St	42	E 12	Bayview Av	47	G 15	Bouck Ct	52	D 18
Aster Ct	53	F 18	Barwell Ct	48	A 17	Beach Pl	41	B 13	Boulevard Ct	52	D 18
Atkins Av	47	H 14	Bassett Av	51	G 17	Beach Walk	52	D 19	Bowery St	52	C 19
Atlantic Av	41	C 13	Bassett Walk	51	G 17	Beach 37th St	52	B 19	Bowne St	41	B 13
Atlantic Av (Sea Gate)	52	B 19	Batchelder St	53	E 18	Beach 38th St	52	B 19	Box St	40	D 10
Atlantic Commons	41	D 13	Bath Av	48	B 17	Beach 40th St	52	B 19	Boynton Pl	52	D 18
Atwater Ct	52	D 19	Battery Av	48	B 17	Beach 42nd St	52	B 19	Bradford St	47	G 14
Auburn Pl	41	D 13	Baughman Pl	50	F 17	Beach 43rd St	52	B 19	Bragg Ct	53	F 19
Aurelia Ct	50	E 16	Bay Av	50	E 17	Beach 44th St	52	B 19	Bragg St	53	F 18
Autumn La	47	J 14	Bay Cliff Ter	48	A 16	Beach 45th St	52	B 19	Branton St	46	F 15
Avenue A	46	F 15	Bay Pkwy	52	C 18	Beach 46th St	52	B 19	Brevoort Pl	42	E 13
			Bay Ridge Av	48	A 16	Beach 47th St	52	B 19	Bridge Plz Ct *(bounded by Concord & Nassau Sts, bet Flatbush Av Ext & Jay St)	41	C 12
			Bay Ridge Pkwy	48	A 16	Beach 48th St	52	B 19			
						Beach 49th St	52	B 19			
						Beach 50th St	52	B 19			
						Beach 51st St	52	B 19			
						Beacon Ct	53	F 18			

STREET	MAP	GRID
Bridge St	41 C	13
Bridgewater St	40 E	11
Brigham St	53 F	18
Brighton Beach Av	52 D	19
Brighton Ct	52 D	18
Brighton 1st La *(off Brighton 1st St)	52 D	19
Brighton 1st Path *(off Brighton 1st St)	52 D	19
Brighton 1st Pl *(off Brighton 1st St)	52 D	19
Brighton 1st Rd	52 D	19
Brighton 1st St	52 D	19
Brighton 1st Ter *(off Brighton 1st St)	52 D	19
Brighton 1st Walk	52 D	19
Brighton 2nd La *(off Brighton 2nd St)	52 D	19
Brighton 2nd Path *(off Brighton 2nd St)	52 D	19
Brighton 2nd Pl *(off Brighton 2nd St)	52 D	19
Brighton 2nd St	52 D	19
Brighton 2nd Walk	52 D	19
Brighton 3rd Ct *(off Brighton 3rd St)	52 D	19
Brighton 3rd La *(off Brighton 3rd St)	52 D	19
Brighton 3rd Pl *(off Brighton 3rd St)	52 D	19
Brighton 3rd Rd	52 D	19
Brighton 3rd St	52 D	19
Brighton 3rd Ter *(off Brighton 3rd St)	52 D	19
Brighton 3rd Walk	52 D	19
Brighton 4th Ct *(off Brighton 4th St)	52 D	19
Brighton 4th La *(off Brighton 4th St)	52 D	19
Brighton 4th Pl *(off Brighton 4th St)	52 D	19
Brighton 4th Rd	52 D	19
Brighton 4th St	52 D	19
Brighton 4th Ter *(off Brighton 4th St)	52 D	19
Brighton 4th Walk	52 D	19
Brighton 5th Ct *(off Brighton 5th St)	52 D	19
Brighton 5th La *(off Brighton 5th St)	52 D	19
Brighton 5th Pl *(off Brighton 5th St)	52 D	19
Brighton 5th St	52 D	19
Brighton 5th Walk	52 D	19
Brighton 6th Ct *(off Brighton 6th St)	52 D	19
Brighton 6th La *(off Brighton 6th St)	52 D	19
Brighton 6th Pl *(off Brighton 6th St)	52 D	19
Brighton 6th St	52 D	19
Brighton 6th Walk	52 D	19
Brighton 7th Ct *(off Brighton 7th St)	52 D	19
Brighton 7th La *(off Brighton 7th St)	52 D	19
Brighton 7th St	52 D	19
Brighton 7th Walk	52 D	19
Brighton 8th Ct *(off Brighton 8th St)	52 D	19
Brighton 8th La *(off Brighton 8th St)	52 D	19
Brighton 8th Pl *(off Brighton 8th St)	52 D	19
Brighton 8th St	52 D	19
Brighton 10th Ct	52 D	19
Brighton 10th La	52 D	19
Brighton 10th Path	52 D	19
Brighton 10th St	53 E	19
Brighton 10th Ter	52 D	19
Brighton 11th St	53 E	19
Brighton 12th St	53 F	19
Brighton 13th St	53 E	19
Brighton 14th St	53 E	19
Brighton 15th St	53 E	19
Brightwater Av	53 E	19
Brightwater Ct	52 D	19
Bristol St	47 G	14
Broadway	40 D	12
Brookdale Plz *(bounded by Rockaway Pkwy, Av A and Linden Blvd)	46 F	15
Brooklyn Av	46 E	14
Brooklyn-Queens Expwy	41 C	12
Brooklyn Terminal Market	46 F	15
Broome St	40 E	11
Brown St	53 E	18
Bryant St	44 B	14
Buckingham Rd (E 16th St)	45 D	15

STREET	MAP	GRID
Buffalo Av	46 F	14
Bulwer Pl	43 G	13
Burnett St	50 E	17
Bush St	41 B	14
Bushwick Av	40 E	12
Bushwick Pl	40 E	12
Butler Pl	41 D	14
Butler St	41 C	13

C

STREET	MAP	GRID
Cadman Plz	41 C	12
Cadman Plz E	41 C	12
Cadman Plz W	41 C	13
Calder Pl	45 C	14
Calhoun St	40 E	11
Calyer St	40 D	11
Cambridge Pl	42 D	13
Cameron Ct	49 C	17
Campus Pl	43 H	13
Campus Rd	50 E	16
Canada Av	53 E	19
Canal Av	52 C	19
Canarsie La	46 F	15
Canarsie Rd	51 G	16
Canarsie Veterans Cir	51 H	16
Canton Ct	53 F	18
Carlton Av	41 D	13
Carlton Ct *(off Surf Av)	52 B	19
Carroll St	41 B	13
Cary Ct	49 D	17
Cass Pl	53 E	19
Catharine St	40 E	11
Cathedral Pl	41 C	12
Caton Av	45 D	15
Caton Pl	45 D	15
Cedar St	49 D	17
Cedar St	42 F	12
Celeste Ct	53 F	18
Central Av	42 F	12
Centre Mall *(Red Hook Housing)	41 B	14
Centre St	41 B	14
Channel Av	53 F	18
Chapel St	41 C	12
Charles Pl	42 F	12
Chase Ct	46 F	15
Chauncey St	42 F	13
Cheever Pl	41 C	13
Cherry St	40 E	11
Chester Av	45 C	15
Chester Ct	45 D	15
Chester St	47 G	14
Chestnut Av	49 D	17
Chestnut St	43 H	13
Christopher Av	47 G	14
Church Av	45 D	15
Church La	51 G	16
Clara St	45 C	15
Clarendon Rd	46 E	15
Clark St	41 C	12
Clarkson Av	46 E	15
Classon Av	42 D	13
Claver Pl	42 D	13
Clay St	40 E	10
Clermont Av	41 D	13
Cleveland St	47 H	14
Clifford Pl	40 E	11
Clifton Pl	42 D	13
Clinton Av	42 D	13
Clinton St	41 C	13
Clinton Wharf	41 B	13
Clove Rd	46 E	14
Clymer St	41 D	12

STREET	MAP	GRID
Cobble Hill St	41 C	13
Cobeck Ct	52 D	18
Coffey St	41 B	14
Colby Ct	52 D	19
Coleman St	50 F	17
Coleridge St	53 E	19
Coles St	41 B	13
Colin Pl	52 D	18
College Pl	41 C	12
Colonial Ct	48 A	16
Colonial Gardens	48 A	17
Colonial Rd	48 A	17
Columbia Ct *(off Nassau Ct)	52 D	19
Columbia Heights	41 C	12
Columbia Pl	41 C	13
Columbia St	41 C	13
Columbus Pl	46 F	14
Commerce St	41 B	13
Commercial St	40 D	10
Commercial Wharf	41 B	13
Concord St	41 C	12
Conduit Blvd (Southern Pkwy)	43 H	13
Coney Island Av	49 D	17
Congress St	41 B	13
Conklin Av	47 G	15
Conover St	41 B	14
Conselyea St	40 E	11
Conway St	43 G	13
Cook St	42 E	12
Cooke Ct	43 G	13
Cooper St	43 G	13
Corbin Pl	53 E	19
Cornelia St	42 F	13
Corso Ct *(at Van Sicklen off Avenue V)	52 D	18
Cortelyou Rd	49 D	16
Court Sq	41 C	13
Court St	41 C	13
Coventry Rd	46 F	15
Covert St	43 F	13
Cox Pl	43 H	13
Coyle St	53 E	18
Cozine Av	47 H	15
Cranberry St	41 C	12
Crawford Av	52 D	18
Creamer St	41 B	14
Crescent St	43 H	14
Crooke Av	45 D	15
Cropsey Av	48 B	18
Crosby Av	43 G	13
Croton Loop	47 H	15
Crown St	46 E	14
Crystal St	43 H	14
Cumberland St	41 D	13
Cumberland Walk *(Walt Whitman Houses)	41 D	13
Cypress Av	40 F	12
Cypress Av (Sea Gate)	52 B	19
Cypress Ct	43 H	13
Cypress Hills St	43 G	12
Cyrus Av	53 F	18

D

STREET	MAP	GRID
Dahill Rd	49 D	16
Dahl Ct	49 C	17

STREET	MAP	GRID
Dahlgren Pl	48 A	17
Dakota Pl	51 G	17
Danforth St	43 H	13
Dank St	52 D	18
Dare Ct	53 F	18
Dean St	41 C	13
Dearborn Ct	46 E	14
Debevoise Av	40 E	11
Debevoise St	42 E	12
Decatur St	42 E	13
Degraw St	41 B	13
De Kalb Av	41 C	13
De Koven Ct	49 D	16
Delavan St	41 B	13
Delamere Pl	50 E	17
Delmar Loop	47 H	15
Delmonico Pl	42 E	12
Dennet Pl	41 C	14
Denton Pl	41 C	14
De Sales Pl	43 G	13
Desmond Ct	53 D	18
Devoe St	40 E	11
Devon Av	53 F	18
Dewey Pl	42 F	14
De Witt Av	47 G	15
Diamond St	40 E	11
Dickinson St	40 E	11
Dictum St	53 F	18
Dikeman St	41 B	14
Dinsmore Pl	43 H	13
Ditmars Pl	42 F	12
Ditmas Av	49 D	16
Division Av	40 D	12
Division Pl	40 E	11
Dobbin St	40 E	11
Dock St	41 C	12
Dodworth St	42 F	13
Dooley St	53 E	18
Doone Ct	53 E	18
Dorchester Rd	49 D	16
Dorset St	46 F	15
Doscher St	43 H	13
Doughty St	41 C	12
Douglass Ct	41 C	13
Douglass St	41 C	13
Dover St	53 E	19
Downing St	42 D	13
Drew St	47 J	14
Driggs Av	40 D	12
Duffield St	41 C	13
Dumont Av	47 G	14
Dunham Pl	40 D	12
Dunne Ct	52 D	18
Dunne Pl	53 E	18
Dupont St	40 E	10
Durland Pl	47 G	15
Duryea Ct	49 C	17
Duryea Pl	46 E	15
Dwight St	41 B	14
Dyker Pl	48 B	17

E

STREET	MAP	GRID
Eagle St	40 D	10
East New York Av	46 E	14
East 1st St	52 D	18
East 2nd St	45 D	16
East 3rd St	45 D	16
East 4th St	45 D	16
East 5th St	45 D	16
East 6th St	52 D	19
East 7th St	49 D	17
East 8th St	49 D	17
East 9th St	49 D	17
East 10th St	49 D	17
East 11th St	52 D	18

STREET	MAP	GRID
East 12th St	49 D	16
East 13th St	49 D	17
East 14th St	49 D	16
East 15th St	49 D	16
East 16th St	49 D	16
East 17th St	49 D	16
East 18th St	49 D	16
East 19th St	49 D	16
East 21st St	45 D	15
East 22nd St	46 E	15
East 23rd St (Delamere Pl)	46 E	15
East 24th St (Mansfield Pl)	50 E	16
East 25th St	50 E	16
East 26th St	50 E	16
East 27th St	50 E	16
East 28th St	50 E	16
East 29th St	50 E	16
East 31st St	46 E	15
East 32nd St	46 E	15
East 33rd St	50 E	17
East 34th St	46 E	15
East 35th St	46 E	15
East 36th St	50 E	16
East 37th St	46 E	15
East 38th St	46 E	15
East 39th St	46 E	15
East 40th St	46 E	15
East 41st St	50 F	16
East 42nd St	46 E	15
East 43rd St	46 E	15
East 45th St	46 F	15
East 46th St	46 F	15
East 48th St	46 F	15
East 49th St	46 F	15
East 51st St	46 F	15
East 52nd St	46 F	15
East 53rd Pl	50 F	17
East 53rd St	46 F	15
East 54th St	46 F	15
East 55th St	46 F	15
East 56th St	46 F	15
East 57th Pl	50 F	17
East 57th St	46 F	15
East 58th St	46 F	15
East 59th Pl	51 G	17
East 59th St	46 F	15
East 60th Pl	51 G	17
East 60th St	50 F	17
East 61st St	50 F	17
East 63rd St	50 F	17
East 64th St	50 F	17
East 65th St	50 F	17
East 66th St	51 G	17
East 67th St	51 G	17
East 68th St	51 G	17
East 69th St	50 F	17
East 70th St	51 G	17
East 71st St	51 G	17
East 72nd St	50 F	16
East 73rd St	50 F	16
East 74th St	51 G	17
East 76th St	50 F	16
East 77th St	50 F	16
East 78th St	50 F	16
East 79th St	50 F	16
East 80th St	50 F	16
East 81st St	50 F	16
East 82nd St	50 F	16
East 83rd St	51 G	16
East 84th St	51 G	16
East 85th St	51 G	16
East 86th St	46 F	15
East 87th St	46 F	15

STREET	MAP	GRID
East 88th St	46 F	15
East 89th St	46 F	15
East 91st St	51 G	16
East 92nd St	51 G	16
East 93rd St	51 G	16
East 94th St	51 G	16
East 95th St	51 G	16
East 96th St	46 F	14
East 98th St	47 G	15
East 99th St	47 G	15
East 100th St	47 G	15
East 101st St	47 G	15
East 102nd St	47 G	15
East 103rd St	47 G	15
East 104th St	47 G	15
East 105th Dr *(off Seaview Av)	51 H	16
East 105th St	47 G	15
East 105th Walk	47 G	15
East 106th St	47 G	15
East 107th St	47 G	15
East 108th St	47 G	15
Eastern Pkwy	45 D	14
Eaton Ct	53 F	18
Ebony Ct	53 F	18
Eckford St	40 E	11
Edwards Ct *(off West 20th St)	52 C	19
Eldert La	43 J	13
Eldert St	43 F	13
Elizabeth Pl	41 C	12
Ellery St	42 E	12
Elm Av	49 D	17
Elm Pl	41 C	13
Elmira Loop	47 H	15
Elmwood Av	49 D	16
Elton St	47 H	14
Emerald St	47 J	14
Emerson Pl	42 D	13
Emmers La	53 E	18
Emmons Av	53 E	19
Empire Blvd	46 E	14
Engert Av	40 E	11
Erasmus St	46 E	15
Eric Pl	48 B	16
Erie Basin	41 B	14
Erskine St	47 H	15
Esplanade	53 E	19
Essex St	47 H	14
Estate Rd	49 D	17
Etna St	43 H	13
Euclid Av	43 H	13
Evans St	41 C	12
Everett Av	53 F	18
Evergreen Av	42 F	13
Everit St	41 C	12
Exeter St	53 E	19

F

STREET	MAP	GRID
Fair St	41 C	13
Fairview Pl	46 E	15
Falmouth St	53 E	19
Fanchon Pl	43 G	13
Fane Ct	53 F	18
Fane Ct S	53 F	18
Farr Pl	50 E	16
Farragut Pl	50 E	16
Farragut Rd	50 E	16
Fayette St	40 E	12
Fenimore St	46 E	15
Ferris St	41 B	13
Ferry Pl	41 B	13
Fillmore Av	50 F	17

STREET	MAP	GRID
Fillmore Pl	40 D	11
Fiske Pl	41 D	14
Flatbush Av	45 D	15
Flatbush Av Ext	41 C	12
Flatlands 1st St	47 G	15
Flatlands 2nd St	47 G	15
Flatlands 3rd St	47 G	15
Flatlands 4th St	47 H	15
Flatlands 5th St	47 H	15
Flatlands 6th St	47 H	15
Flatlands 7th St	51 H	16
Flatlands 8th St	51 H	16
Flatlands 9th St	51 H	16
Flatlands 10th St	51 H	16
Flatlands Av	50 E	17
Fleet Alley	41 C	12
Fleet Pl	41 C	13
Fleet St	41 C	13
Fleet Walk (Raymond V Ingersoll Houses)	41 C	13
Florence Av	53 F	18
Floyd Bennett Field (US Naval Air Station)	54 G	18
Floyd St	40 E	12
Flushing Av	41 D	12
Folsom Pl	43 H	13
Forbell St	43 J	14
Force Tube Av	43 H	13
Ford St	46 F	14
Forest Pl	48 A	17
Forrest St	42 E	12
Fort Greene Pl	41 D	13
Fort Hamilton Pkwy	48 A	17
Fort Hill Pl	48 A	17
Foster Av	49 D	16
Fountain Av	43 H	14
Frank Ct	53 F	18
Franklin Av	42 D	13
Franklin Ct *(off Kent Av)	41 D	13
Franklin St	40 D	11
Fraser Sq	50 E	17
Freeman St	40 E	11
Freeport Loop	47 H	15
Friel Pl	45 D	15
Front St	41 C	12
Frost St	40 E	11
Fuller Pl	45 D	15
Fulton St	41 C	13
Furman Av	43 G	13
Furman St	41 C	13

G

STREET	MAP	GRID
Gain Ct	53 F	18
Gallatin Pl	41 C	13
Garden Pl	41 C	13
Garden St	42 E	12
Gardner Av	40 F	11
Garfield Pl	45 C	14
Garland Ct	53 F	18
Garnet St	41 C	14
Garrison St *(off Front St)	41 C	12
Gates Av	42 E	13
Gatling Pl	48 B	17
Gaylord Dr N	51 G	17
Gaylord Dr S	51 G	17
Gelb Walk *(off West 5th St)	52 D	19
Gelston Av	48 A	17
Gem St	40 E	11

STREET	MAP	GRID	STREET	MAP	GRID	STREET	MAP	GRID	STREET	MAP	GRID
Geneva Loop	47	H 15	Harover Ct *(off			Hunterfly Pl	46	F 14	Kenmore Ter	45	D 15
George St	42	F 12	Rodman St) ...	52	D 19	Huntington St	41	B 14	Kensington St ...	53	E 19
Georgia Av	47	G 14	Harrison Alley			Huron St	40	D 11	Kensington		
Gerald Ct	52	D 18	*(off Evans			Hutchinson Ct ...	52	D 18	Walk	52	C 19
Gerald H			St)	41	C 12	Hyman Ct	53	F 18	Kent Av	40	D 11
Chambers			Harrison Av	42	E 12				Kent St	40	E 11
Sq	53	E 19	Harrison Pl	42	F 12	**I**			Kermit Pl	45	D 15
Gerritsen Av	50	E 17	Hart Pl	52	C 19				Kiely Pl	43	H 13
Gerry St	42	E 12	Hart St	42	E 13	Imlay St	41	B 13	Kimball St	50	F 17
Gibbons St	40	F 11	Harway Av	52	C 18	Independence			King St	41	B 13
Gilmore Ct	52	D 19	Harwood Pl	50	F 16	Av	52	B 18	Kings Hwy	49	C 17
Girard St	53	E 19	Hastings St	53	E 19	India St	40	D 11	Kings Pl	52	D 18
Glen St	43	H 13	Hattie Jones			Indiana Pl	51	G 17	Kingsborough 1st		
Glendale Ct	50	F 16	Ct	42	E 13	Ingraham St	40	F 12	Walk		
Glenmore Av	43	G 14	Hausman St	40	E 11	Interboro Pkwy ..	43	G 13	*(Kingsborough		
Glenmore Plz	47	G 14	Havemeyer St ...	40	D 12	Interstate Hwy 278			Houses)	46	F 14
Glenwood Rd	49	D 16	Havens Pl	43	G 14	(Brooklyn-			Kingsborough 2nd		
Gold St	41	C 12	Hawthorne St	46	E 15	Queens			Walk		
Goodwin Pl	42	F 13	Hazel Ct	53	F 18	Expwy)	41	C 12	*(Kingsborough		
Gotham Av	53	F 18	Heath Pl	43	G 13	Ira Ct	53	F 18	Houses)	46	F 14
Gowanus			Hefferman Sq	45	C 15	Irving Av	42	F 12	Kingsborough 3rd		
Expwy	44	B 15	Hegeman Av	47	G 15	Irving Pl	42	D 13	Walk		
Gowanus			Hemlock St	43	H 13	Irving St	41	B 13	*(Kingsborough		
Expwy	48	B 16	Henderson			Irvington Pl	49	D 16	Houses)	46	F 14
Gowanus			Walk	52	D 19	Irwin St	53	E 19	Kingsborough 4th		
Expwy	45	C 14	Hendrickson Pl ..	50	F 17	Ivan Ct	53	F 18	Walk		
Grace Ct	41	C 13	Hendrickson St ..	50	F 17	Ivy Hill Rd	40	F 11	*(Kingsborough		
Grace Ct Alley ...	41	C 13	Hendrix St	47	H 14				Houses)	46	F 14
Grafton St	46	F 14	Henry St	41	C 13	**J**			Kingsborough 5th		
Graham Av	42	E 12	Herbert St	40	E 11				Walk		
Grand Army			Herkimer Ct	42	E 13	Jackson Ct	48	A 17	*(Kingsborough		
Plz	41	D 14	Herkimer Pl	42	E 13	Jackson Pl	45	C 14	Houses)	46	F 14
Grand Av	42	D 13	Herkimer St	42	E 13	Jackson St	40	E 11	Kingsborough 6th		
Grand St	40	D 11	Herzl St	46	F 15	Jaffray St	53	E 19	Walk		
Grand St Ext	40	E 12	Hewes St	42	D 12	Jamaica Av	43	G 13	*(Kingsborough		
Granite St	43	G 13	Heyward St	42	D 12	Jardine Pl	43	G 14	Houses)	46	F 14
Grant Av	43	H 13	Hicks St	41	C 12	Java St	40	E 11	Kingsborough 7th		
Grant Sq	46	E 14	High St	41	C 12	Jay St	41	C 13	Walk		
Granville Payne			Highland Av	52	B 19	Jefferson Av	42	E 13	*(Kingsborough		
Av (Penn Av) .	47	G 14	Highland Blvd	43	G 13	Jefferson House			Houses)	46	F 14
Grattan St	42	F 12	Highland Pl	43	H 13	*(off Surf Av) ..	52	B 19	Kingsland Av	40	E 11
Gravesend Neck			Highland View			Jefferson St	42	E 12	Kingston Av	46	E 14
Rd	53	E 18	Av	52	C 19	Jerome Av	53	E 18	Kingsway Pl	50	F 16
Green St	40	E 10	Highlawn Av	52	C 18	Jerome St	47	H 14	Knapp St	53	F 18
Greene Av	41	D 13	Hill St	43	H 13	Jewel St	40	E 11	Knickerbocker		
Greenpoint Av ...	40	D 10	Hillel Pl	50	E 16	Jewell McKoy			Av	42	F 12
Greenwood Av ..	45	D 15	Himrod St	42	F 12	La	46	F 13	Knight Ct	53	F 18
Grove Pl	41	C 13	Hinckley Pl	45	D 15	Jewell Sq	43	G 14	Kosciusko St	42	E 13
Grove St	42	F 13	Hinsdale St	47	G 14	Jodie Ct	46	F 15	Kossuth Pl	42	F 13
Guernsey St	40	E 11	Holly St	47	H 14	John Barry			Krier Pl	47	G 15
Guider Av	52	D 19	Holmes La	51	G 16	Blvd	53	E 19			
Gunnison Ct	53	E 19	Homecrest Av ...	53	D 18	John St	41	C 12	**L**		
Gunther Pl	46	F 14	Homecrest Ct ...	53	D 18	Johnson Av	40	E 12			
			Hooper St	42	D 12	Johnson Pl	46	E 15	Lacon Ct	53	F 18
H			Hope St	40	E 12	Johnson St	41	C 13	Lady Moody		
			Hopkins St	42	E 12	Jones Walk	52	D 19	Sq	53	E 18
Hale Av	43	H 13	Hopkinson Av			Joralemon St	41	C 13	Lafayette Av	41	D 13
Hall St	42	D 13	(Thomas S.			Joval Ct	53	F 18	Lafayette St *(off		
Halleck St	44	B 14	Boyland St) ...	43	F 14	Judge St	40	E 12	Debevoise Pl) ...	41	C 13
Halsey St	42	E 13	Horace Ct	45	D 15	Junius St	47	G 14	Lafayette Walk ..	48	A 17
Hamilton Av	41	B 13	Hornell Loop	47	H 15	Just Ct	53	F 18	Lake Pl	52	D 18
Hamilton Pl	45	C 14	Howard Alley	41	C 12				Lake St	52	D 18
Hamilton Walk ...	48	A 17	Howard Av	42	F 13	**K**			Lama Ct *(at		
Hampton Av	53	E 19	Howard Pl	45	C 15				West 5th St off		
Hampton Pl	46	E 14	Hoyt St	41	C 13	Kane Pl	46	F 14	Avenue V)	52	D 18
Hancock St	42	E 13	Hoyt's La	47	G 15	Kane St	41	B 13	Lamont Ct	46	E 14
Hanover Pl	41	C 13	Hubbard Pl	50	E 16	Kansas Pl	51	G 17	Lancaster Av	52	D 18
Hanson Pl	41	D 13	Hubbard St	52	D 19	Karweg Pl	43	H 13	Landis Ct	53	F 18
Harbor Ct	48	A 17	Hudson Av	41	C 12	Kathleen Pl	52	D 18	Langham St	53	E 19
Harbor La	48	A 16	Hudson Walk			Kaufman Pl	51	G 16	Laurel Av	52	B 19
Harbor View			*(Raymond V			Kay Ct	53	F 18	Lawn Ct	53	E 19
Ter	48	A 16	Ingersoll			Keap St	42	D 12	Lawrence Av	49	D 16
Harden St	50	F 17	Houses)	41	C 13	Keen Ct	53	F 18	Lawrence St	41	C 13
Haring St	53	E 18	Hull St	42	F 13	Kenilworth Pl	50	E 16	Lawton St	42	F 13
Harkness Av	53	F 18	Humboldt St	40	E 12	Kenmore Ct *(off			Lee Av	42	D 12
Harman St	42	F 13	Hunt's La	41	C 13	Voorhies Av) ..	53	E 18	Lefferts Av	46	E 14
			Hunter Av	52	C 18	Kenmore Pl	45	D 15	Lefferts Pl	42	D 13

STREET	MAP	GRID	STREET	MAP	GRID	STREET	MAP	GRID	STREET	MAP	GRID
Legion St	46	F 14	Maple St	46	E 14	Montague Ter	41	C 13	North Portland		
Leif Ericson Dr	48	A 16	Marconi Pl	43	F 14	Montana Pl	51	G 17	Av	41	D 13
Leiv Eiriksson			Marcus Garvey			Montauk Av	43	H 14	North 1st St	40	D 11
Sq	48	B 16	Blvd	42	E 13	Montauk Ct	52	D 19	North 2nd St	40	D 11
Lenox Rd	46	E 15	Marcy Av	42	D 12	Montgomery Pl	45	D 14	North 3rd St	40	D 11
Leonard St	40	E 12	Marginal St	44	B 15	Montgomery			North 4th St	40	D 11
Lester St	53	F 18	Marginal St E	43	G 13	St	46	E 14	North 5th St	40	D 11
Lewis Av	42	E 13	Marginal St W	43	G 13	Montieth St	42	E 12	North 6th St	40	D 11
Lewis Pl	45	D 15	Marine Av	48	A 17	Montrose Av	40	E 12	North 7th St	40	D 11
Lexington Av	42	E 13	Marine Pkwy	50	E 17	Monument Walk			North 8th St	40	D 11
Liberty Av	43	G 14	Marion St	42	F 13	*(Raymond V			North 9th St	40	D 11
Lieutenant			Marlborough Ct			Ingersoll			North 10th St	40	D 11
Kenneth E			*(off Foster			Houses)	41	C 12	North 11th St	40	D 11
Aimee			Av)	49	D 16	Moore Pl	50	E 17	North 12th St	40	E 11
Triangle	50	E 17	Marlborough			Moore St	42	E 12	North 13th St	40	E 11
Lincoln Av	43	H 13	Rd	45	D 15	Morgan Av	40	F 12	North 14th St	40	E 11
Lincoln Pl	45	D 14	Marshall St	41	C 12	Morgan St	40	E 11	North 15th St	40	E 11
Lincoln Rd	46	E 14	Martense Ct	45	D 15	Mother Gaston			Norwood Av	43	H 13
Linda Ct	46	F 15	Martense St	46	E 15	Blvd	47	G 14	Nostrand Av	42	E 13
Linden Blvd	46	E 15	Martin Luther			Moultrie St	40	E 11	Nova Ct	53	F 18
Linden St	42	F 13	King Jr. Pl	42	E 12	Murdock Ct	52	D 19			
Linwood St	43	H 13	Maspeth Av	40	E 11	Myrtle Av	41	C 13	**O**		
Little Nassau			Mater Ct *(off						Oak St	40	D 11
St	42	D 12	Brighton			**N**			Oakland Pl	46	E 15
Little St	41	C 12	Beach Av)	53	E 19	Narrows Av	48	A 17	O'Brien Pl	43	H 13
Livingston Plz	41	C 13	Matthews Ct	45	D 15	Nassau Av	40	E 11	Ocean Av	45	D 15
Livingston St	41	C 13	Matthews Pl	51	G 16	Nassau St	41	C 12	Ocean Beachside		
Livonia Av	46	F 14	Maujer St	40	E 12	National Dr	51	G 17	Ct *(off Brighton		
Lloyd Ct	52	D 18	Mayfair Dr N	51	G 17	Nautilus Av	52	B 19	Beach Av)	53	E 19
Lloyd St	46	E 15	Mayfair Dr S	51	G 17	Navy St	41	C 13	Ocean Ct	52	D 18
Locust Av	49	D 17	McClancy Pl	47	H 14	Navy Walk			Ocean Pkwy	45	D 16
Locust St	42	E 12	McDonald Av	49	D 16	*(Raymond V			Ocean View		
Logan St	43	H 14	McDonough St	42	E 13	Ingersoll			Av	52	B 19
Lois Av	53	F 18	McGuinness			Houses)	41	C 13	Oceanic Av	52	B 19
Lombardy St	40	E 11	Blvd	40	E 11	Nelson St	41	B 14	Ohio Walk	51	G 17
Lorimer St	42	E 12	McGuinness			Neptune Av	52	C 19	Old Fulton St		
Loring Av	47	H 14	Blvd S	40	E 11	Neptune Ct *(off			*(Cadman Plz		
Lorraine St	41	B 14	McKeever Pl	46	D 14	West End			W between		
Losee Ter	53	E 19	McKenny St			Av)	53	E 19	Furman St and		
Lott Av	47	G 15	*(off Vine St)	41	C 12	Neptune Ter *(off			Henry St)	41	C 12
Lott Pl	50	E 17	McKibbin St	42	E 12	Neptune Av)	52	D 19	Old Mill Rd	47	H 14
Lott St	46	E 15	McKinley Av	43	H 13	Nevins St	41	C 13	Old New Utrecht		
Lotts La	49	C 16	Meadow St	40	E 12	New Dock St	41	C 12	Rd	49	C 16
Louis Pl	46	F 14	Meeker Av	40	E 11	New Jersey Av	47	G 14	Olean St	50	E 17
Louisa St	45	C 15	Melba Ct	53	F 18	New Lots Av	47	G 14	Olive St	40	E 12
Louise Ter	48	A 16	Melrose St	42	E 12	New Utrecht			Oliver St	48	A 17
Louisiana Av	47	G 15	Menahan St	42	F 13	Av	49	C 17	Opal Ct	53	F 18
Love La	41	C 12	Merceine St *(off			New York Av	46	E 14	Orange St	41	C 12
Lowe Sq	46	F 14	Front St)	41	C 12	Newel St	40	E 11	Orient Av	40	E 11
Ludlam Pl	46	E 14	Merit Ct	53	F 18	Newkirk Av	49	D 16	Oriental Blvd	53	E 19
Luquer St	41	B 13	Mermaid Av	52	C 19	Newkirk Av Plz			Oriental Ct *(off		
Lyme Av	52	B 19	Mesereau Ct *(off			*(off Newkirk			West End Av)	53	E 19
Lynch St	42	D 12	Emmons Av)	53	E 18	Av)	49	D 16	Osborne St	47	G 14
			Meserole Av	40	E 11	Newport St	47	G 15	Otsego St	41	B 14
M			Meserole St	40	E 12	Newton St	40	E 11	Overbaugh Pl	50	E 16
MacDougal St	42	F 13	Metropolitan			Nichols Av	43	H 13	Ovington Av	48	A 16
Mackay Pl	44	A 16	Av	40	D 11	Nixon Ct	52	D 19	Ovington Ct	49	C 17
Mackenzie St	53	E 19	Miami Ct	46	E 14	Noble St	40	D 11	Owls Head Ct	44	A 16
Macon St	42	E 13	Micieli Pl	45	C 15	Noel Av	53	F 18	Oxford St	53	E 19
Madeline Ct	48	A 16	Middagh St	41	C 12	Nolans La	47	G 15			
Madison Pl	50	E 17	Middleton St	40	D 12	Noll St	42	E 12	**P**		
Madison St	42	E 13	Midwood St	46	E 15	Norfolk St	53	E 19	Pacific St	41	C 13
Madoc Av	53	F 18	Milford St	43	H 14	Norman Av	40	E 11	Paerdegat Av		
Main St	41	C 12	Mill Av	50	F 17	Norman Pl	43	G 13	N	51	G 16
Malbone St	46	E 14	Mill Basin	51	G 17	North Conduit			Paerdegat Av		
Malcolm X			Mill La	50	F 17	Av	43	J 14	S	50	F 16
Blvd	42	F 13	Mill Rd	52	C 18	North Elliot Pl	41	D 12	Paerdegat 1st		
Malta St	47	G 14	Mill St	41	B 14	North Elliot Walk			St	50	F 16
Manhattan Av	40	E 12	Miller Av	43	G 13	*(Walt Whitman			Paerdegat 2nd		
Manhattan Av			Miller Pl	43	G 13	Houses)	41	D 13	St	51	G 16
(Sea Gate)	52	B 19	Milton St	40	D 11	North Henry St	40	E 11	Paerdegat 3rd		
Manhattan Ct	52	D 18	Minna St	45	C 15	North Oxford			St	51	G 16
Manor Ct	52	D 18	Moffat St	43	G 13	St	41	D 12	Paerdegat 4th		
Mansfield Pl			Monaco Pl	43	G 14	North Oxford			St	51	G 16
(E 24th)	50	E 17	Monitor St	40	E 11	Walk *(Walt			Paerdegat 5th		
Maple St	52	B 19	Monroe Pl	41	C 13	Whitman			St	51	G 16
			Monroe St	42	E 13	Houses)	41	D 13			
			Montague St	41	C 13						

STREET	MAP	GRID
Paerdegat 6th St	51 G	16
Paerdegat 7th St	51 G	16
Paerdegat 8th St	51 G	16
Paerdegat 9th St	51 G	16
Paerdegat 10th St	51 G	16
Paerdegat 11th St	51 G	16
Paerdegat 12th St	51 G	16
Paerdegat 13th St	51 G	16
Paerdegat 14th St	51 G	16
Paerdegat 15th St	51 G	16
Paidge Av	40 E	10
Palm Ct	46 E	14
Palmetto St	42 F	13
Parade Pl	45 D	15
Park Av	42 E	12
Park Cir	45 D	15
Park Pl	41 D	14
Park St	42 E	12
Parkes Cadman Plz	41 C	12
Parkside Av	45 D	15
Parkside Ct	45 D	15
Parkville Av	49 D	16
Parkway Ct	52 D	18
Parrott Pl	48 A	17
Patchen Av	42 F	13
Pearl St	41 C	13
Pearson St	50 F	17
Pembroke St	53 E	19
Penn St	42 D	12
Pennsylvania Av	47 G	14
Percival St	44 B	14
Peri La	51 G	16
Perry Av	53 E	19
Perry Pl	42 E	13
Perry Ter	48 A	16
Perry Walk	53 E	19
Pierrepont Pl	41 C	13
Pierrepont Plz	41 C	13
Pierrepont St	41 C	13
Pilling St	43 G	13
Pine St	43 H	13
Pineapple St	41 C	12
Pioneer St	41 B	13
Pitkin Av	47 G	14
Plaza St E	41 D	14
Plaza St W	41 D	14
Pleasant Pl	43 G	14
Plumb Beach Av	53 F	18
Plumb 1st St	53 F	18
Plumb 2nd St	53 F	18
Plumb 3rd St	53 F	18
Plymouth St	41 C	12
Poe Pl	40 E	12
Polar St	52 B	19
Polhemus Pl	41 D	14
Poly Pl	48 B	17
Poole La	53 E	19
Pope John Paul II Sq *(sec of Humboldt St bet Driggs Av to Broome St)	40 E	11
Poplar Av	52 B	19
Poplar St	41 C	12
Portal St	46 F	14
Porter Av	40 E	11
Post Ct	53 F	18
Powell St	47 G	14
Powers St	40 E	12
Prescott Pl	42 F	14
President St	41 B	13
Preston Ct	50 F	16
Prince St	41 C	13
Prospect Av	45 D	15
Prospect Expwy	45 C	14
Prospect Park SW	45 D	15
Prospect Park W	45 C	15
Prospect Pl	41 D	13
Prospect St	41 C	12
Provost St	40 E	11
Pulaski St	42 E	13
Putnam Av	42 E	13
Quay St	40 D	11
Quentin Rd	49 D	17
Quentin St	53 F	19
Quincy St	42 E	13
Rabbi Joel Teitelbaum Pl	42 D	12
Radde St	42 F	14
Raleigh Pl	46 E	15
Ralph Av	42 F	13
Randolph St	40 F	12
Rapelye St	41 B	13
Red Cross Pl	41 C	12
Red Hook La	41 C	13
Reed St	41 B	14
Reeve Pl	45 D	15
Regent Pl	45 D	15
Remsen Av	46 F	15
Remsen St	41 C	13
Revere Pl	42 E	14
Rewe St	40 F	11
Richards St	41 B	14
Richardson St	40 E	11
Richmond St	43 H	13
Ridge Blvd	48 A	16
Ridge Ct	48 A	16
Ridgecrest Ter	48 A	16
Ridgewood Av	43 H	13
Ridgewood Pl	43 F	12
Riegelmann Boardwalk	52 C	19
River St	40 D	11
Riverdale Av	46 F	14
Robert Pl	43 G	13
Robert St	43 G	13
Rochester Av	46 F	14
Rock St	42 F	12
Rockaway Av	47 G	14
Rockaway Pkwy	46 F	14
Rockwell Pl	41 D	13
Roder Av	49 D	17
Rodney St	42 D	12
Roebling St	40 D	12
Rogers Av	46 E	14
Roosevelt Ct *(off 30th St)	44 B	15
Roosevelt Pl	42 F	14
Rose St	47 G	15
Ross St	42 D	12
Rost Pl	51 G	16
Royce Pl	51 G	16
Royce St	51 G	16
Rubins La *(off Sea Breeze Av)	52 D	19
Ruby St	47 J	14
Rugby Rd	45 D	16
Russell St	40 E	11
Rutherford Pl	52 B	18
Rutland Rd	46 E	15
Rutledge St	42 D	12
Ryder Av	49 D	17
Ryder St	50 E	17
Ryerson St	41 D	13
S		
Sackett St	41 C	13
Sackman St	43 G	14
Saint Andrew's Pl	42 E	13
Saint Charles Pl	46 E	14
Saint Edward's St	41 D	13
Saint Felix St	41 D	13
Saint Francis Pl	46 E	14
Saint James Pl	42 D	13
Saint Johns Pl	45 D	14
Saint Jude Pl	51 H	16
Saint Mark's Av	41 C	13
Saint Mark's Pl	41 C	13
Saint Nicholas Av	40 F	12
Saint Paul's Ct	45 D	15
Saint Paul's Pl	45 D	15
Sandford St	42 E	13
Sands St	41 C	12
Sapphire St	47 J	14
Saratoga Av	42 F	14
Schaefer St	43 G	13
Schenck Av	47 H	14
Schenck Ct	43 G	13
Schenck Pl	51 G	16
Schenck St	51 G	16
Schenectady Av	46 F	14
Schermerhorn St	41 C	13
Scholes St	40 E	12
School La	47 G	15
Schroeders Av	47 H	15
Schweikerts Walk	52 C	19
Scott Av	40 F	12
Sea Breeze Av	52 D	19
Sea Breeze Ct *(off West End Av)	53 E	19
Sea Gate Av	52 B	19
Sea Pl	52 C	19
Seabreeze Walk	52 D	19
Seabring St	41 B	13
Seacoast Ter	53 E	19
Seaview Av	51 G	16
Seaview Ct	51 H	16
Seaview Loop	47 H	15
Seba Av	53 F	18
Sedgwick Pl	44 A	16
Sedgwick St	41 B	13
Seeley St	45 C	15
Seigel St	42 E	12
Senator St	44 A	16
Seneca Av	40 F	12
Seton Pl	49 D	16
Sharon St	40 E	11
Sheepshead Bay Rd	53 E	18
Sheffield Av	47 G	14
Shell Rd	52 D	19
Shepherd Av	43 H	13
Sheridan Av	47 H	14
Sherlock Pl	43 G	14
Sherman St	45 D	15
Shore Blvd	53 E	19
Shore Ct	48 A	17
Shore Pkwy (Leif Ericson Dr)	48 B	18
Shore Rd	48 A	16
Shore Rd Ext	52 B	18
Shore Road Dr	48 A	16
Shore Road La	48 A	16
Sidney Pl	41 C	13
Siegel St	40 E	12
Sigourney St	41 B	14
Skidmore Av	51 G	16
Skidmore La	51 G	16
Skidmore Pl	51 G	16
Skillman Av	40 E	11
Skillman St	42 D	13
Sloan Pl	52 D	18
Slocum Pl	45 D	16
Smith St	45 C	14
Smith's La	47 G	15
Snediker Av	47 G	14
Snyder Av	46 E	15
Somers St	43 G	13
South Conduit Av	47 J	14
South Elliott Pl	41 D	13
South Oxford St	41 D	13
South Portland Av	41 D	13
South 1st St	40 D	11
South 2nd St	40 D	12
South 3rd St	40 D	12
South 4th St	40 D	12
South 5th Pl	40 D	12
South 5th St	40 D	12
South 6th St	40 D	12
South 7th St	40 D	12
South 8th St	40 D	12
South 9th St	40 D	12
South 10th St	40 D	12
South 11th St	40 D	12
Southgate Ct	52 D	18
Spencer Ct	42 E	13
Spencer Pl	42 E	13
Spencer St	42 E	13
Stagg St	40 E	12
Stagg Walk	40 F	12
Stanhope St	42 F	12
Stanley Av	47 G	15
Stanton Rd	53 F	19
Stanwix St	40 E	12
Starr St	42 F	12
State St	41 C	13
Stephen's Ct	50 E	16
Sterling Pl	41 D	14
Sterling St	46 E	14
Steuben St	42 D	13
Stewart Av	40 F	12
Stewart St	43 G	13
Stillwell Av	52 C	19
Stillwell's Pl	51 G	16
Stockholm St	42 F	12
Stockton St	42 E	13
Stoddard Pl	46 E	14

STREET	MAP	GRID
Stone Ave (Mother Gaston Blvd)	47 G	14
Story Ct *(off Story St)	45 C	15
Story St	45 C	15
Stratford Rd	45 D	16
Strauss St	46 F	15
Strickland Av	50 F	17
Strong Pl	41 C	13
Stryker Ct	52 D	18
Stryker St	52 D	18
Stuart St	50 E	17
Stuyvesant Av	42 F	13
Sullivan Pl	46 D	14
Sullivan St	41 B	13
Summit St	41 B	13
Sumner Av (Marcus Garvey Blvd)	42 E	13
Sumpter St	42 F	13
Sunnyside Av	43 G	13
Sunnyside Ct	43 G	13
Sunset Ct	52 B	19
Surf Av	52 B	19
Sutter Av	47 H	14
Sutton St	40 E	11
Suydam Pl	42 F	14
Suydam St	42 F	12
Sylvan Ter *(off West 33rd St)	52 C	19

T

STREET	MAP	GRID
Taaffe Pl	42 D	13
Tabor Ct *(off 13th Av)	48 B	16
Tampa Ct	46 E	14
Tapscott St	46 F	14
Taylor St	40 D	12
Tech Pl	41 C	13
Tehama St	45 C	15
Temple Ct	45 D	15
Temple Sq	41 C	13
Ten Eyck St	40 E	12
Ten Eyck Walk *(Williamsburg Housing)	42 F	12
Tennis Ct	45 D	15
Terrace Pl	45 C	15
Thames St	42 F	12
Thatford Av	47 G	14
Thatford St	47 G	14
Thomas S Boyland St (Hopkinson Av)	45 F	13
Thomas St	40 F	11
Thornton St	42 E	12
Throop Av	42 E	13
Tieman's La	47 G	15
Tiffany Pl	41 B	13
Tilden Av	46 E	15
Tillary St	41 C	13
Tompkins Av	42 E	13
Tompkins Pl	41 C	13
Townsend St	40 F	11
Troutman St	42 F	12
Troy Av	46 E	14
Troy Pl	50 F	16
Truckleman's La	47 G	15
Truxton St	43 G	13
Tudor Ter *(off West 37th St)	52 B	19
Turner St	45 D	15
Twin Pines Dr	47 H	15

U

STREET	MAP	GRID
Underhill Av	41 D	14
Union Av	40 E	12
Union St	41 B	13
Utica Av	46 F	14

V

STREET	MAP	GRID
Van Brunt St	41 B	13
Van Buren St	42 E	13
Van Dam St	40 E	11
Van Dyke St	41 B	14
Van Sicklen St	52 D	18
Van Siclen Av	43 G	13
Van Siclen Ct	43 G	13
Van Sinderen Av	47 G	14
Vandalia Av	47 H	15
Vanderbilt Av	41 D	13
Vanderbilt St	45 D	15
Vanderveer Pl	50 E	16
Vanderveer St	43 G	13
Vandervoort Av	40 E	11
Vandervoort Pl	42 F	12
Varet St	42 E	12
Varick Av	40 F	12
Varick St	40 E	11
Varkens Hook Rd	51 G	16
Verandah Pl	41 C	13
Vermont Av	43 G	13
Vermont Ct	43 G	13
Vermont St	47 G	14
Vernon Av	42 E	13
Verona Pl	42 E	13
Verona St	41 B	13
Veronica Pl	46 E	15
Veterans Av	50 F	17
Victor Rd	50 E	16
Village Ct	52 D	18
Village Rd E	52 D	18
Village Rd N	52 D	18
Village Rd S	52 D	18
Vine St	41 C	12
Virginia Pl	46 E	14
Visitation Pl	41 B	13
Vista Pl	48 B	16
Voorhies Av	53 E	18

W

STREET	MAP	GRID
Wakeman Pl	44 A	16
Waldorf Ct	49 D	16
Walker St	47 H	15
Wallabout St	42 D	12
Wallaston Ct	49 C	17
Walsh Ct	49 D	16
Walton St	42 E	12
Walworth St	42 E	13
Warren Pl	41 B	13
Warren St	41 C	13
Warsoff Pl	42 E	12
Warwick St	47 H	14
Washington Av	42 D	13
Washington Park	41 D	13
Washington Plz	40 D	12
Washington St	41 C	12
Washington Walk *(Walt Whitman Houses)	41 C	13
Water St	41 C	12
Waterbury St	40 E	12
Watkins St	47 G	14
Waverly Av	42 D	13

STREET	MAP	GRID
Weber's Ct	53 E	19
Weber's Ter	53 E	19
Webster Av	49 D	16
Webster Pl	45 C	14
Weirfield St	43 F	13
Weldon St	43 H	13
Wellington Ct	49 D	16
Wells St	43 H	13
West Av	52 D	19
West Brighton Av	52 D	19
West End Av	53 E	19
West St	40 D	10
West 1st St	49 D	17
West 2nd Pl	52 D	19
West 2nd St	49 D	17
West 3rd St	49 D	17
West 4th St	49 D	17
West 5th St	49 D	17
West 6th St	49 D	17
West 7th St	52 D	18
West 8th St	52 D	18
West 9th St	52 D	18
West 10th St	52 D	18
West 11th St	52 C	18
West 12th St	52 C	18
West 13th St	52 C	18
West 15th Pl	52 C	19
West 15th St	52 C	19
West 16th St	52 C	19
West 17th St	52 C	19
West 19th St	52 C	19
West 20th St	52 C	19
West 21st St	52 C	19
West 22nd St	52 C	19
West 23rd St	52 C	19
West 24th St	52 C	19
West 25th St	52 C	19
West 26th St	52 C	19
West 27th St	52 C	19
West 28th St	52 C	19
West 29th St	52 C	19
West 30th St	52 C	19
West 31st St	52 C	19
West 32nd St	52 C	19
West 33rd St	52 C	19
West 34th St	52 C	19
West 35th St	52 C	19
West 36th St	52 C	19
West 37th St	52 C	19
Westbury Ct	45 D	15
Westerly La	48 A	16
Westminster Rd	45 D	16
Wharton Pl	43 H	13
Whipple St	42 E	12
White St	40 E	12
Whitman Dr	51 G	17
Whitney Av	53 F	18
Whitney Pl	52 D	18
Whitty La	50 F	16
Whitwell Pl	41 C	14
Will Pl	47 G	15
William J Hennesy Sq	52 D	19
Williams Av	47 G	14
Williams Ct	53 E	18
Williams Pl	47 G	14
Williamsburg Pl	42 D	12
Williamsburg St E	42 D	12
Williamsburg St W	42 D	12
Willmohr St	46 F	15
Willoughby Av	41 D	13
Willoughby St	41 C	13
Willow Pl	41 C	13
Willow St	41 C	12

STREET	MAP	GRID
Wilson Av	42 F	12
Wilson St	42 D	12
Windsor Pl	45 C	14
Winthrop St	46 E	15
Withers St	40 E	11
Wogan Ter	48 A	17
Wolcott St	41 B	14
Wolf Pl	52 D	18
Woodbine St	42 F	13
Woodhull St	41 B	13
Woodpoint Rd	40 E	11
Woodrow Ct *(off 30th St)	44 B	15
Woodruff Av	45 D	15
Woods Pl	46 E	15
Woodside Av	49 D	17
Wortman Av	47 G	15
Wortman Dr	47 H	15
Wyckoff Av	42 F	12
Wyckoff St	41 C	13
Wyona St	47 G	14
Wythe Av	40 D	11
Wythe Pl	42 D	12

Y

STREET	MAP	GRID
York St	41 C	12

Numbered Streets

STREET	MAP	GRID
1st Av	44 B	15
1st Ct	52 D	18
1st Pl	41 C	13
1st St *(Fort Hamilton Manor)	48 A	17
1st St	41 C	14
2nd Av	44 B	15
2nd Pl	41 C	13
2nd St	41 C	14
3rd Av	48 A	17
3rd Pl	41 C	13
3rd St	41 C	14
4th Av	48 A	17
4th Pl	41 C	13
4th St	41 C	14
5th Av	48 A	17
5th St	41 C	14
6th Av	48 B	16
6th St	45 C	14
7th Av	48 B	17
7th St	45 C	14
8th Av	45 D	14
8th St	45 C	14
9th Av	48 B	16
9th St	45 C	14
10th Av (John P Devaney Blvd)	48 B	16
10th St	45 C	14
11th Av	48 B	16
11th St	45 C	14
12th Av	48 B	17
12th St	45 C	14
13th Av	48 B	17
13th St	45 C	14
14th Av	49 C	17
14th St	45 C	14
15th Av	49 C	17
15th St	45 C	14
16th Av	49 C	17
16th St	45 C	14
17th Av	48 B	18
17th Ct	52 B	18
17th St	45 C	14

STREET INDEX — BROOKLYN

STREET	MAP	GRID	STREET	MAP	GRID	STREET	MAP	GRID	STREET	MAP	GRID
18th Av	52	B 18	29th St	45	C 15	55th St	44	B 15	79th St	48	A 16
18th St	45	C 14	30th St	45	C 15	56th Dr	51	G 17	80th St	48	A 16
19th Av	49	C 17	31st St	44	B 15	56th St	44	B 15	81st St	48	A 16
19th La	52	B 18	32nd St	44	B 15	57th St	44	B 15	82nd St	48	A 16
19th St	45	C 14	33rd St	44	B 15	58th St	44	B 16	83rd St	48	A 16
20th Av	49	C 17	34th St	44	B 15	59th St	44	B 16	84th St	48	A 16
20th Dr	52	B 18	35th St	44	B 15	60th St	44	B 16	85th St	48	A 16
20th La	52	C 18	36th St	44	B 15	61st St	44	B 16	86th St	48	A 16
20th St	45	C 14	37th St	44	B 15	62nd St	44	B 16	87th St	48	A 17
21st Av	49	C 17	38th St	44	B 15	63rd St	44	B 16	88th St	48	A 17
21st Dr	52	C 18	39th St	44	B 15	64th St	44	B 16	89th St	48	A 17
21st La	52	C 18	40th St	44	B 15	65th St	48	B 16	90th St	48	A 17
21st St	45	C 14	41st St	44	B 15	66th St	48	B 16	91st St	48	A 17
22nd St	45	C 14	42nd St	44	B 15	67th St	48	B 16	92nd St	48	A 17
23rd Av	52	C 18	43rd St	44	B 15	68th St	44	A 16	93rd St	48	A 17
23rd St	45	C 14	44th St	44	B 15	70th St	48	A 16	94th St	48	A 17
24th Av	52	C 18	45th St	44	B 15	71st St	48	A 16	95th Av	43	J 13
24th St	45	C 14	46th St	44	B 15	72nd Ct	48	A 16	95th St	48	A 17
25th Av	52	C 18	47th St	44	B 15	72nd St	48	A 16	96th St	48	A 17
25th St	45	C 14	48th St	44	B 15	73rd St	48	A 16	97th St	48	A 17
26th Av	52	C 18	49th St	44	B 15	74th St	48	A 16	98th St	48	A 17
26th St	45	C 14	50th St	44	B 15	75th St (Bay Ridge Pkwy)	48	A 16	99th St	48	A 17
27th Av	52	C 18	51st St	44	B 15	76th St	48	A 16	100th St	48	A 17
27th St	45	C 15	52nd St	44	B 15	77th St	48	A 16	101st Av	43	J 13
28th Av	52	C 18	53rd St	44	B 15	78th St	48	A 16	101st St	48	A 17
28th St	45	C 15	54th St	44	B 15						

STREET INDEX — STATEN ISLAND

A

STREET	MAP	GRID	STREET	MAP	GRID	STREET	MAP	GRID	STREET	MAP	GRID
A St	59	J 4	Albourne Av E	65	F 10	Amsterdam Pl	58	H 5	Armour Pl	65	F 11
Abbey Rd	62	H 8	Albourne Ct	64	E 10	Amy Ct	58	H 6	Armstrong Av	62	H 8
Abbott St	60	P 4	Albright St	60	N 5	Amy La	59	J 5	Arnedo Pl	57	M 2
Abby Pl	57	M 2	Alcott St	62	F 8	Anaconda St	62	F 9	Arnold St	57	M 2
Abingdon Av	62	H 8	Alden Pl	57	N 2	Anderson Av	56	K 2	Arnprior St	56	J 3
Abingdon Ct	62	H 8	Alderwood Pl	60	M 5	Anderson Pl	55	H 2	Arrowood Ct	61	E 8
Acacia Av	62	J 9	Alexander Av	62	G 8	Anderson St	60	O 4	Arthur Av	60	O 5
Academy Av	64	C 12	Alexandra Pl			Andes Pl	59	L 4	Arthur Ct	56	L 3
Academy Pl	57	O 1	*(connects			Andrea Ct	62	H 8	Arthur Kill Rd	64	B 11
Ackerman St	62	J 9	Gower St to N			Andrea Pl	55	H 3	Arthur Pl	62	G 9
Acorn St	63	L 8	Gannon Av)	59	L 4	Andrease St	60	P 4	Ascot Av	59	K 6
Ada Dr	55	H 3	Alexsandra Ct			Andrews Av	63	K 7	Ash Pl	59	K 4
Ada Pl	57	N 3	*(off Ladd			Andrews St	60	O 6	Ashland Av	64	E 10
Adam Ct	59	J 6	Av)	62	H 8	Andros Av	55	H 2	Ashland Av E	65	F 10
Adams Av	60	M 6	Algonkin St	65	F 10	Androvette Av	65	F 10	Ashley La	61	E 9
Adelaide Av	63	L 8	Allegro St	65	G 10	Androvette St	61	C 9	Ashton Dr	62	F 9
Adele Ct	57	O 3	Allen Ct	56	L 2	Anita St	56	J 3	Ashwood Ct	62	J 8
Adele St	60	N 5	Allen Pl	65	H 10	Ann St	56	K 2	Ashworth Av	58	H 5
Adelphi Av	64	D 11	Allendale Rd	60	O 5	Annadale Rd	62	G 8	Aspen Knolls		
Adlai Cir	62	H 9	Allentown La	64	C 10	Annadale Rd	65	G 10	Way	62	G 8
Adlers La	64	C 12	Allison Av	63	L 7	Annfield Ct	60	M 5	Aspinwall St	64	B 12
Admiralty Loop	64	E 11	Allison Pl	63	L 7	Anthony Pl	56	K 3	Athena Pl	59	L 4
Adrianne La	56	J 3	Almond St	62	G 9	Anthony St	61	E 9	Atlantic Av	60	N 5
Adrienne Pl	62	J 9	Alpine Av	60	M 4	Appleby Av	60	O 6	Atmore Pl	63	K 8
Agda Av	63	M 8	Alpine Ct	56	L 3	Arbutus Av	65	G 10	Auburn Av	59	J 4
Agnes Pl	60	O 6	Alter Av	60	M 5	Arbutus Way	65	G 10	Augusta Av	62	H 9
Ainsworth Av	63	K 9	Altoona Av	63	K 7	Arc Pl	63	L 7	Aultman Av	63	K 7
Akron St	58	H 4	Aluminum Av	58	H 6	Arcadia Pl	56	L 2	Ausable Av	57	M 2
Alabama Pl	56	L 3	Alverson Av	61	E 8	Arden Av	62	F 8	Austin Av	60	O 5
Alan Loop	60	N 4	Alverson Av	61	E 8	Arden Av	65	H 10	Austin Pl	57	N 2
Alaska Pl	62	H 7	Alverson Loop	62	F 9	Ardmore Av	59	K 4	Avenue B	56	K 2
Alaska St	56	L 2	Alvine Av	65	G 10	Ardsley St	63	K 7	Averill Pl	64	C 11
Alban St	57	M 2	Alysia Ct	61	E 9	Area Pl	59	L 4	Aviston St	63	L 8
Albans Pl	62	H 9	Amador St	55	H 3	Argonne St	60	O 5	Avon Green	62	F 9
Albany Av	55	H 3	Amanda Ct	62	G 8	Arielle La	58	H 6	Avon Pl	57	N 2
Albee Av	62	G 9	Amaron La	64	C 12	Arkansas Av	62	J 8	Aye Ct	55	H 3
Albert Ct	55	H 3	Amber St	63	K 7	Arlene Ct	56	L 2	Aymar Av	60	M 4
Albert St	59	L 4	Amboy Rd	64	B 12	Arlene St	55	H 3	Azalea Ct	61	E 8
Alberta Av	58	F 5	Amelia Ct	57	M 1	Arlington Av	55	H 1			
Albion Pl	56	K 2	Amherst St	63	L 8	Arlington Ct	57	M 1	**B**		
Albourne Av	64	E 10	Amity Pl	55	H 2	Arlington Pl	55	H 2	B St	59	J 5
			Amity St	60	O 4	Arlo Rd	57	N 3	Bache Av	63	L 7
			Amsterdam Av	58	H 4	Armand St	56	J 3			

STREET	MAP	GRID	STREET	MAP	GRID	STREET	MAP	GRID	STREET	MAP	GRID
Bache St	56	K 2	Belmont Pl	57	O 1	Boulevard, The	56	K 3	Butler Ct	64	D 11
Baden Pl	63	N 7	Bement Av	56	L 1	Boundary Av	63	M 7	Butler Pl	57	O 3
Bailey Pl	55	H 1	Bement Ct	56	L 1	Bovanizer St	62	H 9	Butler St	64	D 11
Baker St	57	M 2	Benedict Av	56	K 3	Bowden St	60	M 6	Butler Ter	57	N 2
Balfour St	60	O 6	Benedict Rd	60	M 5	Bowdoin St	59	J 6	Butterworth Av	60	M 4
Ballard Av	62	F 9	Benjamin Dr	55	H 3	Bowen St	60	N 4	Buttonwood Rd	60	M 5
Balsam Pl	61	E 9	Benjamin Pl	55	H 2	Bower St	61	E 8	Byrd Pl	65	J 10
Baltic Av	60	N 4	Bennet Pl	65	H 10	Bowles Av	56	J 2	Byrne Av	59	K 4
Baltic St	57	O 2	Bennett Av	65	G 10	Bowling Green Pl	58	H 5			
Baltimore St	62	J 9	Bennett St	56	K 2	Boyce Av	63	K 7	**C**		
Bamberger La	62	H 9	Bennington St	65	J 10	Boyd St	57	O 3	C St	59	J 5
Bancroft Av	59	L 6	Benson St	62	G 8	Boylan St	62	G 8	Cabot Pl	60	O 4
Bang Ter	60	P 4	Bent St	62	H 9	Boyle Pl	63	K 7	Calcutta St	64	D 11
Bangor St	59	J 6	Bentley St	64	B 11	Boyle St	59	L 6	Caldera Pl	57	M 2
Bank Pl	60	N 5	Benton Av	60	N 5	Boynton St	64	E 10	Call St	63	K 7
Bank St	57	N 1	Benton Ct	63	K 8	Brabant St	55	H 2	Callan Av	60	M 5
Barbara St	63	K 7	Benziger Av	57	N 2	Bradford Av	64	E 10	Calvin Pl	57	N 3
Barclay Av	65	H 10	Berglund Av	58	H 4	Bradley Av	59	K 4	Cambria St	60	O 5
Barclay Cir	62	F 8	Berkley St	65	H 10	Bradley Ct	59	K 5	Cambridge Av	56	J 3
Bard Av	57	M 1	Berne Pl	61	E 9	Brady Pl	60	O 5	Camden St	57	O 3
Bard Pl	57	M 3	Berry Av	62	G 8	Braisted Av	59	J 6	Cameron Av	60	O 5
Baring Pl	57	N 3	Berry Av W	62	G 8	Brandis Av	62	H 8	Campbell Av	56	L 2
Barker St	56	L 2	Berry Ct	61	E 8	Brehaut Av	64	C 11	Campus Rd	60	N 4
Barlow Av	62	H 8	Bertha Pl	57	N 3	Brenton Pl	59	L 4	Canal St	57	O 3
Barnard Av	64	C 11	Bertram Av	65	G 11	Brentwood Av	57	M 2	Candon Av	61	E 9
Baron Blvd	58	G 5	Berwick Pl	57	M 3	Brewster St	57	O 2	Candon Ct	61	E 9
Barrett Av	56	K 3	Berwin La	56	L 3	Briarcliff Rd	60	O 5	Cannon Av	58	F 5
Barrett La	56	L 1	Beth Pl	62	J 9	Briarwood Rd	55	H 3	Cannon Blvd	63	L 7
Barrow Pl	61	E 9	Bethel Av	64	C 11	Bridgetown St	59	J 6	Canoe Pl	63	N 7
Barry St	61	E 8	Beverly Av	57	M 3	Brielle Av	59	K 5	Canon Dr	62	H 7
Bartlett Av	62	H 9	Beverly Rd	60	O 5	Brighton Av	57	M 2	Canterbury Av	56	J 3
Barton Av	60	M 6	Bianca Ct	62	G 8	Brighton St	64	C 12	Canton Av	62	F 9
Bartow La	64	D 12	Bidwell Av	56	K 3	Bristol Av	60	M 4	Cappellan St	65	G 11
Bartow St	63	K 9	Billiou Ct	65	F 10	Britton Av	60	N 4	Cardiff St	62	F 9
Bascom Pl	59	J 4	Billiou St	65	G 10	Britton La	63	M 8	Cardinal La	62	J 8
Bass St	59	K 4	Billop Av	64	B 12	Britton St	56	L 2	Carlin St	61	D 9
Bates Av	58	G 5	Biltmore St	59	J 4	Broad St	57	N 3	Carlton Av	64	E 10
Bath Av	60	N 5	Bionia Av	60	O 5	Broadway	56	L 1	Carlton Blvd	62	G 9
Bathgate St	65	H 10	Birch Av	57	M 3	Brokenshell Rd	64	E 11	Carlton Ct	65	F 10
Bay St	57	O 1	Birch La	62	F 8	Brook Av	63	L 8	Carlton Pl	60	M 4
Bay Ter	63	K 8	Birch Rd	55	H 3	Brook St	57	N 2	Carly Ct	64	D 11
Bayard St	62	H 9	Birchard Av	59	K 4	Brookfield Av	62	H 8	Carlyle Green	62	F 8
Bayport Pl	59	J 4	Bishop St	63	K 7	Brooks Pl	56	L 2	Carlyle St	57	N 1
Bayview Av	64	E 11	Bismark Av	57	N 1	Brookside Av	56	L 3	Carmel Av	59	K 4
Bayview Pl	57	N 2	Bismark St	57	N 1	Brookspond Pl	56	L 3	Carnegie Av	58	H 4
Bayview Ter	65	H 11	Blackford Av	56	K 2	Brower Ct	62	J 9	Caro St	59	K 4
Beach Av	63	L 7	Blackhorse Av	59	L 5	Brown Av	62	J 9	Carol Ct	64	E 11
Beach Rd	62	H 9	Blaine St	56	L 3	Brown Pl	60	O 4	Carol Pl	55	H 3
Beach St	57	O 3	Bland Pl	65	G 10	Brownell St	57	O 3	Carolina Ct	59	K 5
Beachview Av	63	M 7	Bleeker Pl	58	H 5	Browning Av	59	L 5	Carolina Pl	56	L 3
Beacon Av	63	L 7	Block St	63	K 8	Bruckner Av	55	H 2	Caroline St	56	L 2
Beacon Pl	63	M 8	Bloomfield Av	58	G 4	Brunswick St	59	J 6	Carpenter Av	59	J 5
Bean St	63	M 8	Bloomfield Rd	58	G 4	Bryan St	64	B 12	Carreau Av	58	H 5
Bear St	60	N 5	Bloomingdale Rd	61	E 9	Bryant Av	63	M 7	Carroll Pl	57	N 1
Beard St	59	J 6	Blue Heron Dr	65	H 10	Bryson Av	56	J 3	Carteret St	64	B 12
Bedell Av	64	C 11	Blueberry La	65	H 10	Buchanan Av	59	K 4	Cary Av	56	L 2
Bedell St	64	E 11	Blythe Pl	63	K 8	Buel Av	60	M 6	Cascade St	60	M 6
Bedford Av	60	M 6	Boardwalk Av	65	H 11	Buffalo St	63	K 8	Cascio Pl	57	M 1
Bedford Pl	62	F 9	Boating Pl	65	F 11	Buffington Av	65	G 10	Case Av	65	F 11
Bee Ct	55	H 3	Bodine St	56	L 2	Bunnell Ct	62	F 8	Casino Pl *(off Staten Island Blvd near Andes Pl)	59	L 4
Beebe St	60	M 4	Bogert Av	59	L 5	Bunnell St	62	F 8	Casper Av	58	G 5
Beechwood Av	57	N 1	Bogota St	59	J 6	Burbank Av	63	L 7	Cassidy Pl	57	M 1
Beechwood Pl	56	L 3	Bolivar St	59	L 5	Burchard Ct	62	G 9	Castleton Av	56	K 3
Beekman Cir	62	F 8	Bombay St	61	E 9	Burden Av	56	K 2	Castleton Ct	57	N 2
Beekman Pl	56	K 2	Bond St	56	K 2	Burgher Av	60	N 5	Castleton Pk E	57	O 1
Beethoven St	60	O 4	Boone St	59	K 5	Burke Av	58	G 5	Castleton Pk N	57	O 1
Behan Ct	63	L 7	Booth Av	65	G 10	Burnside Av	56	K 3	Castleton Pk S	57	O 1
Belair Rd	60	O 4	Borman Av	59	J 5	Burton Av	64	E 11	Castor Pl	62	F 9
Belfast Av	63	L 7	Borough Pl	57	O 1	Burton Ct	59	K 6			
Belfield Av	62	F 9	Boscombe Av	64	C 10	Bush Av	55	H 2			
Bell St	60	O 4	Bosworth St	56	L 3	Butler Av	64	B 11			
Bellhaven Pl	59	J 4	Boulder St	62	F 9	Butler Blvd	64	D 12			
Belmar Dr E	59	J 6									
Belmar Dr W	59	J 6									

STREET	MAP	GRID
Caswell Av	56	J 3
Caswell La	55	H 3
Catharine Ct	56	K 2
Catherine Pl	55	G 1
Catherine St	56	K 2
Catlin Av	57	N 2
Cattaragus St	60	M 4
Cayuga Av	60	M 4
Cebra Av	57	N 2
Cedar Av	60	O 5
Cedar Grove Av	63	L 9
Cedar Grove Beach Pl	63	M 8
Cedar Grove Ct	63	M 8
Cedar St	57	O 3
Cedar Ter	60	N 4
Cedarcliff Rd	57	N 3
Cedarview Av	63	K 7
Cedarwood Ct	55	H 3
Celina La	64	C 12
Celtic Pl	63	M 8
Center Av	57	N 3
Center Pl	63	M 8
Center St	62	J 7
Central Av	57	O 1
Challenger Dr *(off Ladd Av)	62	H 8
Champ Ct	64	D 11
Champlain Av	63	K 8
Chandler Av	59	K 4
Chapin Av	60	M 5
Chappell St	56	L 2
Charles Av	56	K 2
Charles Ct	59	K 6
Charles Pl	56	J 2
Charleston Av	61	E 8
Charter Oaks Rd	60	M 6
Chelsea Rd	58	G 4
Chelsea St	64	C 12
Chemical La	61	D 8
Cherokee St	63	N 7
Cherry Pl	59	K 5
Cherrywood Ct	62	J 8
Cheryl Av	62	G 8
Chesebrough St	62	H 9
Cheshire Pl	57	M 3
Chester Av	65	G 11
Chester Pl	57	N 2
Chesterton Av	63	K 8
Chestnut Av	57	O 3
Chestnut Cir	62	F 8
Chestnut St	57	N 3
Cheves Av	56	K 3
Chicago Av	60	O 5
Chisholm St	65	F 10
Christ St	60	N 5
Christine Ct	65	G 10
Christopher La	56	J 3
Christopher St	55	H 2
Church Av	58	G 5
Church Ct	58	G 5
Church La	60	O 4
Church St	56	K 1
Churchill Av	64	D 10
Circle Loop	60	O 4
Circle Rd	60	M 5
City Blvd	57	M 2
Claire Ct	57	N 3
Claradon La	60	O 5
Clarence Pl	63	L 8
Clark La	57	N 2
Clark Pl	56	K 3
Clarke Av	62	J 7
Clawson St	63	L 7
Clayboard St	63	M 8
Claypit Rd	61	D 9
Clayton St	60	P 4
Clearmont Av	64	E 10
Clermont Av	64	B 12
Clermont Av	64	D 12
Clermont Pl	59	K 4
Cletus St	60	M 6
Cleveland Av	62	J 9
Cleveland Pl	60	O 5
Cleveland St	57	N 1
Cliff Ct *(connects Cliff St and Nautilus St)	60	P 4
Cliff St	60	P 4
Cliffside Av	60	N 4
Clifton Av	60	O 4
Clifton St	58	H 4
Clinton Av	57	M 1
Clinton B Fiske Av	56	K 3
Clinton Ct	57	M 2
Clinton Pl	56	K 2
Clinton Rd	62	J 9
Clinton St	57	O 2
Cloister Pl	63	L 7
Clove Lake Pl	56	L 2
Clove Rd	56	L 2
Cloverdale Av	62	J 9
Clovis Rd	62	J 9
Clyde Pl	57	N 2
Coale Av	59	K 4
Coddington Av	63	L 7
Cody Pl	62	F 8
Cole St	64	D 11
Colfax Av	60	M 6
Colgate Pl	63	L 7
College Av	56	K 3
College Pl	60	M 5
Collfield Av	56	J 3
Collyer Av	65	G 10
Colon Av	65	G 10
Colon St	65	G 10
Colonial Av	59	J 5
Colonial Av	59	K 5
Colonial Ct	56	L 3
Colony St	63	N 7
Colorado St *(connects Kingsley Av and College Av)	56	L 3
Colton St	60	O 4
Columbia Av	60	O 5
Columbus Av	60	N 5
Columbus Pl	56	K 3
Combs Av	63	K 7
Comely St	65	G 10
Commerce St	58	H 4
Commodore Dr	64	E 11
Comstock Av	55	H 3
Concord La	60	M 5
Concord Pl	60	N 4
Confederation Pl	55	H 2
Conger St	60	P 5
Congress Av	57	O 2
Conklin Av	56	J 2
Connecticut St	64	B 12
Connor Av	63	K 7
Connors Av	59	L 6
Constant Av	56	K 3
Continental Pl	55	H 2
Convent Av	61	E 9
Conyingham Av	57	M 2
Cooke St	55	H 3
Coonley Av	56	J 2
Coonley Ct	55	H 2
Cooper Av	60	N 5
Cooper Pl	65	F 11
Cooper Ter	58	H 5
Copley St	59	J 6
Copperflagg La	60	M 6
Copperleaf Ter	60	M 6
Corbin Av	62	J 8
Cordelia Av	64	E 11
Cordes Av	64	E 11
Cornelia Av	65	F 10
Cornelia St	60	N 5
Cornell Av	56	L 2
Cornell Pl	60	N 4
Cornell St	56	K 2
Cornish St	62	J 9
Cornwall Av	60	M 5
Corona Av	63	K 8
Correll Av	61	E 9
Corson Av	57	N 2
Cortelyou Av	62	H 8
Cortelyou Pl	57	N 1
Cortlandt St	56	K 2
Cottage Av	62	J 9
Cottage Pl	56	K 2
Cotter Av	63	K 8
Cottonwood Ct	62	J 8
Coughlan Av	56	L 3
Country Dr E	58	H 5
Country Dr S	58	H 6
Country Dr W	58	H 6
Country La	62	F 8
Country Woods La	62	J 8
Coursen Ct	57	O 3
Coursen Pl	57	O 3
Court Pl *(bet Richmond Hill & Arthur Kill Rds, conn Richmond Rd to Center St)	62	J 7
Court St	57	O 3
Coventry Loop	62	F 9
Coventry Rd	60	M 6
Coverly Av	60	M 4
Coverly Av N *(off Coverly Av)	60	M 4
Coverly St	63	L 7
Cowen Pl	55	H 2
Crabbs La	58	F 5
Crabtree Av	61	D 9
Crafton Av	59	K 4
Craig Av	64	B 12
Crane Ter	64	E 11
Cranford Av	63	K 7
Cranford Ct	63	K 7
Cranford St	63	K 9
Crescent Av	57	N 1
Crest Loop	65	J 10
Creston Pl	57	N 2
Creston St	64	E 11
Crittenden Pl	56	K 2
Croak Av	59	L 4
Crocheron Av	59	J 4
Crocker Ct	62	F 8
Croft Ct	63	K 8
Croft Pl	58	H 4
Cromer St	62	J 8
Cromwell Av	60	M 5
Cromwell Cir	60	M 6
Cross St	57	O 3
Crossfield Av	62	G 8
Crosshill St	57	M 3
Croton Av	57	M 3
Crowell Av	56	K 3
Crown Av	62	G 9
Crown Pl	62	F 9
Crystal Av	56	K 3
Cuba Av	63	M 8
Cubberly Pl	63	L 7
Cunard Av	60	N 4
Cunard Pl	60	N 4
Cunningham Rd	64	D 11
Currie Av	63	K 8
Curtis Av	56	L 3
Curtis Ct	57	M 2
Curtis Pl	57	N 1
Cypress Av	60	M 4
Cypress Loop	61	E 8

D

D St	59	J 5
Daffodil Ct	62	F 8
Daffodil La	58	H 6
Dahlia St	62	F 9
Daisy Way	59	K 6
Dakota Pl	56	K 3
Dale Av	63	L 7
Daleham St	62	J 8
Dalemere Rd	60	M 5
Dallas St	56	L 3
Dalton Av	63	K 7
Damon St	64	D 11
Dana St	57	M 2
Daniel Low Ter	57	N 1
Darcey Av	59	J 4
Darien St	60	N 4
Darlington Av	64	E 10
David Pl	56	J 2
David St	63	J 10
Davidson Ct	55	H 2
Davidson St	55	H 2
Davis Av	57	M 1
Davis Ct	57	M 1
Dawson Cir	58	H 4
Dawson Ct	58	H 4
Dawson Pl	60	N 5
Dawson St	59	K 4
Dayna Dr	60	O 4
Deal Ct	60	O 4
Debbie St	59	J 4
Decatur Av	59	J 4
Decker Av	56	K 3
Deems Av	56	K 3
Deere Park Pl	60	M 4
De Groot Pl	56	L 2
De Hart Av	56	J 2
Deisius St	65	F 10
De Kalb St	60	N 4
De Kay St	57	M 2
Delafield Av	56	L 2
Delafield Pl	56	L 1
De Laine Pl	55	H 3

STREET	MAP	GRID
Delaware Av	60	N 5
Delaware Pl	56	L 3
Delaware St	60	M 5
Delford St	57	N 3
Dellwood Rd	60	N 5
Delmar Av	62	F 9
Delmore St	56	K 3
Delphine Ter	60	O 5
Demopolis Av	62	H 9
Demorest Av	56	K 3
Denise Ct	65	G 10
Denker Pl	59	J 6
Dennis Toricelli		
St	60	P 4
DeNoble La	60	M 4
Dent Rd	62	J 9
Denton Pl	59	J 4
Depew Pl	64	E 10
Deppe Pl	56	J 3
Derby Ct	56	K 2
Dermody Pl	59	K 6
De Ruyter Pl	56	J 2
Deserre Av	62	F 9
Detroit Av	62	G 9
Devens St	56	J 3
Devine St	60	N 5
Devon Loop	58	H 6
Devon Pl	57	M 2
Dewey Av	62	J 8
Dewey Pl	62	J 8
Dewhurst St	59	K 5
Diana Tr	60	N 4
Diaz St	60	O 5
Dickie Av	56	K 3
Dierauf St	62	G 8
Di Marco Pl	63	L 7
Dina Ct	63	K 8
Dinsmore St	58	H 4
Di Renzo Ct	65	F 11
Dissoway Pl	56	L 2
Ditson St	57	O 3
Divine St	60	N 5
Division St	59	J 4
Dix Pl	57	O 3
Dixon Av	56	J 2
Dixwell Av	65	G 11
Doane Av	62	J 8
Dobbs Pl	60	M 4
Dock Rd	58	H 6
Dock St	57	O 3
Doe Ct	58	H 5
Doe Pl	56	L 2
Dogwood Av	60	O 6
Dogwood Dr	62	F 9
Dogwood La	60	O 5
Dole St	65	H 11
Dolson Pl	58	H 2
Domain St	55	H 3
Donald Pl	57	M 1
Dongan Av	59	L 4
Dongan Hills		
Av	60	M 6
Dongan St	56	L 2
Donley Av	60	O 4
Donna Ct	58	H 6
Dora St	59	K 4
Dore Ct	58	H 5
Doreen Dr	55	H 3
Dorothea Pl	63	L 7
Dorothy St	59	K 5
Dorval Av	62	G 8
Dorval Pl	62	G 8
Doty Av	60	P 5
Douglas Av	56	L 3
Douglas Rd	60	N 4
Dover Green	62	F 8
Downes Av	65	G 10
Downey Pl	55	H 2
Dr Martin Luther		
King Jr		
Expwy	56	J 3
Drake Av	56	L 3
Draper Pl	58	H 5
Dresden Pl	59	L 4
Dreyer Av	59	J 4
Driggs St	65	J 10
Driprock St	56	K 2
Drumgoole Rd	62	G 9
Drumgoole Rd		
E	64	E 10
Drumgoole Rd		
W	64	E 10
Drury Av	60	P 5
Dryden Ct	56	K 2
Drysdale St	59	K 5
Duane Ct	57	N 2
Dublin Pl	55	H 2
Dubois Av	56	K 2
Dudley Av	60	M 4
Duer Av	60	P 5
Duer La	57	N 2
Dugdale St	63	L 8
Duke Pl	59	K 4
Dumont Av	60	N 5
Dunbar St	62	J 8
Duncan Rd	57	N 3
Duncan St	60	M 5
Dunham St	64	E 10
Durant Av	63	K 8
Durgess St	60	N 5
Dutchess Av	60	M 5
Dwarf St	55	H 2
Dyson St	57	O 2
E		
Eadie Pl	57	N 1
Eagan Av	65	H 10
Eagle Rd	56	J 3
Earle Av	56	K 3
Earley Pl	64	B 11
East Albourne		
Av	65	F 10
East Ashland		
Av	65	F 10
East Augusta		
Av	62	H 9
East Brandis		
Av	62	H 8
East Broadway	63	K 7
East Buchanan		
St	57	N 1
East Figurea		
Av	62	H 9
East Gurley Av	62	H 8
East Loop Rd	60	M 6
East Macon Av	62	H 8
East Raleigh		
Av	56	L 2
East Reading		
Av	62	H 8
East Scranton		
Av	62	H 8
East Stroud Av	62	H 8
East Tenafly		
Av	65	G 10
Eastentry Rd	60	M 6
Eastman St	65	H 10
Eaton Pl	56	J 2
Ebbitts St	63	M 8
Ebey La	62	F 9
Ebony St	63	L 7
Echo Pl	56	J 3
Eddy St	57	N 3
Edgar Pl	60	N 4
Edgar Ter	57	N 2
Edgegrove Av	65	F 10
Edgewater St	57	O 3
Edgewood Rd	62	J 9
Edinboro Rd	62	J 7
Edison St	63	L 7
Edith Av	65	G 11
Edna Pl	55	H 3
Edstone Dr	57	M 3
Edward Ct	59	J 6
Edward Curry		
Av	58	G 4
Edwin St	65	G 10
Egan Av	59	L 4
Egbert Av	56	L 3
Egbert Av	56	K 3
Egbert Pl	60	P 4
Egbert Sq	56	J 3
Egmont Pl	57	N 1
Elaine Ct	60	M 5
Elbe Av	60	N 4
Elder Av	64	E 11
Eldridge Av	56	K 3
Eleanor La	62	J 9
Eleanor Pl	56	J 3
Eleanor St	59	K 6
Elias Pl	56	K 3
Elie Ct	58	H 6
Elise Ct	63	K 8
Elizabeth Av	56	L 1
Elizabeth St	24	C 11
Elizabeth Grove		
Rd	55	H 2
Elizabeth Pl	65	F 11
Elizabeth St	56	L 2
Elk Ct	63	K 8
Elkhart St	62	J 8
Elks Pl	61	E 9
Ella Pl	63	L 8
Ellicott Pl	57	M 2
Ellington St	60	N 4
Ellis Pl	61	C 9
Ellis St	64	B 11
Ellsworth Av	62	F 9
Ellsworth Pl	59	L 4
Elm Av	65	G 11
Elm Pl	60	M 4
Elm St	56	L 1
Elma Av	60	O 5
Elmbank St	65	H 10
Elmhurst Av	59	L 5
Elmira Av	56	K 3
Elmira St	63	L 8
Elmtree Av	63	M 7
Elmwood Av	62	J 9
Elmwood Park		
Dr	58	H 6
Elson St	55	H 3
Elson St	55	H 3
Eltinge St	60	N 5
Eltingville Blvd	62	H 9
Elverton Av	62	J 8
Elvin St	59	L 4
Elwood Av	58	H 5
Elwood Pl	57	M 2
Ely Av	65	G 10
Ely St	57	N 2
Emeric Ct	56	J 2
Emerson Av	60	M 4
Emerson Ct	60	M 4
Emerson Dr	60	N 4
Emily La	62	G 8
Emmet Av	63	K 8
End Pl	62	G 8
Endor Av	60	M 4
Endview St	62	G 9
Enfield Pl	63	L 7
Engert St	61	E 8
Englewood Av	64	D 10
Erastina Pl	56	J 2
Eric La	62	J 8
Erie St	64	E 10
Errington Pl	57	O 3
Escanaba Av	62	H 9
Esmac Ct	60	M 5
Essex Dr	59	J 6
Esther Depew		
St	59	K 6
Eton Pl	58	H 4
Eugene Pl	65	G 10
Eugene St	64	D 11
Eunice Pl	56	J 3
Eva Av	63	M 8
Evan Pl	62	G 8
Evans St	59	J 6
Evelyn Pl	60	P 4
Everett Pl	64	E 11
Evergreen Av	60	N 5
Evergreen St	62	J 8
Everton Av	62	F 9
Excelsior Av	64	E 11
Exeter St	62	J 8
Eylandt St	65	F 11
Eylandt St	65	H 10
F		
Faber St	56	K 2
Fabian St	62	G 9
Fahy Av	55	H 3
Fairbanks Av	63	K 8
Fairfield St	62	J 8
Fairlawn Av	63	K 9
Fairview Av	56	L 3
Fairview Pl	60	M 6
Fairway Av	57	O 3
Fairway Dr	57	M 3
Falcon Av	63	L 8
Fancher Pl	55	H 1
Fanning St	59	L 4
Farraday St	56	J 3
Farragut Av	55	H 3
Father		
Capodanno		
Blvd	63	N 7
Fawn La	62	J 8
Fayette Av	60	N 5
Federal Pl	55	H 1
Feldmeyers La	58	F 5
Felton St	55	H 3
Fenway Cir	62	H 8
Fern Av	62	H 9
Ferndale Av	58	H 5
Ferndale Ct	59	J 5
Ferry St	56	K 1
Ficarelle Dr	64	E 11
Fiedler Av	57	N 2
Field St	59	K 5
Fields Av	59	K 5
Fieldstone Rd	55	H 3
Fieldway Av	62	J 9
Figurea Av	62	H 9

STREET	MAP	GRID
Filbert Av	60	N 6
Filer St	62	G 9
Filipe La	65	J 10
Fillat St	59	K 4
Fillmore Av	59	K 4
Fillmore Pl	60	O 4
Fillmore St	57	M 1
Fine Blvd	59	L 4
Fingal St	65	H 10
Fingerboard Rd	60	O 5
Finlay Av	64	E 11
Finlay St	64	B 12
Finley Av	63	M 8
Firth Rd	58	H 4
Fisher Av	64	C 11
Fisk Pl	59	J 4
Fiske Av	56	K 3
Fitzgerald Av	65	J 10
Flagg Ct	60	M 6
Flagg Pl	60	M 6
Flagship Cir	64	E 11
Fletcher St	60	O 4
Flint St	63	L 8
Florence Pl	64	E 11
Florence St	62	J 9
Florida Av	60	P 5
Florida Ter	59	K 6
Flower Av	64	D 12
Floyd St	56	K 2
Foch Av	60	O 5
Fonda Pl	64	E 10
Foote Av	60	M 4
Ford Pl	56	L 2
Fordel St	60	O 4
Forest Av	55	H 2
Forest Ct	55	H 2
Forest Green	62	F 8
Forest Hill Rd	59	K 4
Forest Rd	60	M 5
Forest St	58	H 4
Fornes Pl	65	G 10
Forrestal Av	62	G 8
Forrestal Ct	62	G 8
Fort Hill Cir	57	N 1
Fort Hill Park	57	N 1
Fort Pl	57	O 1
Foster Av	59	L 5
Foster Rd	61	E 9
Four Corners Rd	60	M 5
Fox Hill Ter	60	O 4
Fox Hunt Ct	57	M 3
Fox La	63	L 9
Foxbeach Av	63	L 9
Foxholm St	63	L 7
Francesca La	55	H 3
Francine Ct	63	L 7
Francine La	59	J 4
Francis Pl	60	M 5
Franklin Av	57	N 1
Franklin D Roosevelt Boardwalk	60	O 7
Franklin La	62	J 7
Franklin Pl	59	L 4
Fraser Av	62	F 8
Fraser St	59	J 6
Frean St	57	N 3
Frede St *(bet. Felton St and Elson St, Connects Gauldy Av and Caswell Av)	55	H 3

STREET	MAP	GRID
Frederick St	59	K 4
Freeborn St	63	N 7
Freedom Av	58	H 5
Freeman Pl	56	L 3
Fremont Av	60	M 6
Fremont St	57	N 2
Front St	57	O 2
Fuller Ct	63	K 8
Fulton St	57	N 3
Furman St	65	G 10
Furness Pl	59	J 6
Futurity Pl	62	G 8
G		
Gadsen Pl	58	H 5
Gail Ct	63	L 7
Gales La	56	K 1
Galesville Ct	60	P 5
Gall Ct	60	N 5
Galloway Av	56	K 3
Gannon Av	59	J 4
Gansevoort Blvd	59	K 4
Garden Ct	60	M 5
Garden St	59	L 4
Gardenia La	58	H 6
Garfield Av	60	O 4
Garibaldi Av	63	M 8
Garretson Av	60	M 6
Garrison Av	56	K 3
Garth Ct	63	K 8
Gary Ct	58	H 4
Gary Pl	58	H 5
Gateway Dr	60	N 5
Gauldy Av	55	H 3
Gaynor St	64	D 10
Geissel Pl	55	H 2
Geldner Av	63	L 7
Genesee Av	62	G 9
Genesee St	60	M 4
George La	64	E 11
George St	64	C 12
Gervil St	61	E 9
Getz Av	62	H 8
Geyser Dr	62	F 9
Gibson Av	62	J 8
Gibson Pl	62	J 8
Giegerich Pl	64	C 12
Giffords Glen	62	J 9
Giffords La	62	J 8
Gigi St	56	J 2
Gil Ct	62	H 9
Gilbert Pl	64	E 11
Gilbert St	63	K 7
Giles Pl	60	N 4
Gill Pl	57	M 2
Gillard Av	62	H 9
Gilroy St	62	F 9
Gina Ct	59	J 6
Giordan Ct	56	J 2
Girard St	64	B 11
Gladwin Av	61	D 9
Glascoe Av	56	K 3
Glen Av	57	N 2
Glen Rd	59	J 4
Glen St	58	G 4
Glendale Av	60	N 5
Glenwood Av	60	M 4
Glenwood Pl	56	L 3
Globe Av	55	J 3
Glover St	65	J 10
Goethals Rd N	55	G 2

STREET	MAP	GRID
Goff Av	64	E 10
Gold Av	62	G 8
Golf View Ct	59	J 6
Goller Pl	58	H 4
Goodall St	65	J 10
Goodell Av	59	L 4
Goodrich St	55	H 2
Goodwin Av	56	K 3
Gordon Pl	57	M 1
Gordon St	57	N 3
Gothic Pl	62	H 8
Governor Rd	59	L 4
Gower St	59	L 4
Grace Ct	57	M 1
Grace Rd	63	L 7
Grafe St	61	E 8
Graham Av	58	H 4
Graham Blvd	63	N 7
Grand Av	57	M 3
Grandview Av	55	H 1
Grandview Ter	62	J 9
Granite Av	56	J 2
Grant Pl	63	M 7
Grant St	57	O 2
Grantwood Av	62	G 8
Grasmere Av	60	N 4
Grasmere Dr	60	O 4
Grattan Av	63	K 9
Graves St	59	K 4
Gray St	57	O 3
Grayson St	63	L 8
Great Kills La	63	M 9
Great Kills Rd	62	J 9
Greaves Av	62	J 8
Greaves Ct *(connects Exeter St and Greaves Av)	62	J 8
Greeley Av	59	L 6
Green St	57	M 2
Green Valley Rd	62	F 9
Greencroft Av	63	K 9
Greencroft La	63	K 9
Greenfield Av	57	O 3
Greenfield Ct	57	O 3
Greenleaf Av	56	L 3
Greenport St	60	M 5
Greentree La	58	H 4
Greenway Dr	57	M 3
Greenwood Av	57	M 2
Gregg Pl	57	M 2
Gregory La	58	H 6
Greta Pl	57	N 3
Gridley Av	55	H 2
Grille Ct	61	D 9
Grimsby St	63	N 7
Grissom Av	58	H 5
Griswold Ct	57	M 3
Groton St	65	J 10
Grove Av	56	K 2
Grove Pl	56	K 2
Grove St	57	O 3
Grymes Hill Rd	57	N 3
Guilford St	60	P 5
Guillard Av	62	H 9
Gulf Av	55	G 3
Gulf Av	59	K 5
Gunton Pl	61	E 8
Gurdon St	59	K 4
Gurley Av	62	H 8
Guyon Av	63	K 8

STREET	MAP	GRID
H		
Hafstrom St	63	K 8
Hagaman Pl	56	K 2
Hale St	64	C 11
Hales Av	65	H 10
Hallister St	64	E 10
Halpin Av	62	G 9
Hamden Av	60	M 6
Hamilton Av	57	N 1
Hamilton St	60	N 4
Hamlin Pl	56	K 3
Hammock La	62	F 9
Hampton Green	62	F 8
Hampton Pl	61	E 8
Hancock St	60	N 6
Hank Pl	65	F 11
Hannah St	57	O 2
Hanover Av	65	F 11
Hanover Av	60	N 4
Harbor La	56	J 2
Harbor Rd	55	H 2
Harbor View Ct	57	N 2
Harbor View Pl E	60	P 4
Harbor View Pl N	60	P 4
Harbor View Pl S	60	P 4
Harbour Ct	65	J 10
Hardin Av	56	L 3
Hardy Pl	62	J 9
Hardy St	57	N 3
Harold Av	65	H 10
Harold St	59	K 5
Harris Av	59	K 4
Harris La	61	E 9
Harrison Av	56	K 2
Harrison Pl	56	L 1
Harrison St	57	O 3
Hart Av	57	M 2
Hart Blvd	57	M 2
Hart Loop	63	K 8
Hart Pl	64	C 11
Hartford Av	57	M 3
Hartford St	62	J 9
Harvard Av	57	N 1
Harvest Av	56	L 3
Harvey Av	59	K 4
Harvey St	60	O 4
Hasbrouck Hill Rd	60	N 5
Hastings St	60	O 5
Hatfield Pl	56	K 2
Haughwout Av	56	K 2
Haven Av	60	M 6
Haven Esplanade	57	N 2
Havenwood Rd	57	N 2
Haverford Av	58	H 6
Hawley Av	65	F 10
Hawthorne Av	56	J 3
Hay St	60	N 4
Haynes St	65	F 10
Haywood St	64	C 11
Hazel Pl	56	J 3
Heaney Av	55	H 2
Heberton Av	56	K 2
Hecker St	64	C 11
Heenan Av	62	G 9
Heffernan St	62	G 8
Heinz Av	65	J 10
Helena Av	60	M 5

STREET	MAP	GRID	STREET	MAP	GRID	STREET	MAP	GRID	STREET	MAP	GRID
Helene Ct	64	E 10	Howard Av	60	M 4	Jacobs St	64	C 11	Kenneth Pl	64	E 11
Helios Pl	61	E 9	Howard Cir	57	N 3	Jacques Av	63	L 7	Kennington St	62	J 8
Hemlock Ct	61	E 8	Howard Ct	56	L 1	Jaffe St	56	J 3	Kenny Rd	64	D 11
Hemlock St	61	E 9	Howe St	56	L 3	Jaime La	62	G 8	Kensico St	63	K 7
Hempstead Av	63	N 7	Howton Av	62	J 8	James Ct	56	J 3	Kensington Av	60	O 5
Henderson Av	56	L 2	Hoyt Av	57	M 2	James Pl	60	O 4	Kent Av	59	L 5
Hendricks Av	57	N 2	Hudson Pl	56	J 2	Jansen Ct	65	G 10	Kent St	59	K 6
Henning St	59	L 4	Hudson St	57	O 3	Jansen St	65	H 10	Kenwood Av	65	G 11
Henry Pl	60	N 6	Huguenot Av	62	F 8	Jardine Av	58	H 4	Keppel Av	64	C 12
Herbert St	65	F 11	Huguenot Av	65	G 10	Jarvis Av	65	G 11	Kermit Av	60	N 5
Hereford St	62	J 8	Hull Av	60	M 6	Jasper St	59	K 5	Kerry La	64	C 12
Herkimer St	57	M 3	Humbert St	60	O 5	Jean Pl	55	H 3	Keune Ct	60	M 5
Hervey St	61	E 8	Humbolt St (now			Jeanette Av	62	G 9	King St	65	J 10
Hett Av	63	M 8	Raily St)	62	F 8	Jefferson Av	60	M 6	Kingdom Av	65	G 10
Heusden St	56	J 2	Hunt La	60	M 5	Jefferson Blvd	62	G 9	Kinghorn St	65	H 10
Hewitt Av	60	M 4	Hunter Av	60	M 6	Jefferson St	60	M 6	Kingsbridge Av	55	H 3
Hickory Av	60	O 5	Hunter Pl	57	M 2	Jeffrey Pl	64	C 11	Kingsland St	65	F 11
Hickory Cir	62	F 8	Hunter St	60	N 5	Jennifer La	63	M 8	Kingsley Av	56	K 3
Hickory Ct	61	E 8	Hunton St	60	N 5	Jennifer Pl	58	H 4	Kingsley Pl	57	N 2
High Point Rd	60	M 5	Hurlbert St	60	N 6	Jerome Av	60	O 5	Kinsey Pl	55	H 2
High St	60	P 4	Huron Pl	57	M 2	Jerome Rd	60	N 5	Kirby Ct	57	N 1
Highland Av	57	M 3	Hurst St	56	K 2	Jersey St	57	N 1	Kirshon Av	55	H 3
Highland La	65	J 10	Husson St	60	M 6	Jewett Av	56	K 2	Kissam Av	63	L 8
Highland Rd	62	J 9	Hyatt St	57	O 1	Jillian Ct	56	K 3	Kissel Av	57	M 2
Highmount Rd	62	J 9	Hygeia Pl	57	O 3	Joan Pl	56	K 2	Kiswick St	63	M 7
Highview Av	57	N 1	Hylan Blvd	64	B 12	Joel Pl	63	K 7	Klondike Av	58	H 5
Hill St	57	O 3	Hylan Pl	63	M 7	Johanna La	65	F 11	Knapp St	58	H 5
Hillbrook Ct	60	O 4				John St	56	K 2	Knauth Pl	60	O 5
Hillbrook Dr	60	O 5	**I**			Johnson Av	64	B 11	Knesel St	61	E 8
Hillcrest Av	62	J 9				Johnson Pl	60	N 5	Knollwood Ct	55	H 3
Hillcrest Ct	60	N 4	Ibsen Av	62	G 8	Johnson St	61	D 8	Knox Pl	59	L 4
Hillcrest Rd	57	N 3	Ida Ct	65	G 10	Johnston Ter	64	E 11	Knox St	65	F 11
Hillcrest St	65	J 10	Idaho Av	64	E 10	Joline Av	64	C 11	Koch Blvd	65	H 10
Hillcrest Ter	60	N 5	Idlease Pl	63	N 7	Joline La	64	C 12	Kraft Pl	65	G 10
Hilldale Ct	60	O 4	Ilion Pl	63	L 7	Jones Pl	57	M 2	Kramer Av	61	E 9
Hillis St	65	G 10	Ilyse Ct	63	K 8	Jones St	58	H 4	Kramer Pl	56	K 2
Hillman Av	58	H 4	Ilyssa Way	62	G 8	Joseph Av	59	K 5	Kramer St	60	O 5
Hillridge Ct	60	O 4	Ina St	63	M 8	Joseph La	60	O 5	Kreischer St	61	C 9
Hillside Av	57	N 3	Indale Av	64	E 11	Josephine St	59	L 4	Kruser St	63	L 7
Hillside Ter	62	J 9	Independence			Journeay Av	62	F 9	Kyle Ct	62	F 8
Hilltop Pl	62	J 9	Av	62	H 7	Journeay St	55	H 2			
Hilltop Rd	65	J 10	Industrial Loop			Joyce La	64	C 11	**L**		
Hilltop Ter	60	M 5	E	61	D 8	Joyce St	60	M 6			
Hillview La	60	M 5	Industrial Loop			Jules Dr	55	H 3	Labau Av	60	M 4
Hillview Pl	60	M 5	W	61	D 8	Julie Ct	59	K 4	Laconia Av	60	N 6
Hillwood Ct	60	O 4	Inez St	65	F 11	Jumel St	62	J 8	Ladd Av	62	G 8
Hinton St	62	G 8	Ingram Av	59	K 4	Juni Ct	59	J 6	Lafayette Av	57	M 1
Hitchcock Av	63	K 7	Innis St	56	J 2	Juniper Pl	60	M 6	Lafayette St	64	B 11
Hoda Pl	65	G 10	Interstate Hwy			Jupiter La	55	H 2	LaForge Av	56	K 2
Hodges Pl	59	L 4	278	55	F 2	Justin Av	63	K 8	LaForge Pl	56	K 2
Holbernt Ct	56	K 2	Interstate Hwy						LaGrange Pl	56	K 2
Holcomb Av	62	F 9	278	60	N 4	**K**			LaGuardia Av	59	L 4
Holden Blvd	59	K 4	Inwood Rd	60	N 4				Lake Av	56	J 2
Holdridge Av	65	H 10	Iona St	63	N 7	Kaltenmeier La	60	O 4	Lakeland Rd	56	L 3
Holgate St	59	J 4	Ionia Av	65	F 10	Kalver Pl	56	J 2	Lakeside Pl	60	O 5
Holiday Dr	56	J 3	Iowa Pl	59	K 4	Karen Ct	56	K 3	Lakeview Ter	60	N 5
Holiday Way	56	J 3	Irma Pl	57	M 3	Katan Av	62	H 9	Lakewood Rd	57	M 3
Holland Av	55	H 1	Iron Mine Dr	60	M 6	Katan Loop	62	J 9	Lamberst La	55	G 3
Holly Av	62	J 9	Ironwood St	62	J 8	Kathleen Ct	64	C 12	Lambert St	55	H 3
Holly Pl	63	L 7	Iroquois St	63	N 7	Kathy Pl	58	H 6	Lamberts La	55	H 3
Holly St	60	N 5	Irving Pl	57	N 3	Kay Pl *(off			Lamoka Av	62	H 9
Holsman Rd	60	N 4	Irvington St	65	G 11	Maryland Av)	60	O 4	Lamont Av	64	E 10
Holton Av	65	F 11	Isabella Av	63	L 8	Keating Pl	59	J 5	Lamped Loop	58	H 6
Home Av	60	P 4	Isernia Av	63	M 8	Keating St	65	F 11	Lamport Blvd	60	O 5
Home Pl	56	J 3	Islin St	56	K 2	Keats St	62	J 9	Lander Av	55	H 3
Homer St	57	O 2	Islington St	62	J 8	Keegans La	63	K 9	Landis Av	60	O 5
Homestead Av	56	K 2	Ismay St	50	K 5	Keeley St	60	P 4	Langere Pl	57	O 3
Hooker Pl	56	J 2	Isora Pl	63	L 8	Keiber Ct	56	K 3	Lansing St	60	O 6
Hooper Av	63	K 8	Ivy Ct	61	E 9	Kell Av	59	K 4	Larch Ct	61	E 8
Hope Av	60	O 4				Keller Av	65	F 10	Laredo Av	62	H 9
Hopkins Av	63	K 8	**J**			Kelly Blvd	63	K 8	Larkin St	56	K 1
Hopping Av	64	B 11				Kelvin Av	63	K 8	LaSalle St	56	J 2
Houseman Av	56	J 2	Jackson Av	60	O 5	Kemball Av	59	K 4	Latham Pl	61	E 9
Houston St	56	J 3	Jackson St	57	O 2	Kenmore St	62	G 8	Lathrop Av	56	K 3

STREET	MAP	GRID	STREET	MAP	GRID	STREET	MAP	GRID	STREET	MAP	GRID
Latimer Av	58	G 5	Lockwood Pl	56	K 3	Mallard La	64	E 10	Maryland Av	60	O 4
Latourette St	64	E 11	Locust Av	63	L 7	Mallory Av	60	O 5	Maryland La *(off		
Laurel Av	57	N 3	Locust Ct	61	E 9	Mallow St	61	E 9	Maryland Av)	60	O 4
Lava St	60	O 6	Locust Pl	62	J 9	Malone Av	63	K 8	Maryland Pl *(off		
Law Pl	56	L 3	Logan Av	60	M 4	Malvine Av	61	E 9	College Av)	56	L 3
Lawn Av	63	K 7	Lois Pl	57	M 2	Manchester Dr	62	F 9	Mason Av	63	M 7
Lawrence Av	57	M 2	Lola St *(off			Manee Av	64	E 11	Mason Blvd	61	E 9
Lawton Av	58	F 5	Quincy Av			Manhattan St	64	C 12	Mason St	60	N 5
Layton Av	57	N 1	opposite Pinto			Manila Av	63	M 8	Massachusetts		
Leason Pl	59	J 6	St)	63	N 7	Manila Pl	63	M 8	St	64	B 12
Ledyard Pl	60	N 5	Lombard Ct	62	F 8	Manley St	61	C 9	Mathews Av	57	M 3
Lee Av	64	C 11	London Ct	59	K 6	Mann Av	59	K 4	Maxim St *(now		
Leeds St	63	L 8	London Rd	59	K 6	Manor Ct	62	J 7	Court Pl)	63	K 7
Legate Av	62	G 8	Long Pond La	60	O 4	Manor Rd	56	L 3	Maxine La	56	J 3
Leggett Pl	58	H 4	Longdale St	55	H 3	Manorville Ct	60	O 5	Maxwell Av	65	G 11
Legion Pl	60	O 4	Longfellow Av	60	M 4	Mansion Av	63	K 9	May Av	55	H 3
Lehigh St	64	C 11	Longview Rd	60	N 4	Maple Av	56	K 1	Mayberry		
Leigh Av	55	H 3	Loret Ct	56	L 2	Maple Ct	62	F 8	Promenade	65	H 10
Lenevar Av	61	E 9	Loretto St	64	C 12	Maple Pkwy	56	J 2	Maybury Av	62	J 9
Lenhart St	64	C 11	Loring Av	62	G 8	Maple Ter	63	M 8	Maybury Ct	63	K 9
Lennon Ct	62	H 8	Lorraine Av	62	G 9	Mapleton Av	63	N 7	Mc Arthur Av	62	G 8
Lenore Ct	56	J 3	Lorraine Loop	61	E 9	Maplewood Av	63	K 7	Mc Baine Av	61	E 9
Lenzie St	65	H 10	Lortel Av	59	L 4	Maplewood Pl	63	M 7	Mc Clean Av	60	O 5
Leo St	56	J 3	Louis St	57	N 2	Marble St	59	K 4	Mc Cormack		
Leona St	58	H 4	Louise La	60	M 4	Marc St	56	J 3	Pl	60	N 5
Leonard Av	56	J 3	Louise St	65	G 10	Marcie La	63	K 9	Mc Cully Av	63	K 7
LeRoy St	58	G 5	Lovelace Av	62	H 8	Marcy Av	62	F 9	Mc Dermott		
Leslie Av	60	N 5	Lovell Av	59	J 5	Maretzek Ct	64	E 10	Av	60	N 6
Lester St	59	L 4	Lowell St	59	K 6	Margaret St	62	J 9	Mc Divitt Av	59	J 5
Leverett Av	62	H 8	Lower Sharrott			Margaretta Ct	56	K 3	Mc Donald St	59	K 5
Leverett Ct *(off			Rd *(near			Maria La	62	H 9	Mc Farland Av	60	O 5
Leverett Av bet			Sharrotts Rd)	61	D 9	Marianne St	56	K 3	Mc Gregor St	65	F 11
Miles Av and			Lucille Av	61	E 9	Marie Pl	60	N 5	Mc Kee Av	63	K 9
Greaves Av)	62	J 8	Ludlow St	62	G 9	Marie St	60	N 4	Mc Kinley Av	63	K 7
Levit Av	56	J 3	Ludwig La	55	H 3	Marine Dr	64	E 11	Mc Laughlin St	60	O 6
Levit Pl	56	J 3	Ludwig St	56	L 2	Marine Way	63	M 8	Mc Veigh Av	59	J 6
Lewiston St	59	J 6	Luigi Ct	63	L 7	Mariners La	56	J 2	Meade Loop	64	D 11
Lexa Pl	65	G 10	Luigi Pl	63	L 7	Marion Av	57	N 2	Meade St	64	D 11
Lexington Av	56	K 2	Luke Ct	62	J 8	Marion St	56	K 2	Meadow Av	60	N 4
Lexington La	62	J 8	Lukes Av	61	E 8	Marisa Cir	61	E 9	Meadow Ct	61	E 8
Leyden Av	55	H 2	Luna Cir	65	H 10	Mark St	60	N 5	Meadow La	62	J 8
Liberty Av	60	N 6	Lundi Ct	59	J 6	Market St	56	L 2	Meadow Pl	60	N 6
Lighthouse Av	63	K 7	Lundsten Av	61	D 9	Markham Ct			Medford Rd	60	M 5
Lightner Av	59	L 4	Lupton St	59	K 5	*(in Edwin			Medina St	63	L 8
Lilac Ct	55	H 2	Luten Av	65	F 10	Markham			Meeker St	59	K 6
Lillian Pl	65	J 10	Lyle Ct	63	K 8	Housing)	56	L 1	Meisner Av	59	K 6
Lily Pond Av	60	P 5	Lyman Av	60	P 4	Markham Dr			Melba St	59	L 4
Lincoln Av	63	M 7	Lynch St	65	G 11	*(in Edwin			Melhorn Rd	59	L 4
Lincoln Pl	60	O 4	Lyndale Av	62	H 9	Markham			Melissa St	56	J 3
Lincoln St	59	L 4	Lyndale La	62	H 9	Housing)	56	L 1	Melrose Av	57	M 3
Linda Av	60	P 5	Lynhurst Av	57	O 3	Markham La			Melrose Pl	62	J 9
Lindbergh Av	63	L 7	Lynn Ct	56	J 3	*(in Edwin			Melville St	65	F 11
Linden Av	65	G 11	Lynn St	63	L 8	Markham			Melvin Av	58	G 5
Linden Av	56	J 2	Lynnhaven Pl	56	L 3	Housing)	56	L 1	Melyn Pl	62	J 9
Linden Pl	60	P 4	Lyon Pl	56	J 3	Markham Pl	56	K 3	Memo St	65	F 11
Linden St	57	M 1				Markham Rd			Memphis Av	62	H 9
Lindenwood Pl	62	J 9	**M**			*(in Edwin			Mendelsohn St	60	O 4
Linton Pl	62	J 8				Markham			Mercer Pl	62	J 9
Linwood Av	60	O 5	Mace St	63	K 7	Housing)	56	L 1	Mercury La	59	J 6
Lion St	64	C 11	Mackay Av	58	F 6	Markham Walk			Meredith Av	58	F 4
Lipsett Av	65	G 10	Macon Av	62	G 8	*(in Edwin			Merkel Pl	63	L 9
Lisa La	62	F 9	Macormac Pl	55	H 2	Markham			Merle Pl	60	O 4
Lisa Pl	58	H 4	Mada Av	57	M 2	Housing)	56	L 1	Merrick Av	59	L 5
Lisbon Pl	60	M 6	Madera St	65	F 11	Marne Av	62	H 8	Merrill Av	58	H 4
Lisk Av	55	H 3	Madison Av	56	J 3	Marscher Pl	65	F 11	Merriman Av	56	L 3
Liss St	65	H 10	Madsen Av	64	C 11	Marsh Av	58	H 6	Merry Mount		
Little Clove Rd	60	M 4	Magnolia Av	60	N 6	Marshall Av	59	L 5	St	58	H 6
Littlefield Av	65	J 10	Maguire Av	61	E 9	Martha St	60	M 4	Mersereau Av	55	H 1
Livermore Av	56	K 3	MaGuire Ct	64	E 10	Martin Av	59	K 4	Metcalfe St	57	N 3
Livingston Av	59	K 4	Maiden La	64	C 11	Martineau St	55	H 1	Metropolitan		
Livingston Ct	57	M 1	Main St	64	B 11	Martling Av	56	L 3	Av	57	M 3
Llewellyn Pl	56	K 2	Maine Av	56	K 3	Marvin Rd	64	E 10	Meyer La	60	O 4
Lloyd St	56	L 3	Major Av	60	O 5	Marx St	59	L 4	Meyer La	60	O 4
Lockman Av	55	H 2	Malden Pl	63	L 8	Mary St	60	N 4	Michelle Ct	56	J 2

STREET	MAP	GRID
Michelle La	63	M 8
Middle Loop		
Rd	62	H 8
Midland Av	60	M 6
Midland Rd	62	J 9
Midway Pl	60	N 5
Milbank Rd	63	M 8
Milburn Av	63	L 7
Milburn St	63	L 7
Milden Av	60	M 4
Mildred Av	58	G 5
Miles Av	62	J 8
Milford Av	60	M 4
Milford Dr	60	M 4
Mill Rd	63	L 8
Miller St	56	L 3
Mills Av	60	O 5
Milton Av	63	M 8
Mimosa La	62	F 8
Minerva Pl	57	N 1
Miniturn Av	64	E 10
Minna St	60	N 5
Minthorne St	57	O 2
Minturn Av	64	E 10
Mobile Av	63	K 7
Moffett St	62	G 9
Mohn Pl	60	M 4
Monahan Av	59	J 5
Monroe Av	57	O 2
Monroe Pl	59	K 5
Monsey Pl	56	J 3
Montauk Pl	59	J 4
Montell St	56	K 2
Monterey Av	62	H 8
Montgomery Av	57	O 2
Monticello Ter	62	J 9
Montreal Av	63	K 8
Montvale Pl	62	J 9
Moody Pl	57	M 2
Moore St	63	K 7
Morani St	59	J 4
Moreland St	63	M 7
Morgan La	58	H 4
Morley Av	63	K 7
Morningstar		
Rd	56	J 2
Morris Pl	62	J 9
Morris St	61	E 8
Morrison Av	56	L 2
Morrow St	55	H 2
Morse Av	59	L 5
Morton St	63	K 7
Mosel Av	60	N 4
Mosel Loop	60	N 4
Mosely Av	65	G 10
Motley Av	59	L 4
Mott St	62	H 9
Mountainside		
Rd	60	N 5
Mountainview		
Av	59	L 4
Mulberry Av	58	H 5
Mulberry Cir	58	H 5
Muldoon Av	62	F 7
Muller Av	56	K 3
Mundy Av	56	K 3
Murdock Pl	56	J 2
Murray Hulbert		
Av	57	O 2
Murray Pl	57	N 3
Murray St	64	C 11
Myle St	64	C 10
Myrna La	62	F 9
Myrtle Av	56	L 2

N

STREET	MAP	GRID
Nadal Pl	58	H 4
Nadine St	63	K 7
Nahant St	62	J 8
Nancy Ct	62	J 8
Nancy La	64	C 12
Narrows Rd N	60	N 4
Narrows Rd S	60	N 4
Nash Ct	62	J 9
Nashville St	64	C 11
Nassau Pl	64	C 11
Nassau St	57	N 1
Natalie Pl	56	J 3
Nathan Ct	64	E 10
Natick St	63	K 7
Naughton Av	60	M 6
Nautilus Ct	60	P 4
Nautilus St	60	P 4
Navesink Pl	63	M 8
Neal Dow Av	56	K 3
Neckar Av	60	N 4
Nedra La	62	F 8
Nehring Av	58	H 6
Nelson Av	62	J 9
Neptune Pl	59	J 4
Neptune St	63	M 8
Nesmythe Ter	57	N 3
Netherlands		
Av	55	H 2
Neutral Av	63	M 8
Nevada Av	59	K 6
New Dorp La	63	L 7
New Dorp Plz	63	L 7
New La	60	P 4
New St	56	K 2
New York Pl	56	K 3
Newark Av	56	K 2
Newberry Av	60	N 5
Newfolden Pl	64	C 11
Newkirk Av	56	K 2
Newton St	65	G 11
Newvale Av	62	J 7
Niagara St	60	M 4
Nicholas Av	56	K 1
Nicholas St	57	N 1
Nicolosi Dr	65	G 11
Nicolosi Loop	65	G 11
Nightingale St	59	L 6
Niles Pl	59	K 5
Nina Av	59	J 4
Nippon Av	62	F 9
Nixon Av	57	O 2
Noble Pl	56	L 2
Noel St	65	H 10
Nolan Av	62	J 9
Nome Av	58	H 5
Norden St	60	M 5
Norma Pl	57	M 3
Normalee Rd	60	O 5
Norman Pl	65	F 11
North Av	56	K 3
North Bridge		
St	64	C 10
North Burgher		
Av	56	L 1
North Clove		
Rd	57	M 3
North Gannon		
Av	59	K 4
North Mada Av	57	M 2
North Pine Ter	65	G 10

STREET	MAP	GRID
North Railroad		
Av	60	N 6
North Railroad		
St	65	G 10
North Randall		
Av	57	M 2
North Rhett Av	62	J 9
North Saint		
Austin's Pl	57	M 2
North St	56	K 1
North St	56	L 1
North Tremont		
Av	56	J 3
Northcote Av	60	N 4
Northcote Pl		
*(near		
Northcote		
Av)	60	N 4
Northentry Rd	60	M 6
Northern Blvd	60	M 4
Northfield Av	55	H 2
Northfield Ct	55	H 1
Northport La	58	H 6
Norwalk Av	59	L 4
Norway Av	60	O 5
Norwich St	59	K 5
Norwood Av	57	O 3
Norwood Ct	57	N 3
Nostrand Av	58	H 4
Notre Dame		
Av	62	H 9
Notus Av	62	G 9
Nubro St	65	F 10
Nugent Av	63	N 7
Nugent St	63	K 7
Nunley Ct	60	N 4
Nutley Pl	57	M 3
Nutwood Ct	62	J 8

O

STREET	MAP	GRID
Oak Av	63	L 8
Oak Ct	62	J 9
Oak La	62	G 8
Oak St	60	O 4
Oakdale Av	60	M 5
Oakdale St	65	H 10
Oakland Av	56	L 2
Oakland Ter	57	N 3
Oakley Pl	63	L 7
Oakville St	59	K 5
Oakwood Av	57	M 2
Oban St	65	H 10
Oberlin St	60	O 5
Occident Av	57	N 2
Ocean Av	60	P 5
Ocean Drive		
Way	65	H 11
Ocean Rd	62	J 9
Ocean Ter	59	L 5
Oceanic Av	65	J 10
Oceanside Av	60	O 6
Oceanview Av	65	H 11
Oceanview Pl	62	J 9
O'Connor Av	59	K 4
Oder Av	60	N 4
Odin St	63	L 7
Ogden St	65	H 10
O'Gorman Av	63	K 8
Ohio Pl	56	K 3
Old Amboy Rd	62	H 9
Old Farmers		
La	60	M 5
Old Mill Rd	62	J 7

STREET	MAP	GRID
Old Mill Rd	63	L 8
Old Town Rd	60	N 5
Oldfield St	63	M 7
Olga Pl	60	O 4
Olive St	56	L 2
Oliver Av	64	E 10
Oliver Pl	58	H 4
Olympia Blvd	63	N 7
Omaha St	55	G 1
Oneida Av	60	M 4
Ontario Av	60	M 4
Opp Ct	62	H 8
Opp St	62	H 8
Orange Av	56	K 2
Orange St *(off		
Union Av)	56	J 2
Orchard La	65	H 10
Orchard St	62	G 9
Orchid La	58	H 6
Ordell Av	56	K 3
Oregon Rd	60	N 5
Orinoco Pl	56	J 2
Orlando St	60	O 6
Ormond Pl	57	O 3
Ormsby Av	65	F 11
Osage La	65	H 10
Osborn Av	62	J 9
Osborne St	65	H 10
Osgood Av	57	N 3
Oswald Pl	64	E 11
Oswego St	60	M 4
Otis Av	63	L 7
Otsego Av	60	M 4
Outerbridge Av	64	E 10
Oval, The	60	M 6
Ovas Ct	62	H 9
Overlook Av	60	M 5
Overlook Dr	60	N 4
Overlook Ter	60	O 5
Ovis Pl	63	K 8
Ox Ct	58	H 5
Oxford Pl	57	N 2
Oxholm Av	57	M 3

P

STREET	MAP	GRID
Pacific Av	62	H 9
Page Av	64	C 11
Palisade St	60	P 5
Palma Dr	60	N 4
Palmer Av	56	K 2
Pamela La	60	N 5
Pan St	64	C 11
Paradise Pl	64	C 12
Parish Av	58	F 5
Park Av	56	K 2
Park Ct	57	M 3
Park Dr N	58	H 5
Park Hill Av	57	O 3
Park Hill Cir	57	O 3
Park Hill Ct	57	O 3
Park Hill Dr *(off		
Park Hill Ct)	57	O 3
Park Hill La	57	O 3
Park La	57	N 3
Park Pl	57	N 1
Park Rd	65	H 10
Park St	63	K 7
Parker St	64	C 11
Parkinson Av	60	N 5
Parkview Loop	59	J 4
Parkview Pl	57	M 3
Parkwood Av	64	E 10
Parsons Pl	57	M 3

STREET	MAP	GRID	STREET	MAP	GRID	STREET	MAP	GRID	STREET	MAP	GRID
Patten St	64	B 11	Pommer Av	57	N 2	Raily St	62	F 8	Ridgefield Av	60	N 4
Patterson Av	63	N 7	Pompey Av	62	H 9	Rainbow Av	56	K 2	Ridgeway Av	58	G 5
Patty Ct	62	H 9	Pond Way	55	H 1	Raleigh Av	56	L 3	Ridgewood Av	62	H 8
Paulding Av	58	H 4	Pontiac St	56	K 3	Ralph Av	62	G 9	Ridgewood Pl	57	M 2
Pauw St	57	N 2	Poplar Av	61	E 8	Ralph Pl	60	N 4	Riedel Av	63	K 8
Pawling Av	65	F 10	Port Richmond			Ramapo Av	61	E 9	Riegelman St	56	K 3
Payne St	58	H 6	Av	56	K 2	Ramble Rd	62	J 9	Riga St	63	L 9
Pearl St	57	N 3	Portage Av	59	K 5	Ramblewood			Rigby St	62	J 7
Pearle Pl	65	H 10	Portland Pl	57	M 2	Av	62	J 9	Riley Pl	56	K 2
Pearsall St	60	O 6	Portsmouth Av	60	M 4	Ramona Av	64	E 10	Ring Rd	58	H 6
Pearson St	58	G 5	Post Av	56	K 2	Ramsey Pl	57	N 3	River Rd	58	F 4
Peck Ct	63	K 8	Post La	55	H 1	Randall Av	57	M 2	Rivington Av	58	H 5
Peel Pl	63	L 8	Potter Av	56	L 3	Rankin St	65	H 10	Roanoke St	59	K 5
Pelton Av	56	L 1	Pouch Ter	60	O 5	Ransom St	65	F 10	Roberts Dr	63	M 8
Pemberton Av	62	J 8	Poultney St	63	M 7	Raritan Av	60	M 5	Robin Rd	60	O 5
Pembrook			Powell St	62	F 9	Raritan Bay	65	J 10	Robinson Av	62	H 9
Loop	64	E 10	Prall Av	65	F 10	Rathbun St	65	F 10	Rochelle Pl	62	H 9
Penbroke Av	57	M 2	Pratt Ct	62	F 8	Ravenhurst Av	56	K 3	Rochelle St	60	M 5
Pendale St	63	L 8	Prescott Av	59	L 6	Ravenna St	65	H 10	Rochelle St	63	L 9
Pendleton Pl	57	N 1	President St	59	K 4	Rawson Pl	58	G 5	Rockaway St	64	C 12
Penn Av	63	L 7	Presley St	62	J 9	Ray St	62	H 9	Rockland Av	59	J 6
Penton St	64	E 11	Preston Av	62	H 9	Raymond Av	59	L 4	Rockne St	58	H 6
Percival Pl	64	E 11	Prices La	58	F 5	Raymond Pl	56	L 2	Rockport St	65	G 10
Percival St	64	E 11	Primrose Pl	63	L 8	Reading Av	62	H 8	Rockville Av	58	H 5
Perkiomen Av	62	H 8	Prince La	61	E 9	Rebecca Ct	64	C 10	Rockwell Av	60	O 4
Perry Av	59	K 4	Prince St	57	N 3	Rector St	56	L 2	Rodeo La	60	O 4
Pershing Cir	57	O 2	Princess La	56	J 2	Redgrave Av	63	K 8	Roderick Av	60	O 5
Pershing St	60	O 5	Princess St	56	J 2	Redmond St	60	M 5	Rodman St	56	J 3
Perth Amboy			Princeton Av	63	L 7	Redwood Av	62	J 8	Roe St	56	L 2
Pl	64	B 12	Princeton La	62	F 8	Redwood Loop	61	E 9	Roff St	57	N 3
Peter Av	63	L 8	Princewood Av	65	F 10	Regan Av	57	M 2	Rogers Pl	65	G 10
Peter St	56	J 3	Prol Pl	65	J 10	Regent Cir	62	F 8	Rokeby Pl	57	M 2
Peterson St	64	E 10	Promenade Av	63	L 8	Regina La	62	G 8	Rolling Hill		
Petrus Av	62	H 9	Property St	62	J 9	Regis Dr	55	H 3	Green	62	F 8
Pfluger Pl	65	G 10	Prospect Av	57	M 2	Reid Av	60	N 5	Rolling Hill		
Phelps Pl	57	N 1	Prospect Pl	63	L 7	Reiss La	60	M 5	Green	62	F 9
Philip Av	65	G 10	Prospect St	57	O 2	Remsen St	60	N 5	Roma Av	63	M 8
Phylis Ct	61	E 9	Providence St	60	N 5	Rene Dr	63	K 8	Roman Av	55	H 3
Piave Av	60	O 5	Public Pl			Renee Pl	55	H 3	Roman Ct	64	C 12
Pickersgill Av	60	O 5	*(intersection of			Renfrew Pl	56	J 2	Rome Av	60	N 5
Piedmont Av	60	O 5	Wright St and			Reno Av	63	L 7	Romer Rd	60	M 5
Pierce St	60	N 4	Canal St)	57	O 3	Rensselaer Av	64	E 10	Ronald Av	56	J 2
Pierpont Pl	59	J 6	Pulaski Av	56	J 2	Renwick Av	60	M 4	Roosevelt Av	59	K 4
Pierre Pl	65	G 11	Pulaski St	55	G 2	Reon Av	59	L 4	Roosevelt Ct	59	K 4
Pike St	57	N 2	Purcell St	56	L 3	Retford Av	62	H 9	Roosevelt St	60	N 4
Pilcher St	59	K 5	Purdue Ct	58	H 6	Retner St	60	O 5	Rose Av	63	L 7
Pine Pl	57	O 3	Purdue St	58	H 6	Revere La	62	J 7	Rose Ct	57	M 3
Pine St	57	N 2	Purdy Av	59	K 4	Revere St	57	M 3	Rose La	65	G 10
Pine Ter	65	G 10	Purdy Pl	65	F 12	Rewes Av	63	L 9	Rosebank Pl	60	O 4
Pinewood Av	63	K 7	Purroy Pl	57	N 3	Reynaud St	60	O 6	Rosecliff Rd	55	H 3
Pitney Av	64	D 10	Putnam Pl	57	N 2	Reynolds St	60	O 4	Rosedale Av	62	F 9
Pitt Av	59	L 5	Putnam St	62	H 9	Rhett Av	62	J 9	Rosewood Pl	57	N 2
Pittsville Av	64	B 12	Putters Ct	57	M 3	Rhine Av	60	N 4	Ross Av	63	L 7
Plank Rd	58	H 4				Rice Av	56	L 3	Ross La	65	H 10
Platinum Av	58	H 6	**Q**			Richard Av	64	D 11	Rossville Av	61	E 8
Platt St	63	K 8				Richard La	59	J 4	Roswell Av	58	F 5
Plattsburg St	60	M 6	Queen St	59	K 4	Riche Av	58	G 5	Row Pl	62	G 8
Plaza, The	60	M 6	Queensdale St	65	F 10	Richmond Av	62	H 7	Rowan Av	63	L 7
Pleasant Ct	57	O 3	Quimby Av	58	G 4	Richmond Ct	55	H 1	Roxbury St	55	H 2
Pleasant Pl	57	O 3	Quincy Av	63	N 7	Richmond Hill			Royal Oak Rd	56	L 3
Pleasant Plains			Quinlan Av	59	K 4	Rd	58	H 6	Rubenstein St	60	O 4
Av	64	D 11	Quinn St	57	O 3	Richmond			Rudyard St	63	M 7
Pleasant St	62	J 9	Quintard St	60	O 5	Pkwy	62	G 9	Rugby Av	57	M 3
Pleasant Valley						Richmond			Ruggles St	65	G 1C
Av	57	N 3	**R**			Pkwy	64	E 10	Rumba Pl	62	F 9
Plymouth Rd	58	H 5				Richmond Rd	63	K 7	Rumson Rd	62	H 7
Poe Ct	64	C 11	Racal Ct	58	H 6	Richmond Ter	56	J 2	Rupert Av	59	K 5
Poe St	64	C 11	Radcliff Rd	60	O 5	Richmond Valley			Russek Dr	62	F 9
Poets Cir	62	F 8	Radford St	58	H 5	Rd	64	C 11	Russell St	65	J 10
Poi Pl	58	H 6	Radigan Av	61	E 9	Ridge Av	60	M 5	Rustic Pl	62	J 9
Poillon Av	65	G 10	Rae Av	65	G 10	Ridge Ct	57	M 3	Ruth Pl	60	N 5
Poland Pl	59	L 4	Railroad Av	61	E 9	Ridge Loop	60	M 5	Ruth St	56	K 3
Polk Walk	60	P 4	Raily Ct	62	F 8	Ridgecrest Av	62	H 9	Ryan Pl	65	H 10
									Rye Av	62	H 9

STREET	MAP GRID	STREET	MAP GRID	STREET	MAP GRID	STREET	MAP GRID
S		Schubert St	60 O 4	Silver Ct	57 M 3	Spruce St	63 K 7
		Schuyler St	57 O 1	Silver Lake Rd	57 M 2	Stack Dr	62 F 9
Sable Av	60 N 4	Scott Av	60 O 5	Simmons La	58 G 5	Stadalbert Pl	56 J 2
Sable Loop	62 J 8	Scranton Av	62 H 9	Simmons Loop	58 G 5	Stafford Av	61 E 9
Saccheri Ct	62 J 9	Scranton St	60 N 5	Simonson Av	56 J 2	Stage La	60 O 4
Saint Adalbert		Scribner Av	57 N 2	Simonson Pl	56 K 2	Stanley Av	57 M 2
Pl	56 J 2	Scudder Av	64 E 10	Simpson St	60 N 6	Stanley Cir	62 H 9
Saint Andrews		Sea Gate Rd	60 P 4	Sinclair Av	62 F 9	Stanwich St	60 N 5
Ct	62 J 7	Seabreeze La	64 C 12	Sioux St	63 N 7	Star Ct	62 H 9
Saint Andrews		Seacrest Av	65 J 10	Sky La	60 O 4	Starbuck St	60 N 4
Pl	64 C 11	Seacrest La	64 C 12	Skyline Dr	60 O 4	Stark Ct	57 N 2
Saint Andrews		Seafoam St	63 M 8	Slaight St	60 N 6	Starlight Rd	60 N 4
Rd	62 J 7	Seagate Ct	60 P 5	Slater Blvd	60 N 6	Starr Av	57 M 3
Saint Anthony		Seaside La	60 P 5	Slayton Av	59 J 5	State Hwy 440	64 D 10
Pl	56 K 3	Seaver Av	60 M 6	Sleepy Hollow		State St	56 L 2
Saint Austins		Seaview Av	60 M 6	Rd	58 H 5	Staten Island	
Pl	57 M 2	Seeley La	62 J 9	Sleight Av	64 C 12	Blvd	60 M 4
Saint George		Seguine Av	65 F 11	Sloane Av	59 K 6	Staten Island	
Dr	60 M 5	Seidman Av	65 H 10	Slosson Av	56 L 3	Expwy	55 G 2
Saint George		Seldin Av	55 H 3	Slosson Ter	57 O 2	Staten Island	
Rd	62 J 7	Selkirk St	61 E 8	Smith Av	56 L 3	Expwy	60 M 4
Saint George		Selvin Loop	55 H 3	Smith Ct	59 K 4	Station Av	64 D 11
Rd	63 K 7	Seneca Av	60 M 4	Smith Pl	56 K 3	Stebbins Av	57 M 1
Saint James		Seneca Loop	59 J 4	Smith St	60 O 4	Stecher St	65 G 10
Av	60 M 5	Seneca St	56 L 2	Smith Ter	57 O 2	Steele Av	63 L 7
Saint John Av	56 K 3	Serrell Av	62 H 9	Smyrna Av	62 G 9	Steers St	59 K 5
Saint Johns Av	60 O 4	Seth Ct	57 N 3	Sneden Av	62 G 9	Steinway Av	58 H 5
Saint Josephs		Seven Gables		Snug Harbor		Stephen Loop	58 H 5
Av	56 K 2	Rd	60 N 4	Rd	57 M 1	Stepney St	59 J 6
Saint Julian Pl	57 O 2	Seward Pl	59 K 4	Sobel Ct	60 N 4	Sterling Av	63 L 7
Saint Lukes Av	61 E 8	Seymour Av	56 K 2	Sommer Av	58 H 4	Stern Ct	62 J 9
Saint Marks Pl	57 N 1	Shadow La	63 K 7	Sommers La	59 L 4	Steuben St	60 N 4
St Mary Av	60 O 4	Shadyside Av	64 E 11	Soren St	59 K 5	Stevenson Pl	64 E 11
Saint Patricks		Shafter Av	62 J 8	South Av	55 H 1	Stewart Av	56 J 3
Pl	62 J 7	Shale St	59 J 6	South Beach		Stieg Av	62 J 8
Saint Pauls Av	57 O 2	Sharon Av	57 M 2	Av	60 O 5	Stobe Av	60 M 6
Saint Peter's		Sharon La	64 E 10	South Bridge		Stone La	58 H 6
Pl	57 N 1	Sharpe Av	56 K 2	St	64 C 10	Stone St	57 N 3
Saint Stephens		Sharreti Pl	56 K 2	South Ct *(off		Stonecrest Ct	62 J 9
Pl	63 L 7	Sharrott Av	64 E 11	Cleveland		Stonegate Dr	60 N 5
Sampson Av	62 J 8	Sharrotts Rd	61 C 9	Alley)	60 O 5	Stoneham St	63 L 8
Samuel Pl	55 H 2	Shaughnessy		South Drum St	64 E 10	Storer Av	61 C 9
Sand La	60 O 5	La	60 O 4	South Gannon		Stratford Ct	58 H 6
Sandalwood		Shaw Pl	56 K 3	Av	59 J 4	Stratford Rd	57 N 3
Dr	62 J 8	Shawnee St	57 M 3	South Goff Av	64 E 11	Strauss St	60 O 4
Sandborn St	65 H 10	Sheffield St	56 L 2	South Greenleaf		Strawberry La	65 H 11
Sanders St	56 J 3	Sheldon Av	62 F 9	Av	56 L 3	Stroud Av	62 H 8
Sandgap St	65 H 10	Shelley Av	58 G 5	South Hawthorne Av	59 J 4	Studio La	60 O 4
Sands St	57 O 2	Shelterview Dr	57 N 3	South Mann		Sturges St	56 L 3
Sandywood La	61 E 9	Shepard Av	59 J 5	Av	59 K 4	Stuyvesant Av	62 H 9
Sanford Pl	59 L 4	Sheraden Av	59 K 4	South Railroad		Stuyvesant Pl	57 O 1
Sanford St	64 C 11	Sheridan Av	60 N 4	Av	63 K 8	Suffolk Av	59 K 4
Sanilac St	63 M 7	Sheridan Ct	63 K 8	South Railroad		Summer St	60 P 4
Satterlee St	64 B 12	Sheridan Pl	65 G 10	St	65 G 10	Summerfield	
Saturn La	59 J 6	Sherman Av	57 N 1	South Saint		Pl	55 H 2
Saunders St	60 N 4	Sherrill Av	62 G 8	Austin's Pl	57 M 2	Summit Av	63 L 7
Savin Ct	60 N 5	Sherwood Pl	62 J 9	South Service		Summit Pl	65 G 10
Savoy St		Shiel Av	61 E 9	Rd	64 D 11	Summit Rd	64 B 12
*(connects		Shield Pl	59 M 4	South St	56 L 2	Summit St	64 C 12
Hafstrom St		Shift Pl	62 F 9	South Woodbine		Sumner Av	56 J 3
with Montreal		Shiloh St	58 H 5	Av	59 J 4	Sumner Pl	57 N 2
Av)	63 K 8	Shirley Av	65 H 10	Spar Av	61 E 9	Sunfield Av	62 G 8
Sawyer Av	56 K 3	Shirra Av	59 J 5	Spark Pl	58 G 4	Sunnyside Ter	60 M 4
Saxon Av	58 H 5	Shore Acres		Sparkill Av	60 N 5	Sunrise La *(off	
Saybrook St	58 H 4	Rd	60 P 4	Spartan Av	55 H 2	Woods of Arden	
Scarboro Av	60 P 4	Shore Av	65 G 11	Speedwell Av	58 H 4	bet Shirley Av	
Scarsdale St	62 J 9	Shore Rd	64 B 12	Spencer St	58 F 4	and Osage	
Scenic La	60 O 4	Short Pl	65 G 11	Sperry Pl	62 F 9	La)	65 H 10
Scheffelin Av	59 K 6	Shotwell Av	62 G 8	Sprague Av	64 C 11	Sunrise Ter	57 N 2
Schley Av	62 J 8	Sideview Av	58 H 4	Spratt Av	63 K 8	Sunset Av	59 K 4
Schmidts La	59 L 4	Signal Hill Rd	57 N 3	Spring St	60 M 5	Sunset Hill Dr	57 M 3
Schoharie St	60 N 4	Signs Rd	58 H 4	Springfield Av	56 K 3	Sunset La	64 C 12
School Rd	60 P 4	Silver Beach		Springhill Av	57 M 2	Surf Av	64 C 12
School St	62 J 9	Dr	60 M 4			Surf Ct	64 D 12

STREET	MAP	GRID	STREET	MAP	GRID	STREET	MAP	GRID	STREET	MAP	GRID
Surfside Plz	64	C 12	Tompkins Av	57	O 3	Van Cortlandt			Wales Pl	57	M 1
Susan Ct	57	O 3	Tompkins Cir	57	O 2	Av	60	M 4	Walker Ct	62	G 8
Susanna La	62	G 8	Tompkins Ct	56	L 1	Van Duzer St	57	N 3	Walker Dr	56	J 2
Sussex Green	62	F 9	Tompkins Pl	57	O 3	Van Name Av	56	J 2	Walker Pl	62	F 9
Sutton Pl	62	F 9	Tompkins St	57	O 3	Van Pelt Av	56	J 2	Walker St	56	J 2
Swaim Av	65	G 11	Tone La	60	O 4	Van Riper St	56	J 2	Wall St	57	O 1
Swan St	57	O 2	Tonking Rd	59	K 6	Van St	56	L 1	Wallace Av	60	O 5
Sweetbrook			Toscany Ct	60	O 6	Van Tuyl St	57	N 2	Walloon St	56	J 2
Rd	62	H 8	Tottenville Pl	64	B 12	Van Wyck Av	65	F 11	Walnut Av	65	J 10
Sweetwater Av	65	J 10	Towers La	58	G 5	Vanderbilt Av	57	N 3	Walnut Pl	63	L 7
Swinnerton St	64	B 12	Townley Av	59	L 4	Vassar St	58	H 6	Walnut St	57	M 1
Sycamore St	65	H 10	Townsend Av	57	O 3	Vaughan St	60	O 4	Walters Av	59	L 4
Sydney Pl	63	L 7	Trantor Pl	56	J 2	Vedder Av	56	J 3	Wandel Av	60	N 4
Sylva La	60	P 4	Travis Av	58	G 4	Veith Pl	65	G 11	Ward Av	57	N 2
Sylvan Ct	64	C 12	Travis Av	58	H 5	Veltman Av	56	K 3	Wards Point		
Sylvan Pl	55	H 2	Treadwell Av	56	K 2	Venice Av	60	N 5	Av	64	B 12
Sylvaton Ter	57	O 3	Treetz Pl	59	K 4	Venus La	59	J 6	Wardwell Av	56	K 3
Sylvia St	62	H 9	Tremont Av	56	J 3	Vera St	60	M 6	Waring Av	62	G 8
			Trent St	63	K 9	Vermont Av	60	O 4	Warren St	57	N 3
T			Trenton Ct	65	F 11	Vermont Ct	59	K 5	Warwick Av	59	K 4
			Trinity Pl	56	L 2	Vernon Av	65	F 10	Washburn Av	55	H 2
Tabb Pl	56	K 2	Trossach Rd	57	N 3	Vespa Av	62	F 9	Washington Av	59	K 5
Tacoma St	60	N 5	Trout Pl	65	G 11	Veterans Rd E	64	D 10	Washington Pl	56	K 2
Taft Av	57	N 1	Troy St	62	J 8	Veterans Rd W	61	D 9	Watchogue Rd	56	J 3
Taft Ct	59	K 4	Truman St	64	C 11	Victoria Rd	62	F 9	Water St	57	O 3
Talbot Pl	57	O 3	Trumbull Pl	57	N 2	Victory Blvd	58	F 6	Waterbury Av	64	E 11
Tallman St	65	H 10	Tuckahoe Av	65	G 10	Villa Av	56	J 2	Waterford Ct	60	P 5
Tanglewood Dr	62	J 7	Tudor St	62	J 8	Villa Nova St	58	H 6	Waters Av	56	J 3
Tappen Ct	57	O 3	Tulip Cir	62	F 9	Village La	62	H 9	Waterside		
Targee St	57	N 3	Turf Ct	59	J 6	Vincent Av	63	K 7	Pkwy	63	K 9
Tarlee Pl	62	J 9	Turf Rd	59	J 6	Vine St	57	N 1	Waterside St	63	M 8
Tarlton St	63	L 9	Turner St	61	D 9	Vineland Av	62	G 9	Waterview		
Tarring St	63	L 8	Tuttle St	56	J 3	Viola Pl	56	J 3	Loop	57	O 2
Tarrytown Av	63	L 8	Twin Oak Dr	60	M 4	Violet St	64	E 11	Watkins Av	62	G 8
Tarter Pl	57	O 2	Twombley Av	63	K 8	Virginia Av	60	O 4	Watson Av	58	G 5
Tate St	56	J 2	Tyler St	56	L 3	Virginia Pl	56	K 3	Wave St	57	O 2
Tatro St	63	K 8	Tynan St	62	G 8	Vista Av	60	N 5	Wavecrest St	63	M 8
Taunton St	63	K 8	Tyndale St	65	H 10	Vista Pl	60	O 5	Waverly Pl	57	N 3
Taylor Ct	56	L 2	Tyron Av	62	G 9	Vivian St	60	O 6	Wayne Ct *(in		
Taylor St	56	L 2	Tyrrell St	64	B 11	Vogel Av	64	E 10	Edwin		
Teakwood Ct	62	J 8	Tysen Ct *(bet			Vogel La	59	K 4	Markham		
Teleport Dr	58	G 4	Richmond Hill &			Vogel Loop	59	K 4	Housing)	56	L 1
Temple Ct	58	G 5	Arthur Kill Rds,			Vogel Pl	64	E 10	Wayne Pl *(in		
Tenafly Pl	65	G 10	connects Center			Von Braun	62	G 8	Edwin		
Tennyson Dr	65	J 10	St to Clarke			Vreeland St	56	K 2	Markham		
Teri Ct	59	J 6	Av)	62	J 7	Vulcan St	60	O 6	Housing)	56	L 1
Terrace Av	64	E 10	Tysen St	57	M 1				Wayne St	56	L 2
Terrace Ct	59	K 6	Tysens La	63	L 7	**W**			Wayne Ter *(in		
Thames Av	57	M 3							Edwin		
Thayer Pl	63	K 8	**U**			Waddell Av	64	D 10	Markham		
Theatre La	60	O 4				Wade St	56	K 3	Housing)	56	L 1
Thelma Ct	57	O 3	Uncas Av	64	E 10	Wadsworth Av	60	P 4	Weaver St	65	H 10
Thelma Dr	55	H 3	Union Av	56	J 2	Wadsworth Rd	60	P 4	Webster Av	57	N 2
Theresa Pl	57	N 3	Union Ct	56	J 2	Wadsworth Ter	60	O 4	Weed Av	60	N 4
Thollen St	63	K 8	Union Pl	57	O 3	Wagner College			Weiner St	64	D 11
Thomas Pl	63	L 8	University Pl	57	M 2	Rd *(near			Weir La	64	C 11
Thomas St	63	K 7	Upton St	60	N 5	Wagner			Wellbrook Av	59	K 4
Thompson Pl	60	O 4	Urbana St	60	N 5	College)	60	N 4	Welles Ct	56	M 2
Thompson St	57	O 3	Utah St	64	B 11	Wagner College			Wellington Ct	59	J 6
Thornycroft Av	62	H 9	Utica St	64	E 11	St *(near			Wellington		
Thurston St	59	J 4	Utter Av	56	L 3	Wagner			Green	62	F 9
Tiber Pl	60	M 4	Uxbridge St	59	K 4	College)	60	N 4	Wemple St	55	H 2
Tiger Ct	56	J 3				Wagner St	60	O 4	Wendy Dr	65	G 10
Tilden St	57	N 2	**V**			Wahler Pl	63	N 7	Wenlock St	56	J 2
Tillman St	59	L 4				Waimer Pl	62	H 9	Wentworth Av	60	O 6
Tilson Pl	60	O 4	Vail Av	64	E 11	Wainwright Av	62	H 8	Weser Av	60	N 4
Timber Ridge			Valdemar Av	65	F 10	Wakefield Av	58	G 5	West Buchanan		
Dr	62	J 8	Valencia Av	57	M 2	Wakefield Rd	65	J 10	St	57	N 1
Tioga St	60	M 4	Valley Green			Walbrooke Av	57	M 2	West Castor Pl	62	F 9
Titus Av	63	M 8	Rd	62	F 9	Walch Pl	65	F 11	West Caswell		
Toddy Av	58	H 5	Valleyview Pl	59	L 4	Walcott Av	59	K 5	Av	56	J 3
Todt Hill Rd	59	L 4	Van Allen Av	62	G 8	Walden Av	59	L 6	West Cederview		
Token St	62	G 8	Van Brunt St	62	H 9	Waldo Pl	59	L 4	Av	62	J 7
			Van Buren St	57	M 1	Waldron Av	57	M 3			

STREET	MAP	GRID	STREET	MAP	GRID	STREET	MAP	GRID	STREET	MAP	GRID
West Ct *(off Cleveland Alley)	60	O 5	Wildwood La	64	C 12	Winter Av	57	N 2	Yeomalt Av	65	G 11
			Wiley Pl	63	L 7	Winthrop Pl	59	L 4	Yetman Av	64	C 11
West Fingerboard Rd	60	N 5	Willard Av	56	K 3	Wirt Av	61	E 9	York Av	57	N 1
			Willard Pl	56	K 3	Wirt La	61	E 9	York Ter	57	N 1
West Raleigh Av	56	L 3	William Av	65	J 10	Witteman Pl	60	M 4	Young St	57	N 3
			William St	57	O 2	Woehrle Av	62	G 8	Yucca Dr	62	F 9
West Shore Expwy	58	G 4	Willis Av	57	N 2	Wolcott Av	62	G 9	Yukon Av	62	H 7
			Willow Av	57	O 3	Wolcott St	59	K 5			
West Shore Expwy	64	D 10	Willow Brook Ct	56	J 3	Wolkoff La	55	H 3	**Z**		
West St	56	L 2	Willow Brook Pkwy	59	K 6	Wolverine St	63	K 7	Zachary Ct	56	K 3
West Ter	65	F 10				Wood Av	64	C 11	Zebra Pl	61	E 8
Westbrook Av	56	J 2	Willow Brook Rd	56	J 3	Wood Ct	61	E 8	Zeck Ct	56	J 3
Westbury Av	57	M 2	Willow La	62	J 8	Woodbine Av	56	J 3	Zeni Pl	63	M 7
Westcott Blvd	56	K 3	Willow Pond Rd	60	M 5	Woodbridge Pl	56	K 3	Zephyr Av	65	G 11
Westentry Rd	60	M 6	Willow Rd E	56	J 3	Woodcliff Av	55	H 2	Zoe St	60	M 6
Western Av	55	G 1	Willow Rd W	56	J 3	Woodcrest Rd	55	H 3	Zwicky Av	63	M 7
Westervelt Av	57	N 1	Willow Wood La	62	J 8	Woodcutters La	63	K 8			
Westfield Av	61	E 8	Wills Pl	60	O 6	Wooddale Av	59	L 5	**Numbered Streets**		
Westminster Ct	60	M 5	Wilson Av	62	H 9	Woodhaven Av	60	M 5			
Westport La	58	H 6	Wilson St	60	N 5	Woodhull Av	65	F 10	1st Av	59	J 4
Westport St	58	H 6	Wilson Ter	60	N 4	Woodland Av	62	J 8	1st Ct	65	H 11
Westwood Av	59	J 4	Wiman Av	62	J 9	Woodlawn Av	60	N 5	1st St (New Dorp)	63	L 7
Wetmore Rd	60	N 4	Wiman Pl	60	P 4	Woodrow Rd	61	E 9	1st St (Oakwood)	63	L 8
Wheeler Av	59	K 4	Winans St	64	D 11	Woodruff La	56	L 2	2nd Av	59	J 5
Wheeling Av	64	E 10	Winant Av	61	E 8	Woods Of Arden Rd	65	H 10	2nd Ct	65	H 11
Whirt La	61	E 9	Winant La	61	C 9	Woodside Av	57	N 3	2nd St (New Dorp)	63	L 7
Whitaker Pl	60	N 5	Winant Pl	61	C 9	Woodstock Av	57	N 2	2nd St (Oakwood)	63	L 8
White Ct	62	H 9	Winant St	56	J 2	Woodvale Av	64	E 11	3rd Av	59	J 4
White Pl	56	L 2	Winchester Av	62	H 9	Woodvale Loop	64	E 11	3rd Ct	65	H 11
White Plains Av	60	O 4	Windemere Av	63	K 8	Woodward Av	59	J 4	3rd St (New Dorp)	63	L 7
White St	60	P 4	Windermere Rd	60	O 5	Woolley Av	59	K 4	4th Av	59	K 4
Whitehall St	63	L 8	Windham Loop	58	H 6	Wrenn St	65	F 10	4th Ct	65	H 11
Whitewood Av	57	M 3	Winding Woods Loop	64	C 12	Wright Av	56	J 2	4th St (New Dorp)	63	L 7
Whitlock Av	59	L 5	Windom Av	60	P 5	Wright St	57	O 3	7th St (New Dorp)	63	L 7
Whitman Av	62	J 9	Windsor Ct	59	L 4	Wygant Pl	56	K 2	8th St (New Dorp)	63	L 7
Whitney Av	60	N 5	Windsor Rd	59	L 4	Wyona Av	59	J 4	9th St (New Dorp)	63	L 7
Whitwell Pl	59	L 5	Windy Hollow Way	60	M 6				10th St (New Dorp)	63	L 8
Wiederer Pl *(off Price St)	57	N 3	Winfield Av	60	N 5	**X**					
Wieland Av	61	E 9	Winfield St	60	O 6	Xenia St	60	N 6			
Wilbur Pl	59	K 4	Wingham St	60	O 4						
Wilbur St	65	F 11	Winham Av	63	M 8	**Y**					
Wilcox St	56	J 3	Winslow	65	H 10	Yafa Ct	56	J 3			
Wild Av	58	F 5				Yale St	55	H 3			
Wilder Av	63	K 7									

Notes